'2-
History

D0118880

ALSO BY BARRY STRAUSS

*What If?: The World's Foremost Military Historians Imagine
What Might Have Been*
(contributor)

Western Civilization: The Continuing Experiment
(with Thomas F. X. Noble and others)

*War and Democracy: A Comparative Study of the Korean War
and the Peloponnesian War*
(with David McCann, co-editor)

Rowing Against the Current: On Learning to Scull at Forty

*Fathers and Sons in Athens: Ideology and Society
in the Era of the Peloponnesian War*

Hegemonic Rivalry: From Thucydides to the Nuclear Age
(with Richard Ned Lebow, co-editor)

*The Anatomy of Error: Ancient Military Disasters
and Their Lessons for Modern Strategists*
(with Josiah Ober)

Athens After the Peloponnesian War: Class, Faction and Policy, 403–386 B.C.

THE BATTLE

OF SALAMIS

The Naval Encounter

That Saved Greece—

and Western Civilization

BARRY STRAUSS

SIMON & SCHUSTER

NEW YORK · LONDON · TORONTO · SYDNEY

SIMON AND SCHUSTER
Rockefeller Center
1230 Avenue of the Americas
New York, NY 10020

Copyright © 2004 by Barry Strauss
All rights reserved,
including the right of reproduction
in whole or in part in any form.

SIMON & SCHUSTER and colophon are registered trademarks
of Simon & Schuster, Inc.

For information about special discounts for bulk purchases,
please contact Simon & Schuster Special Sales:
1-800-456-6798 or business@simonandschuster.com

Designed by Dana Sloan

Manufactured in the United States of America

3   5   7   9   10   8   6   4   2

Library of Congress Cataloging-in-Publication Data

Strauss, Barry
The battle of Salamis : the naval encounter that saved Greece—and western civilization /
Barry Strauss.
p. cm.
Includes bibliographical references and index.
1. Salamis, Battle of, Greece, 480 B.C. I. Title.
DF225.6.S76 2004
938'.03—dc22
2004045341

ISBN 0-7432-4450-8

FOR SYLVIE

CONTENTS

Contents

THE RETREAT

A NOTE ON SPELLING
AND ABBREVIATIONS

Greek, Persian, and other ancient names are spelled and abbreviated following the style of the standard reference work, *The Oxford Classical Dictionary*, 3rd ed. (Oxford: Oxford University Press, 1999).

I have translated all ancient Greek quotations myself unless otherwise noted. Citations from Old Persian have been translated by others as noted.

TIMETABLE OF EVENTS RELATING TO THE BATTLE OF SALAMIS, 480 B.C.

Note: All dates approximate except full moon and eclipse.

May: Xerxes begins to move troops across the Hellespont.

June: Xerxes begins march from the Hellespont to Athens.

Third week of August: Greek men and ships take up positions at Thermopylae and Artemisium.

August 19, full moon: End of the Olympic Games and the Carnea Festival.

ca. August 27–29: Battles of Thermopylae and Artemisium.

ca. September 1: Greek fleet returns from Artemisium and arrives at Phaleron Bay and at Salamis; Persian army begins march southward.

Early September: Peloponnesian armies in full force begin building wall at Isthmus of Corinth.

ca. September 1–6: Evacuation of Athens.

ca. September 4: Persian fleet moves southward.

ca. September 5: Persian advance guard reaches Attica.

ca. August 31–September 20: Persian army conquers Phocis and Boeotia and regroups in Athens.

ca. September 7: Persian fleet reaches Phaleron Bay.

ca. September 21–23: Siege of Athenian Acropolis.

ca. September 23: Persian army takes Athenian Acropolis; Greek war council on Salamis votes for fleet to retreat to Isthmus of Corinth.

Night of ca. September 23–24: Mnesiphilus, Themistocles, and Eurybiades force Greek war council to change plans and remain at Salamis; debate between Themistocles and Adimantus.

Dawn, ca. September 24: Earthquake.

Evening of ca. September 24: Sicinnus's mission to the Persians.

Midnight, ca. September 24: Persian fleet enters straits of Salamis.

ca. September 25: Battle of Salamis.

End of September: Persians begin to withdraw from Athens.

October 2, partial eclipse of the sun: Spartan army leaves Isthmus.

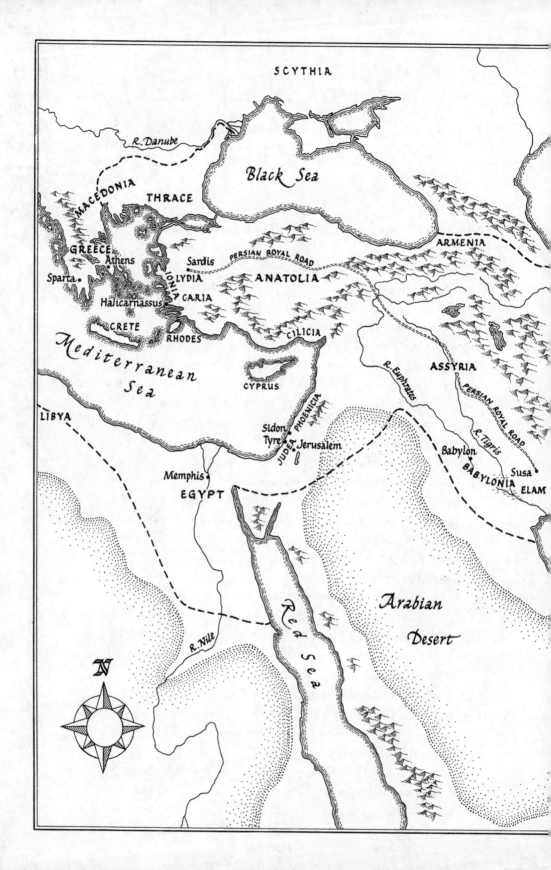

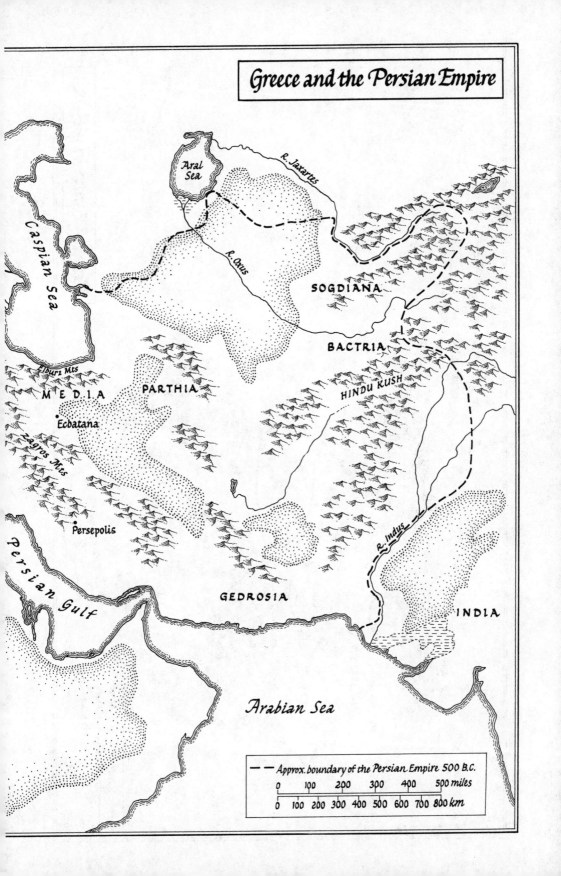

Greece and the Persian Empire

Aral Sea

Caspian Sea

R. Jaxartes

R. Oxus

SOGDIANA

BACTRIA

Elburz Mts

MEDIA

PARTHIA

HINDU KUSH

Ecbatana

Zagros Mts

Persepolis

R. Indus

Persian Gulf

GEDROSIA

INDIA

Arabian Sea

– – – Approx. boundary of the Persian Empire 500 B.C.

0   100   200   300   400   500 miles

0   100 200 300 400 500 600 700 800 km

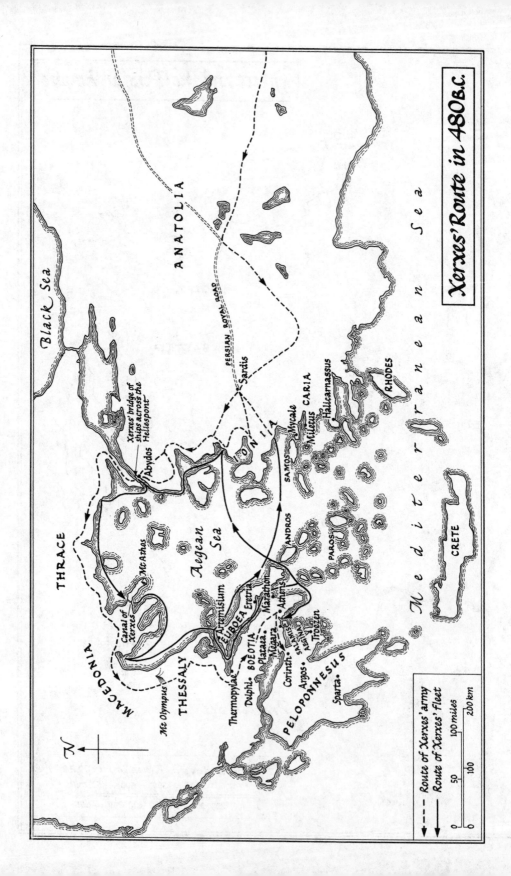

Xerxes' Route in 480 B.C.

Black Sea

ANATOLIA

THRACE

PERSIAN ROYAL ROAD

Sardis

Xerxes' bridge of
ships across the
Hellespont

Abydos

Mt. Athos

MACEDONIA

Canal of
Xerxes

Mt. Olympus

THESSALY

Aegean
Sea

IONIA

SAMOS
Mycale
Miletus
CARIA
Halicarnassus

RHODES

Artemisium

EUBOEA Eretria

Thermopylae

Delphi   BOEOTIA
         Plataea   Marathon
         Megara   Athens
      Corinth   SALAMIS
         AEGINA
   Argos   Troezen
PELOPONNESUS

Sparta

ANDROS

PAROS

Mediterranean Sea

CRETE

N

‒ ‒ ‒ Route of Xerxes' army
⟶ Route of Xerxes' fleet

50   100 miles

100   200 km

0

AN IMPORTANT NOTE
ABOUT THE SHIPS

The battle of Salamis was fought with triremes, wooden warships. Triremes could be powered either by oar or by sail, but in battle only oars were used, because speed and maneuverability were everything. "Trireme" comes from the Greek *triērēs*, which means "three-rower" ship, referring to the three levels of rowers seen in profile when looking along each side of the ship. The trireme represents an innovation in shipbuilding, probably dating to the century before Salamis. In 480 B.C., the trireme embodied state-of-the-art naval technology in the Mediterranean. For two centuries, the trireme would reign as the queen of the seas; Salamis was its greatest battle.

Our information about the trireme is plentiful if incomplete. Unfortunately for the student of Salamis, most of that information comes from the period ca. 430–320 B.C., that is, at least fifty years after the Persian Wars. Fortunately, what little indications we have suggest that what was true of triremes in the later period was, by and large, true of the earlier period as well.

Triremes were sleek ships. A Greek trireme was about 130 feet long and about 18 feet wide (or about 39 feet wide with the oars extended) and sat about 8¼ feet above the waterline. The bottom two levels of oarsmen rowed on oars that extended through openings in the hull and gunwale, while the top level rowed on oars that extended through an outrigger—that is, in the late fifth century B.C., when the outrigger was well established. It is plausible that Greek triremes in 480 B.C. had outriggers as well.

The prow was tipped with a ram, a squat wooden structure encased in bronze and armed with three cutting blades in the fore. The ram sat on the waterline and extended about seven feet off the stem.

The Phoenicians prided themselves on being the greatest sailors in the Mediterranean and followed their own boat-building traditions. Phoenician triremes were about the same length as their Greek counterparts but were wider. Some historians argue that Phoenician triremes were higher than Greek triremes and lacked an outrigger. To carry extra marines, Phoenician triremes had wide decks, lined with a bulwark to protect the tightly packed men from falling overboard. Along the outside of the deck hung a row of shields. The Phoenician ram was long and tapered instead of short and pronged. Both Phoenician and Greek triremes were decorated but in different ways.

It is estimated that a Greek trireme under oar would normally travel at a speed of five or six nautical miles per hour or an average of seven or eight nautical miles an hour when in a hurry. For short bursts of speed, for example during battle, it is estimated that the rowers could move a trireme at a rate of nine or ten nautical miles per hour.

A trireme was narrow for its length, which made the ship as fragile as it was fast. So trireme fleets avoided the open water and hugged the coast. They preferred not to spend the night at sea.

In Athens, whose ships we know most about, a trireme usually contained a crew of 200: 170 oarsmen, 10 marines, and 4 archers, as well as various seamen and petty officers, including the rowing master, the purser, the bow officer, the shipwright, the piper, and men to work the sails. Each trireme had a captain (in Athens called the trierarch), who was usually a wealthy man and sometimes a mere figurehead. The single most important man aboard was the helmsman, also known as the pilot, who worked the double rudders in the stern. A skilled pilot could steer a ship to victory.

Oarsmen were unarmed. They probably had no uniforms and, in the hot, relatively airless space below deck, often wore only a loincloth. Archers carried bows and arrows, while Greek marines wore bronze helmets and breastplates, carried large, round shields, and fought with javelins and swords. Most of the marines in the Persian fleet were similarly equipped, but others used a variety of weapons, from sickles and axes to daggers and long knives.

Experienced crews fought by means of maneuver: they used the ram to strike the enemy and then quickly retreated before he could fight back. Inexperienced crews often preferred to board the enemy and have the marines and archers fight it out. Fleets that used boarding tactics rather than ramming tactics might increase the number of fighting men on deck, sometimes carrying as many as forty per ship.

In the Greek fleet of 480 B.C., it appears that each trireme held ten marines and four archers. In the Persian fleet, each trireme carried forty marines and archers, including a mixed group of thirty Iranians (Persians or Medes) and Sacae (a nomadic people of Central Asia). All of the ships in the Greek fleet were Greek, but none of the ships in the Persian fleet was Persian: every Persian ship had been supplied by a Persian subject state, including Phoenicians, Egyptians, Carians, and Greeks, among others. The Persians supplied only marines, archers, and admirals. The Phoenicians were considered to have the best squadrons in the Persian fleet, followed by the Carians and the Ionian (eastern) Greeks.

The presence of so many Iranians and Sacae on every ship probably reflected Persian unease. Persia was a land power. Persian nobles had a horseman's contempt for sea people. With their marines and archers, they attempted to turn naval battles into land battles at sea. Their armed presence also made it difficult for restive allies to switch to the Greek side.

The three levels of rowers on an Athenian trireme were known as follows; the top level of rowers was called *thranitai* (in English, thranites), "men on the beams"; the middle level was called *zygitai* (in English, zygites), "men on the transverse benches"; and the bottom level was called *thalamioi* (in English, thalamians), "men in the hold" or, equally, "men in the bedroom." The latter may refer to the practice of using the hold to nap or sleep in. A fully manned rowing crew of an Athenian trireme consisted of 58 zygites and 52 thalamians, divided into groups of, respectively, 29 and 26 rowers per side; plus 60 thranites, in two files of 30 rowers, for a total of 170 rowers.

Marines, archers, the pilot, the captain, and the lookouts all sat on deck. All these men had to remain seated as much as possible, especially in battle, because even small movements could unbalance the boat and upset the rowing. On Greek triremes in 480 B.C., the deck was a flimsy affair, a narrow, wooden canopy open in the center for a gangway that ran from bow to stern. There was no deck rail. The trireme's deck also served as a sunscreen for the rowers below.

Athenian triremes in 480 B.C. had been built for "speed and wheeling about." Nonetheless, at Salamis they were heavier than triremes in the Persian fleet. This seems odd, given the large number of marines and the bulwarks on Persian triremes, but it may reflect a conscious Athenian decision to build heavy ships in order to counterbalance the Persian fleet's superiority in numbers and experience. Heavier ships outperform lighter ships under certain conditions; if Athens could manage to fight under those conditions, it had a chance of prevailing. The weight differential might also reflect the greater opportunity of the Persians in the weeks before Salamis to beach their triremes and dry out the hulls in the sun. Athenian triremes might have been relatively more waterlogged and hence heavier.

Since triremes, under battle conditions, were powered by human beings, victory depended in large part on training and toughening the men, on giving them plenty of food (salt fish and barley groats were staples), water (an estimated 1.85 gallons per man per day), and rest on shore (commonly at midday and at night). Morale mattered, and the successful leader had to be as much a coach and psychologist as he was a naval commander.

It was essential to keep all 170 men rowing in unison. The difficult task of keeping time fell on each boat to the rowing master. He stood in the gangway, midway between prow and stern, and called out instructions to the men. They could barely hear him, given the din of the oars and the absorption of sound by so much human flesh. So the rowing master had the help of the bow officer, who faced him and, following the rowing master's signals, called out to the men in the bow. Another man might have done the same thing in the stern.

Meanwhile, a piper kept time by playing on a shrill double pipe. Sometimes the entire crew would join in a rhythmic cry, repeating it over and over, to mark time. The cries *O opop, O opop* and *ryppapai*, each one mimicking the rhythm of the oar stroke, are both attested for Athenian crews. It is also possible that the crews marked time by humming. Each stroke consisted of a quick, hard pull and a longer recovery. The comic writer Aristophanes compared the beat to a chorus of croaking frogs: *"Bre-ke-ke-kex, ko-ax, ko-ax."*

With 170 men rowing as one, the view on either side of a trireme under oar—if you were sitting in the stern and looking toward the prow—might have been hypnotic. And yet a trireme was not very big.

At 130 feet long, it was just over twice the length of an eight-oared rowing boat used by today's athletes. That makes a trireme roughly the length of a modern schooner or an oceangoing tug; a little more than half the length of a World War II German U-boat; about one-fourth the length of an early-twentieth-century armored cruiser; about one-seventh the size of a World War II American aircraft carrier. In short, a trireme crowded two hundred or more men in a small space.

It required ingenuity to maintain control of so many men crowded onto one ship, and it was even harder to keep order within a fleet of hundreds of ships and tens of thousands of men. Advance planning, visual and auditory signals, and constant training were all required.

Every trireme depicted on its prow a pair of eyes and a name, although the name might have been denoted only by a symbol rather than by writing. Some triremes were lavishly outfitted and orna- mented. So if triremes sometimes seemed as complicated as human beings, it is no wonder. The following pages will have a great deal more to say about triremes and their intricacies. For now, we need note the presence of only one other kind of oared ship in both fleets of 480 B.C.: the penteconter. This was a fifty-oared ship with twenty-five men on each side, arranged on one or two levels. It played only a very small role at Salamis.

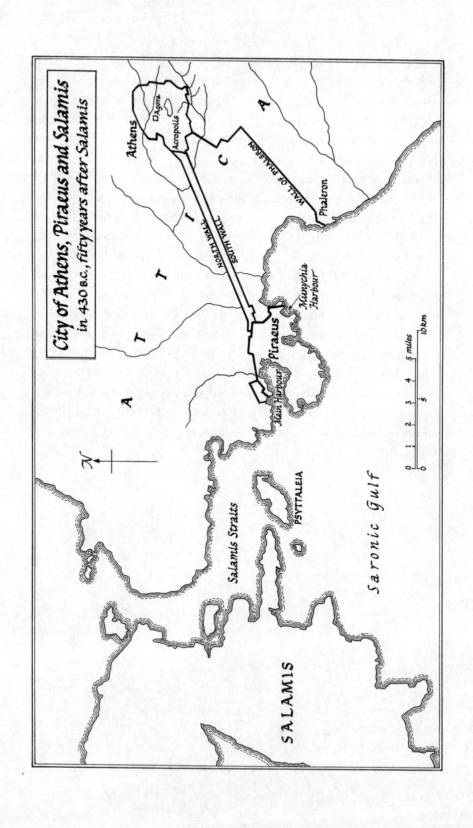

City of Athens, Piraeus and Salamis
in 430 B.C., fifty years after Salamis

Athens
Agora
Acropolis

A T T I C A

WALL OF PHALERON
Phaleron

NORTH WALL
SOUTH WALL

Munychia
Harbour

Piraeus

Main Harbour

N

Salamis Straits

PSYTTALEIA

SALAMIS

Saronic Gulf

0   1   2   3   4   5 miles
0   5   10 km

≈

PIRAEUS

He was the last Athenian. That is, if a box of bones may be considered an Athenian. Alive, he had been Themistocles, architect of the greatest sea battle ever fought. Now his remains were secretly reburied here in Athenian soil, perhaps, as rumored, along the shore outside the wall of Piraeus harbor. Themistocles' family, they said, had dug up the bones from their first grave abroad under the noses of the authorities.

It was a ploy to bring a grin to the skeleton's mouth, for of all the clever Greeks, who was more cunning than Themistocles? No one except perhaps the traveler whose ship passed Themistocles' grave site on this summer morning in 430 B.C. The observer was a man who put the clever in their place, and who now might thank the gods as he stood on the breezy deck and looked toward the last Athenian he might ever see.

Herodotus, as the observer was named, had seen no end of Athenians. Athens ruled the sea, and he had spent his life on waterways. And here, Herodotus could look from his ship toward Athens's most fateful naval battlefield. Across the channel from the great man's bones lay the spot where, fifty years earlier, Themistocles had staked Athens's very existence on the outcome of a single day. Herodotus had only to turn westward on the deck to see it, rising like a rock: Salamis.

It looked more like a fortress than an island, separated from the mainland by only a moatlike strip of blue water, the Salamis straits.

1

Once independent, the island had long belonged to Athens, whose rule extended across the narrow channel. In these straits in 480 B.C., a battle took place just where Themistocles had planned. In the early autumn, when night and day are of equal length, a thousand warships fought over the future of Greece. An invading Persian armada aimed to add Greece to the greatest empire the world had ever seen; the stubborn natives rowed for liberty or death. The day dawned white; when twelve hours later the sun went down red, the remnants of one fleet came flooding out of the straits pursued by another.

If the battle had gone the other way, Greece would be ruled by kings and queens. One was Xerxes, the Great King of Persia, who watched the battle from shore. Another was Artemisia, queen of Halicarnassus (today the city of Bodrum, Turkey), a captain-queen, who fought in the thick of combat—one of the very few women in all of recorded history to have commanded ships in battle.

Now, fifty years later, Athens was bleeding. Only an escape artist of Herodotus's experience could have found the rare merchant ship to put in at the port of Piraeus during a plague and the even rarer place on board. Herodotus had learned more than a little resourcefulness in a life spent traveling. A man in his fifties, he had a long beard, a thin, weather-beaten face, and a receding hairline that revealed a wrinkled forehead. Herodotus wore a cloak draped over a tunic, as well as sturdy boots and a broad-brimmed hat.

When he had arrived in Athens to find the city under siege by an enemy army, Herodotus had probably shrugged the matter off. This war was just the latest in a series of Athens's struggles with its rivals in Greece. Herodotus knew that impregnable walls connected Athens to the harbor at Piraeus, three miles away. The Athenian fleet ruled the sea and conveyed whatever the city needed. Sicilian fish, Crimean grain, Lydian luxuries: nothing was too dear or distant to resist the pull of a port gleaming with gold coins and guarded by three hundred warships. Herodotus had not counted on the epidemic, however.

Men were dying under the marble porticoes, beside the gilded statues, and within the fashionable groves. Having completed the job that had brought him to Athens, Herodotus seized a berth on a merchantman. He had escaped by a hair's breadth. Yet as he took a last look at

Athens, Herodotus might have felt as much awe as relief. The view from the deck was no ordinary one. In fact, between the salt air and the smell of smoke, the distant moaning of the afflicted and the nearby crash of oars in the harbor, the panorama all but brought Herodotus's work to life.

Herodotus had devoted his career to an epic book of enquiries, to use the literal meaning of what he called *Historiai* and we call *Histories*. Some dub him the Father of History, others the Father of Lies. But as he pursued his enquiries from Babylonia to Ukraine and from Egypt to Italy, Herodotus shone on everyone he met the harsh light of a mind without illusions. Even today, 2,500 years later, his analysis has the simple power of Archimedes' lever.

As Herodotus looked back across the deck of his ship, turning eastward he saw the city of Athens, crowned by its Acropolis. This rocky hill, the historic heart of the city, featured the then new temple of Athena Parthenos, today known as the Parthenon. Northward from the Acropolis stretched the best-stocked farmland in Greece, but what caught the visitor's eye were black columns of smoke in the blue summer sky. The farms of Athens's countryside were on fire. They had been put to the torch by an invading Greek army, led by Athens's archrival, Sparta. It was the second year of the Peloponnesian War (431–404 B.C.), the beginning of a bloody inter-Greek struggle for power.

From his viewpoint aboard ship, Herodotus might have turned westward again to the sight that had been dubbed "divine Salamis." There, Athens and Sparta had put aside their differences in 480 B.C. to unite against the Persian invader like two oxen harnessed to one yoke. After the great naval battle, the victors erected two trophies on the island of Salamis and a third on the islet at the entrance to the straits. They gave a part of the Persian spoils, captured in and after the battle, as thank-offerings to the gods. These included three Phoenician triremes, one of which was still there in Herodotus's day. In holy Delphi, Persian spoils financed a huge statue of the god Apollo, seventeen and a half feet tall, holding the stern post of a captured warship in his hand.

In the straits in 480 B.C. the gods of battle had to decide whether to give their favors to the Persian navy or the Greek fleet. The Persians had come in overwhelming force by land and sea to punish Athens for having attacked a Persian city in western Anatolia (modern Turkey) a generation earlier. At least that was the excuse; they really wanted to conquer Greece. In the three months before the battle of Salamis, the Persians had marched through northern and central Greece, crushed the Spartan army at Thermopylae, fought the Athenian navy to a standstill at Artemisium, and entered Athens in triumph. They had burned the old temples of the Acropolis to the ground. With their vast armada the Persians expected victory at Salamis, but the gods had always disapproved of an excessive taste for vengeance, and the Persian emperor Xerxes had a parched throat when it came to Greek blood.

The world had never seen a battle like it. A channel only a mile wide held the fighting men of the three continents of the Old World: Africa, Asia, and Europe. The Persian fleet included not only Iranians and men from Central Asia, but Egyptians, Phoenicians, Cypriots, Pamphylians, Lydians, Cilicians, and even Greeks from Anatolia and the Aegean islands. On the other side, the Hellenic fleet commanded contingents from two dozen separate city-states, most from the Greek mainland, but some from the Aegean and Ionian islands and one lone ship from Italy.

Salamis represented a huge demographic fact. More than 200,000 men fought in the battle. Perhaps 20,000 soldiers lined the shores of the straits, to help or hinder survivors, depending on whose side they fought. In addition, about another 100,000 women, children, and old men had left Athens as refugees. In all, 300,000 combatants and civilians were involved in the battle of Salamis. This was an enormous number of people in the world of 480 B.C. In today's statistical terms, it is equivalent to about 20 million people.

The sailors at Salamis were certainly diverse: they ranged from redheaded Thracians to swarthy Phoenicians to dusky Egyptians. They included citizens and slaves, kings and commoners, cavaliers turned ships' captains as well as lifelong mariners. They spoke a hodgepodge of languages, and Greek was heard on both sides. As many Greeks fought for Persia as against it. These rival Greeks read the same epic poetry and worshipped the same gods, and yet they prayed for each other's defeat.

On the decks of the ships at Salamis sat heavily armed marines, ready to clash when the ships locked. Greek marines on both sides

4

wore metal breastplates and helmets and carried swords and javelins. Persian marines included men in turbans and linen breastplates, soldiers equipped with billhooks and daggers or with spears, battle-axes, and long knives. Most of the contingents incorporated archers, too, waiting to shoot down men even in the water.

The devious Athenian who set traps with the care of a surgeon setting bones; the Persian king who thought he could thunder through the watery world of Hellas the way his horses pounded across the high plain of Iran; the scheming Halicarnassian queen who fought for her place in a world of men but fought against everyone else's freedom; the eunuchs, the slaves, the pipers, the marines, the wives and concubines ashore and the myriad oarsmen on ship; the taste of too many meals of salt fish and barley groats; the perfume of Iranian grandees, the reek of tens of thousands of sweating men who rarely bathed, and the stench of corpses washing up ashore. The days in which, in rapid sequence, Athens was evacuated, invaded and burned, and the ships of two star-crossed nations struggled over empire in the straits. It had all happened here, within a span that a fast trireme could cross in ten minutes. And it had all been part of Herodotus's life since boyhood, in dozens of anecdotes told over and over again. And now, as his ship rounded the coast of the island of Salamis, the tale had become his to tell.

The ships at Salamis were the most important wooden structures in the history of Greece since the Trojan horse. Yet it would not be easy for Herodotus to recount their story. The war memorials were mute. The Athenian state, whose archives were rudimentary, kept few official records of its battles, nor did Persian scribes publish their accounts.

Greek poets, to be sure, proved eager to tell the tale. So a virtual literary industry about the Persian invasion existed in the fifth century B.C. The most important verse work that survives today is *The Persians*, a play about Salamis by the great Athenian tragedian Aeschylus, who probably fought in the battle himself. We also have a good chunk of a poem, written ca. 410 B.C. by one Timotheus of Miletus, which offers a vivid if sometimes over-the-top picture of the battle. But little survives of other poems that patriotic schoolboys once learned by heart.

Herodotus knew Aeschylus's play and had read Athens's inscriptions. But he also knew that the best way to find out about Salamis was to talk to the men who had fought there. Only a child when Artemisia and her ships returned to his hometown of Halicarnassus, Herodotus was too young to interview the commanders of 480 B.C. But he could meet their sons and daughters and learn their families' lore. And he had the chance to speak with other veterans of both sides during his travels through Greece and the Persian Empire. He was able to sail the Salamis channel, and he examined ships with the discerning eye of a lifelong voyager.

What had the battle in the fatal straits really been like? How had victory fallen to an Athens that had become less a city than an encampment of two hundred warships and a hundred thousand exiles? How could defeat become the lot of the Persians, who had sacked Athens and made the mountains and valleys of Greece tremble?

These are the questions that Herodotus pondered. His answers to them are extensive, but they do not preserve every last detail of the battle of Salamis. Herodotus had the luxury of picking and choosing. So information that appears in another source can be considered even when Herodotus does not mention it. And yet it is worth being cautious about anything that *contradicts* Herodotus, because Herodotus was an excellent historian. He was one of the shrewdest and most skeptical students of the past who ever wrote, and also one of the most honest. After decades of being dismissed as a lightweight, Herodotus has of late been appreciated again, as he deserves to be, as a savvy and mainly reliable historian.

In the years after Herodotus finished his book shortly after 430 B.C., other ancient prose writers took on the subject of Salamis. They include one famous name, Plutarch, but they are mostly a collection of little-known or obscure writers. Most lived in the Roman era, but some of them did careful research in earlier Greek writings. Light is thrown on the battle from other, even more out-of-the-way evidence, drawn from Greek inscriptions, art, and archaeology. Then there is topographical, nautical, and meteorological information about the Salamis area today, often still of use for understanding ancient conditions, some of which—the winds, for example—have changed little since antiquity.

Meanwhile, far less data about the Persian Wars survives from the

Persian side. It is the Greek Herodotus who is our main source of information about Persian policy in the wars. And yet, today, by delving into the history of Salamis, we can present a new picture of the battle. It is not that Herodotus was wrong. Rather, he and other ancient sources have been misunderstood. If now they can be read right, it is for three reasons.

After years of being underestimated, ancient Persia is, thanks to new research, now viewed as Herodotus intended. A huge amount of data about Persia of indirect relevance to the Persian invasion of Greece has survived, and recent scholarship has exploited it well. This research shows that Persia was neither decadent nor dull but a formidable and innovative power from which the ancient Greeks—and the modern West—borrowed much.

As for the Greeks, they have long been celebrated as the noble sons of liberty. Now, however, we acknowledge them as the founders of imperial democracy. We can appreciate the Greeks' knowledge of the painful compromises a good society needed to make in order to survive in a hostile world.

Finally, a new focus in military history on the experience of battle, as well as a mass of evidence accruing from the hypothetical reconstruction of an ancient Greek warship, allows us to understand what happened at Salamis in a vivid way. We can hear the trumpets, we can feel the crash of the rams, and we can see the blood in the water.

Legend has it that Herodotus read his *Histories* aloud to audiences at Athens, Olympia, and elsewhere. Certainly, the book seems to have been composed with the spoken as well as the written word in mind. So it is not difficult to imagine that, shortly before he boarded a vessel in Piraeus, Herodotus addressed the public in Athens. A large audience might have gathered in the Odeon, a performance hall on the south slope of the Acropolis, which was said to have been built to resemble Xerxes' royal tent. The men, interspersed with the few women in attendance—courtesans and a smattering of aristocratic grandes dames, as no ordinary Athenian woman dared mix in public with men—would have looked forward to a virtuoso recital.

In a season of the present war and plague, the Athenian audience wanted to forget. They craved a story of the heroic past. As the speaker sat ready on the dais, the audience lent their ears to the eloquent old man.

The master stood up and began reciting:

What follows is an exhibition of the enquiries of Herodotus of Hali-carnassus. I write so that what men have done should not be erased by time and so that great and astonishing achievements of both Greeks and barbarians should not be without renown; among the matters covered is, in particular, the cause of the hostilities between Greeks and barbarians.*

* The Greeks called all non-Greeks barbarians, even very civilized peoples.

THE ADVANCE

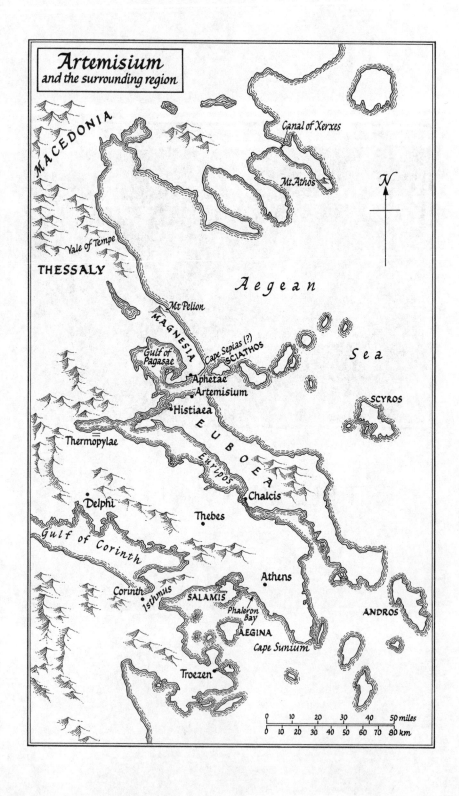

Artemisium
and the surrounding region

MACEDONIA

Canal of Xerxes

Mt.Athos

Vale of Tempe

THESSALY

Aegean

Mt Pelion

MAGNESIA

Gulf of Pagasae

Cape Sepias (?)

SCIATHOS

Aphetae

Artemisium

Sea

SCYROS

Histiaea

EUBOEA

Thermopylae

Euripos

Delphi

Chalcis

Thebes

Gulf of Corinth

Athens

Corinth

Isthmus

SALAMIS

Phaleron Bay

ANDROS

AEGINA

Cape Sunium

Troezen

N

| 0 | 10 | 20 | 30 | 40 | 50 miles |
| 0 | 10 | 20 | 30 | 40 | 50 | 60 | 70 | 80 km |

CHAPTER ONE

≈

ARTEMISIUM

Stifling in the August heat, even at night, Artemisium is a hub of activity. Seen by the light of bonfires, fifty thousand men are at work: here racing to patch damaged equipment, there hauling the bodies of the dead onto pyres, at one point filling water jugs and wineskins at the spring, at another point leaving messages as disinformation for the enemy, who is close behind them. Some men are buckling on bronze helmets, others are tightening the leather straps of the arrow cases they carry on their backs, while most are holding nothing more than a seat pad made of sheepskin. As the men work, the area's familiar scents of brine, thyme, and pine needles mix with the odor of sweat and the stink of corpses.

The cove is lined, at the shore's edge, with about 250 triremes, moored stern first. From each ship, a pair of ladders comes down and a horde of blistered hands grabs onto the rungs, as the rowers pull themselves up toward their seats. The rowers' grunts mix with the crackle of firewood, while the cries of the rowing masters drown out other sounds. The Greek navy is pulling out.

Of all the men crowding the beach, only one could fully make sense of the scene. Chief strategist of the Greeks, that man had planned for years for war with Persia, and now his hour had come. That man was Themistocles.

He cut a forceful presence that night. At about forty-five years of age, Themistocles of Athens, son of Neocles, was a veteran warrior. He would have worn a bronze helmet, a bronze breastplate over a linen tunic that reached to midthigh, greaves (bronze shin guards), and boots. Without his helmet he would have had a fleshy face framed by close-cropped hair and a thick beard and mustache. His forehead was deeply creased; his eyes were large, prominent, and a bit off-kilter. His high cheekbones flanked a blunt nose. His jaw was dominated by a mouth that represented the triumph of utility over grace.

It was the face of a monk or a mercenary. It is preserved in an ancient portrait bust whose inscription identifies this far-from-classical countenance as that of Themistocles. We do not know whether it is an accurate likeness, but if it is an invented portrait, it is inspired. The bust conveys irresistible force, as if of a powerful and intelligent man who needed only his will to wrest an enemy into submission.

For three days, from August 27 to 29, Themistocles led the Greek navy in its first test against the much more experienced Persians. The Greeks were based at Artemisium on the northern tip of the island of Euboea; the Persians were about ten miles away, across the channel, on the mainland. Although outnumbered more than two to one, the Greeks held the enemy to a standstill. Never mind the need to retreat, now that the defenses of the nearby pass of Thermopylae were pierced and the Spartan king Leonidas was dead; never mind the problem of evacuating more than a hundred thousand people from Athens; never mind the smoke and ruin of the Persians' advance: Themistocles had reason to be happy.

In three years he had turned Athens from a backwater into the first sea power in Greece, the proud possessor of two hundred triremes. He had built a fleet and hammered out a plan to save the city from the Persian invasion that he saw coming. And he had turned himself into both the first man in Athens and the kingpin of the Greek navy. Not bad for a man who came from outside the charmed circle of the Athenian aristocracy, a man who put his pragmatism bluntly:

I may not know how to tune the lyre or to handle the harp but I know how to take a small and unknown city and make it famous and great.

Not bad for a man who appalled the old guard, a man about whom the philosopher Plato later complained that he turned the Athenians from steadfast infantrymen into a sailors' rabble. But then, Themistocles was a champion in the game of broad-shouldered, no-holds-barred fighting that was Athenian politics. It was a new game, invented when Themistocles was just a teenager. In 508 B.C., a revolution had turned Athens into one of history's first democracies.

Only a democracy could have put together the manpower to staff two hundred triremes—forty thousand men—and the willpower to use them well. As Herodotus says, democracy energized Athens:

When the Athenians lived under a tyranny they were no better at war than any of their neighbors, but after they got rid of the tyrants they were the first by far. This proves that when they were oppressed they fought badly on purpose as if they were slaving away for a master, but after they were liberated they each were eager to get the job done for his own sake.

Themistocles was that rare thing in a democracy, a leader. He had no fear of speaking truths to the people. By the same token, he knew that a straight line is not always the shortest distance between two points. He was known for his shrewdness and his shock tactics, or what the Greeks called *deinotēs* (pronounced "day-NO-tays"). *Deinotēs* can mean a quick remark or a catastrophe; it can be applied to an orator or a lightning bolt; it can be used as a compliment or a criticism. All of these shades of meaning fitted Themistocles.

Themistocles was brilliant, farsighted, creative, tireless, magnanimous, courageous, and eloquent. Yet it is also true that during the course of his career he lied, cheated, blustered, and threatened; grabbed credit for others' ideas; manipulated religion; took bribes and extorted protection money; served up insult and pursued vendetta; and ended his days in exile, a traitor. In short, Themistocles was no angel, but seraphim could not have saved the Greeks.

In the spring of 480 B.C., the members of the Greek alliance against Persia, the Hellenic League, met at the Isthmus of Corinth to chart strategy. The Persians were coming, invading Greece in force. It was the latest stage in a war that had already lasted a generation.

The war began when Athens insulted the mighty Persian Empire by promising to become its ally around 508 B.C. but then reneged. Athenian ambassadors to the empire made a symbolic gift of earth and water as a sign of submission, but the Athenian government refused to support them. The quarrel worsened when Athens later threw two Persian ambassadors into a pit for condemned criminals, which was probably the prelude to execution. Much worse, Athens next provided military aid to the Ionian Revolt of 499 to 494 B.C., a rebellion of Persia's Greek and Carian subjects in western Anatolia. The Greeks had lived in Anatolia for centuries; the Carians went back even further, and might have been related to the Trojans. In the Ionian Revolt, the Athenians briefly captured the Persian provincial capital of Sardis and started a fire there that burned out of control and destroyed the temple of the goddess Cybele.

Persia put down the Ionian Revolt in 494 B.C. The decisive battle was fought at sea near Lade, an island off the coast of Anatolia and near the Greek city-state of Miletus, the ringleader of the revolt. Now it was time for revenge on Athens. King Darius of Persia sent an armada across the Aegean Sea to invade Athens in 490 B.C. But at the battle of Marathon, in Athenian territory twenty-four miles from the city of Athens, Athenian infantrymen crushed Persia's soldiers and saved their country. Themistocles was one of the Athenians in the line of battle.

Now, ten years later, the Persians were coming back, this time in massive numbers. The Greeks who met at the Isthmus of Corinth in the spring of 480 B.C. came up with a defense strategy that had three basic elements. First, since Persia would attack both by land and sea, the Greeks would respond with an army and a navy. The Peloponnese would provide most of the infantrymen, since Athens would devote all its manpower to its big navy. Second, since Persia was attacking Athens via northern Greece rather than by island-hopping across the Aegean, the allies would mount a forward defense in northern Greece. It was better to try to stop Persia there than at the gates of Athens. Third, time was on the Greeks' side. For political reasons, the Persian king wanted a quick victory, and for practical reasons, the Persian quartermasters could not supply their huge force for very long. Therefore, the Greeks might well have intended to drag out the war until the Persians gave up.

The Greeks began their defense in the north. Their first thrust consisted of an army of ten thousand men to hold the mountain pass known as the Vale of Tempe, which runs between Macedonia and Thessaly. Themistocles led the force. But when he got to Tempe in June or July of 480 B.C., he discovered two other passes nearby. Since it would be impossible to close all three passes to Persia, he withdrew southward. Tempe had been a failure of intelligence—a sign of how little the Greeks knew about their own country and how much darkness ancient strategists often worked in.

But Artemisium was a strategist's triumph. If Themistocles did not choose it as a base, he quickly grasped its importance. It was close enough to Thermopylae to allow a coordinated land-sea strategy. The Greek fleet at Artemisium would keep Persian reinforcements from arriving by sea and cutting off the Greek army holding the pass at Thermopylae.

The Greeks could have stationed their fleet closer to Thermopylae, which is forty miles away from Artemisium. But nearness was not the only issue. Nor was the potential battlefield, since the straits at Artemisium are ten miles wide, and the Greeks might have preferred fighting in narrower waters, where Persia could not deploy its full number of ships. Yet Artemisium offered other advantages.

Artemisium was the region's best harbor because it was large, sheltered, and rich in sources of drinking water. By occupying it themselves, the Greeks denied Artemisium to the enemy. That meant that the Persians could not land on the strategic island of Euboea without a challenge from the Greek fleet. Nor could the Persian fleet bypass the island without risking a Greek challenge.

Since triremes were both too fragile and too uncomfortable for a long stay at sea, trireme fleets did not mount blockades in the modern sense of the word. Rather, they moored in a harbor near the enemy and ventured out to challenge him. In order to be ready, they used scouts both on land and sea to follow enemy movements and to signal information.

From Artemisium the Greeks could challenge the Persian fleet's southward advance in either of two directions. The rocky east coast of the island of Euboea is hostile to sailors, so the Persians were likely to avoid it. The west coast of Euboea is gentler. Its harbors open onto an inland waterway between Euboea and the Greek mainland, a sheltered passage for the Persian navy from northern Greece to Athens. It is completely navigable even if, at about its midpoint, the channel narrows to a width of forty yards of water, a sound called the Euripos. Hence, the Greeks at Artemisium expected a Persian move to the southwest.

Recognizing the Greeks' plan, the Persians coordinated their attack on Artemisium and on Thermopylae. Although they had not planned matters quite so precisely, the land and sea battles there turned out to be fought on precisely the same three days in late August, 480 B.C.

The Greeks would have rejoiced to stop Persia via the joint operations at Thermopylae and Artemisium. But they did not need to fulfill that tall order; merely bloodying Persia and slowing it down would be a Greek success. To force casualties and delay would shake Persia's resolve while it would give the Greeks a taste of Persian tactics—invaluable knowledge for use in the next battle. And so, the Greek navy sat at Artemisium and waited for the barbarian.

Artemisium was usually a sleepy place: a scene of blue water, a sandy beach, and dark green and silver-gray groves of pine and olive, in August dotted with orange clumps of late-blooming crocuses. The nearest town was eight miles away, but on a hill beside the bay (today's Pevki Bay) stood a little temple of Artemis Prosēoia, that is, Artemis Who Looks Toward the East, and the name suited Greece's chief naval base against the threat from the East.

Yet like all forward bases, Artemisium offered advantage and danger in equal measure. If the Greek fleet faltered, its men would be adrift in hostile country. That is, if they survived. Persia wanted to smash the enemy navy and gain control of the sea-lanes southward, which meant crippling Greece's boats and killing its sailors. The Persians wanted to wipe out every last Greek, down to the Spartan priest whose job it was to keep alight the sacred fire brought from the altar of Zeus back in Sparta.

The Greeks' exposed position was risk enough, but worse still was the Greek navy's size. In 480 B.C., the Greek world stretched from Anatolia to the Bay of Naples; there was even a smattering of Greeks as far east as the Caucasus and as far west as Spain. All told, there were fifteen hundred Greek city-states. Yet only a relative handful—only thirty-one city-states—joined the coalition against Persia.

In fact, more Greek city-states fought on the other side. Persia was too strong and loyalty to the idea of Greece too weak to make the Hellenic League any more powerful. Athens, Sparta, and the few other city-states that stood up to Persia spoke harshly of Greek traitors, but most Greeks would have shrugged their shoulders at the charge.

Of the thirty-one members of the Hellenic League, a mere fourteen city-states manned the warships at Artemisium, for a total of 280 warships—271 triremes and 9 penteconters. Later, Athens sent 53 ships as reinforcements, making a total of 333 warships. Athens provided 180 ships at Artemisium, by far the largest contingent; the ships were partly manned by Athens's allies in Plataea. The next largest unit was the 40 ships from Corinth, followed by 20 from Megara, 20 more from Athens manned by crews from Chalcis, 18 from Aegina, and eight smaller contingents.

Opposite the Greeks sailed a navy that vastly outnumbered them. The Persians had no fewer than 1,207 triremes when they set out on their expedition, and another 120 joined them as they added new allies on their advance through northern Greece toward Artemisium—for a total of 1,327 ships.

Both fleets had to cope with the strains and cracks of multinational armadas. But the differences among the Greek city-states were small compared to the contrasts in the floating tower of Babel that was the Persian fleet. It combined Phoenicians, Egyptians, Greeks, Cypriots, and various non-Greek peoples of Anatolia, from Carians to Pamphylians. With all its different languages, communication alone was no small problem for the fleet, let alone coordinating operations at sea.

Four Persian nobles, including two princes, held the supreme command. Yet there was not a single Persian ship in their navy. Every ship carried a mix of marines and archers, including some Persians, but not one of the rowers or seamen was Persian. The Persians were not seafarers.

The Greeks, by contrast, practically had salt water running in their veins, so wedded were they to the sea. The *Odyssey*, that quintessential sailor's story, was one of the two national epics known to every Greek boy. But the Greek coalition against Persia was led by a land power—Sparta. By tradition Greece's greatest city-state, Sparta prided itself on its military virtue. The Greek alliance was known as the Hellenic League. Sparta insisted on holding the supreme command at sea, as it did on land. In the interests of Greek unity, Athens agreed. Yet with its two hundred warships, Athens had by far the largest and strongest Greek navy. Although a Spartan named Eurybiades son of Eurycleides was commander of the Greek fleet, Themistocles amounted to its main strategist.

But his genius was hardly evident at the outset. In the first naval clash of the war, the Greeks sent three ships north to reconnoiter; they were based on the island of Sciathos, about fifteen miles northeast of Artemisium. A Persian contingent advanced toward them, and the Greek ships fled at the first sight of it. Two of them were captured, and the third was beached and abandoned by its crew. The abandoned ship was Athenian, and the two captured ships were from Aegina and Troezen. The Persians focused on the Troezenian ship, because it was the first captured Greek vessel of the war. They picked through the dozen marines until they found the best-looking one. Then they hauled him to the prow and slit his throat. They considered it lucky to sacrifice the best-looking man among their first prisoners. Besides, the victim's name was Leon, "lion," and it was auspicious to kill the king of the beasts.

The fleet at Artemisium learned the news via fire signals transmitted from a mountaintop on Sciathos to a mountaintop on Euboea. In the clear skies of the Mediterranean, fire signals could be seen from far off. They were visible as smoke signals during the day and as beacons at night. Modern tests show that the signals were visible between mountaintops up to a distance of two hundred miles.

Having seen the signal, the fleet withdrew southward into the Euboean channel, all the way to the city of Chalcis. They left scouts in the hills above Artemisium to report Persian movements to them. Scouts had to be fast runners and good horsemen—for those occasions when horses were available. They had to travel light and not call attention to themselves, so they might be armed only with a dagger.

Where, we wonder, was the bold Themistocles? Herodotus says that the Greek move was just plain panic. If he is right, then presumably Themistocles had been overruled by the other generals. But there may be other explanations of the Greek withdrawal. Perhaps the Greeks suspected a bold Persian move via Sciathos down the east coast of Euboea, and they were racing to beat them. Another possibility might be that, with their local knowledge, the Greeks could tell that a dangerous storm was brewing and so had withdrawn to a sheltered position.

Meanwhile, the Persians were heading toward Artemisium, sailing southward down the coast of northeastern Greece, opposite Mount Pelion. The rugged Pelion peninsula rises abruptly from the sea. Unable to find a harbor large enough for all their ships, the Persians were forced to moor their fleet in eight lines parallel to the coast, near Cape Sepias. That in turn left them vulnerable to what Herodotus calls a "monster storm." It lasted three days, until the heavens bowed to the prayers of Persia's priests. Most Greeks saw the storm as the work of Boreas, god of the north wind.

For months after the storm, gold and silver cups and even treasure chests washed up on shore, making one local Greek landowner a millionaire. Herodotus reports that, by conservative estimates, the Persians lost four hundred warships and innumerable sailors. The size of the fleet had been reduced from 1,327 to about 927 warships. It was a terrific blow, but the Persian fleet was still enormous.

Having recovered, the Persian fleet rounded the Pelion peninsula and arrived opposite Artemisium, at a harbor called Aphetae, the legendary starting point of Jason and the Argonauts. Aphetae is probably best thought of as the Persians' naval command post; their fleet was too bulky for any one harbor and so was probably spread out over several.

By now their scouts had rushed news to the Greeks at Chalcis of the disastrous storm. No doubt, the tale grew with the telling. Convinced that the Persians were ruined, the Greeks said a prayer of thanksgiving to the god of the sea, Poseidon, whom they now dubbed Poseidon the Savior. Then they hurried back north to Artemisium. They were in for a shock.

When the Greeks at Artemisium looked across the straits at the enemy and saw how big Persia's fleet remained in spite of the storm, they panicked. There was talk of a retreat, and that, in turn, galvanized the local Euboeans. Unable to convince Eurybiades to stay long enough for them to evacuate women and children, the Euboeans turned to Themistocles. He proved willing to stay—for a price. The Euboeans paid him the huge sum of thirty talents of silver, enough money to employ a hundred workmen for six years, or to buy a thousand slaves, or to pay the crews of thirty triremes for a season's work. After turning over five talents to Eurybiades and three talents to the Corinthian commander, Adimantus son of Ocytus, Themistocles had twenty-two talents left for himself, a fact that he did not advertise. The Greek fleet stayed at Artemisium.

We might say that the Euboeans paid Themistocles and his colleagues a bribe, but the ancient Greeks would have called it a gift. Their language had no word for bribe, but their culture valued gift-giving. Homer's heroes heaped up gold, bulls, and women for their feats of prowess; Herodotus's politicians expected to have their palms greased. Contemporaries accepted the practice; indeed, Athenian law winked at a public servant who took private money as long as he used it in the best interests of the people.

Around this time, the Greeks at Artemisium got a windfall. Fifteen Persian stragglers mistakenly made for Artemisium instead of Aphetae and so sailed right into enemy hands. The Greeks got not only fifteen triremes but also three important Persian commanders, including the governor of Aeolis, a region in northwest Anatolia that included the city of Cyme, a major naval harbor, as well as a Carian tyrant and a commander from Cyprus. After interrogation, they were shipped off in chains to the Isthmus of Corinth.

Meanwhile, the Persians at Aphetae came up with a battle plan. They needed a stratagem, they reasoned, because if they simply came out and fought, the terrified Greeks would turn and flee. So, to prevent a Greek escape, the Persians set a trap. The Persians would send two hundred ships around the east coast of Euboea; once they rounded the southern tip of the island, they would double back along the west coast and emerge west of Artemisium. Then, at a signal, the main Persian fleet would pounce.

Clever though it seems, their plan betrays a landlubber's mentality. It was one thing to turn an enemy's flank on a level plain, quite another to do so along Euboea's windswept and treacherous eastern coast. Besides, a deserter warned the Greeks what Persia was up to. Scyllias of Scione was a northern Greek in Persia's service who was known as the best diver of his day. Herodotus scoffs at reports that he swam the ten-mile straits—underwater!—to reach the Greeks; instead, he says, Scyllias probably stole across in a boat. But the Greeks had primitive snorkels, and perhaps by surfacing every now and then, Scyllias did manage what was mainly an underwater swim. In any case, he delivered the news both of Persia's losses in the storm and of the dispatch of the two hundred ships.

Before deciding on their next move, the Greeks went through a long and barely decisive debate. They finally agreed to launch their ships at midnight to meet the Persian contingent of two hundred ships. Presumably they planned to sail southward and attack the ships in isolation. That was a bad idea because it would have drawn the main Persian fleet out after them, and fortunately, the Greeks never followed through. By the afternoon, with no sign of the two hundred Persian ships, the Greeks changed their minds. They would attack the main body of the Persian fleet.

It was a crazy plan, or so it seemed. Ancient navies rarely chose to fight without a friendly shore nearby, but the Greek fleet had purposely left its base at Artemisium to head across the channel. The Greeks, moreover, had 271 warships, the Persians over 700, plus the menacing 200 ships from the south. On top of that, Persian triremes were faster than Greek triremes.

Supreme in numbers and speed, the Persians could hardly believe their eyes when they saw the Greeks bearing down on them. The Persians quickly manned their ships to meet the attack. The Persian crews were confident of success, and they competed for the honor of being the first to capture an enemy ship, especially a ship from the best Greek contingent, the Athenians. The Ionian Greeks in the Persian fleet pitied their fellow Greeks on the other side. The way the Ionians saw it, not a single man in the Greek navy would make it home.

The Greek attack was as crazy as it was cunning and calculated and courageous. It bears the hallmark of that master tactician Themistocles. The Athenian single-handedly overcame all opposition and talked the Greeks into taking the offensive. Who else could have conceived such a brilliant use of timing, precision, and shock?

Themistocles carefully planned the attack for the evening. Ancient navies reluctantly *traveled* in the dark, but they dared not *fight* in the dark, so the engagement would be brief. It would, in fact, be less of a battle than a raid, and indeed, an experiment. Under carefully controlled conditions, the Greeks would be able to test the enemy's battle skills, particularly at the maneuver known as the *diekplous*.

Diekplous means "rowing through and out." In this dangerous maneuver, a single trireme or, preferably, a line of triremes rowed through a gap in the enemy line and attacked. The decks would be lined with soldiers and archers at the ready, but their role was mainly defensive. The main weapon was the attacking ship's ram: it was used to smash into the quarter (the stern part) of the enemy trireme. The Phoenicians were especially good at this maneuver, as an ancient source notes:

> *When the Phoenicians are lined up opposite the enemy face-to-face,*
> *in line abreast, they bear down as if to ram head-on, but instead of*
> *doing so they row through the enemy's line and turn and attack the*
> *exposed sides of the enemy ships.*

Another tactic in the *diekplous* was to shear off the oars of one side of an enemy trireme, thereby crippling it. The inertial force would wound or possibly kill rowers on the enemy vessel. Meanwhile, the rowers of the attacking ship had to pull in their own oars at the crucial last minute in order to keep from damaging them.

The *diekplous* was a deadly dance and as complex as any ballet. The Greek fleet needed to stop the enemy's dance and to answer it with a maneuver of its own. Success came only with experience, and few rowers in the Athenian fleet had ever executed maneuvers in battle. They had no doubt practiced during the two summers since the building of Athens's new fleet, but those were only rehearsals. Nor had the entire Greek fleet fought together before. That first evening at Artemisium marked the debut of the Greek fleet—and it was brilliant.

Just before launching their ships, the Greeks no doubt took care of the customary pre-battle rituals. The priests who took part in every city-state's forces—just as chaplains accompany modern armies—sacrificed animals in order to gain the gods' approval. Then, as they launched their ships and rowed toward the enemy, the trumpets sounded, and some if not all of the crews bucked up their spirits by singing a battle hymn, or, as the Greeks called it, a paean.

A well-rowed and carefully coordinated fleet would have made a stunning impression. Themistocles was in the thick of things. Ancient generals did not lead from the rear. As an Athenian commander, Themistocles would have directed the attack from a well-marked flagship, perhaps flying a purple flag at the stern. He would have sat in a raised position on the quarterdeck, from which he could follow events and issue orders. But it was a vulnerable position: in a battle at a later date, for example, a Spartan general was thrown from the deck when his ship was rammed, and he drowned.

It was the general's responsibility to make a battle plan and then to see that his ships carried it out. He had to see to it that the ships stayed in line. A general gave the orders to advance and to retreat, to spread out or to pull into a more compact formation. If the enemy behavior proved to be different from what had been expected, it was up to the general to change battle plans and to inform his lieutenants to spread the word.

As surprised by the Greek attack as they were contemptuous of it, the Persians, a superior force, did the obvious thing: they surrounded the enemy. With their huge numbers and a channel ten miles wide, they could easily outflank the Greek line. In fact, as Herodotus reports, the Persians actually encircled the Greeks. But they had played right into Themistocles' hands.

The Greek commanders ordered a prearranged signal. Signaling at sea was often done by flashing sunlight off a burnished shield; a mirror or even a cutlass could be used as well. If the sun was too low at this late hour, and if the light was wrong for waving a white or scarlet linen flag—another means of signaling—then the signal was probably called by the sound of trumpets rising above the din.

At the signal, the Greeks followed their plan and arranged their boats in a defensive circle. They might have carried out the maneuver by having each of the two wings of their line back water, that is, to continue to force the enemy but row backwards, stern first; meanwhile the center maintained its position. Now every boat faced prow out, with the sterns drawn close together. The ring was too tight for the Persians to penetrate. Meanwhile, the self-assured Persians probably felt no need to keep their ships in so strict an order.

The ships of the two fleets could hardly have been closer to each other; they stood prow to prow or, to use the ancient Greek expression, mouth to mouth. To put it differently, the two fleets would fight in an artificially created narrow space. Themistocles had maneuvered the enemy precisely where he wanted it, where Athens's heavier ships could do the most damage. We can only speculate as to whether Themistocles had also chosen a moment when the wind was favorable.

On deck, the soldiers and archers kept at the ready, careful not to shift position and unbalance the boat. The pilot loosely held the two rudder oars, waiting for a call to action. Meanwhile, below deck, the rowers, arranged on three levels, sat silently on their benches, ears pricked for the piper, whose rhythm their strokes would soon follow.

The rowers sitting on the top level might catch glimpses of the scene outside by peering between the ship's wooden posts and the horsehair screens set up for the battle to protect them from enemy arrows. The lower two levels of rowers could only imagine what lay outside. As they headed for an appointment with death, their world consisted only of the 170 men within the wooden walls. It was a world permeated by the odors of pine, from the resin pitch used to protect the hold from seawater, and of mutton, from the sheep tallow used to lubricate the leather sleeves through which the oars passed. And everywhere was the smell of sweat and flatulence and occasionally of vomit.

Now came Themistocles' coup. At a second signal, selected Greek triremes darted out of the circle, went through the loose enemy line, picked off vulnerable Persian triremes, and escaped. The preferred Greek tactics were either to ram a Persian vessel and then back off or to shear off the enemy's oars on one side and then turn and flee. In either case, this superbly executed countermaneuver stopped the enemy's *diekplous* and yielded the Greeks thirty enemy vessels as well as another important captive, a notable man in the Persian forces named Philaon son of Chersis, the brother of King Gorgus, king of the city of Salamis in Cyprus (a different place from Athens's island of Salamis). An Athenian captain, one Lycomedes son of Aeschraeus of the deme of Phyla, won the prize for bravery because he was the first Greek to capture a Persian warship. A Greek ship in Persian service, captained by Antidorus of the island of Lemnos, defected to the Greek side. Two years of hard training had paid off for the Athenians. The Persians probably never knew what hit them.

The dispirited Persians headed back to their base at Aphetae, but their troubles were not over. That night saw a loud and violent thunderstorm, unseasonable in the Greek summer. The weather played havoc with Persian morale, as Herodotus reports:

Corpses and the wreckage of the ships were carried to Aphetae, where they clustered around the prows of the ships and got in the way of the blades of the oars. The crews grew frightened when they heard about this, and they expected that they were going to die, given all the troubles they had encountered.

The morning brought worse news. The same rainstorm that frightened the men at Aphetae had also wrecked the two-hundred-ship Persian contingent that had been sent around Euboea's east coast. Survivors hurried back to Aphetae with the news. There would be no entrapment of the Greeks at Artemisium.

As if to drive the point home, the Greeks attacked the Persians again that very afternoon, waiting once more until the hour was late. Greek spirits were buoyed by the news of Persia's disaster around Euboea and by the arrival of fifty-three triremes from Athens as reinforcements. Information is scanty about the second engagement off Artemisium, but we may speculate that the Greeks pounced on a Persian squadron rather than the whole fleet. At any rate, the Greeks destroyed some ships from Cilicia (a region in southern Anatolia) and then sailed back to Artemisium.

Finally, on the third day, Persia's frustrated commanders initiated their own attack. By now they were worried about soon having to face the anger of their absent king, who was off directing the fighting at Thermopylae but would hear the news from Artemisium. They sailed out around midday. The commanders exhorted their men: "Destroy the Greek fleet and gain control of the waterway!"

As the Persians rowed across in battle order, the Greeks kept calm, embarked on their ships, and kept close to Artemisium. Their generals too exhorted their men: "The barbarians shall not pass into the heart of Greece!"

The Persians arranged their ships in a semicircle, hoping to surround the Greeks and crush them. But it did not work out. We do not know precisely how they did it, but somehow the outnumbered Greeks once again made their quality equal the quantity of the enemy. Maybe the battle took place at the entrance to the bay where the Greek triremes were moored; a narrow space that worked to the advantage of the heavy Athenian vessels. Maybe the Greeks arranged their ships in a double line as a defense against the enemy's *diekplous*. The ships in the second line would try to pick off any Persian ship that broke through before it could turn and ram a Greek ship in the front line. We know that a man named Heraclides of Mylasa, a refugee from Persian rule, used precisely this tactic against Phoenician ships in a battle of Artemisium. But Artemisium was a common name, and we do not know if the anecdote about Heraclides refers to *this* battle.

However they did it, the Greeks managed to put the enemy off balance. Instead of helping, Persia's superiority in number of ships hurt. The ships of the enormous fleet kept falling afoul of themselves, as boats could not avoid colliding with one another.

Still, the Persians refused to yield. They were too proud to let so small a fleet make them turn tail. The battle continued until nightfall, when both sides were bruised enough to be eager to end it. Herodotus reports that both sides lost many ships and men. But there was bad news for Persia even so. Their losses far outnumbered the Greeks'.

Tactically, the battle of the third day was a draw, but in terms of strategy, it was a Greek victory. At Artemisium, Persia had hoped to knock the Greek fleet out of the war. Yet the Greek fleet had not just survived the worst Persia had to offer but had actually won two out of the three engagements. It was a blow to Persia's naval pride.

There would be a rematch between the two fleets, of course, but that would take place further south, near Athens or the Peloponnese. There, the Greeks would have the great advantage of familiar waters. The Persians, meanwhile, would be ever further from their base, ever deeper in hostile territory, ever more troubled by the food supply.

And as important as the battles off Artemisium were, they took second place to the storms that had buffeted the Persian fleet. The Persians had left northern Greece with 1,327 triremes. They suffered the staggering loss of 600 ships to storms; add battle losses, and the Persians probably had only about 650 ships left after Artemisium. As Herodotus commented on the storm that wrecked 200 Persian ships off Euboea, "it was all done by the god so that the Greek force would be saved and the Persian force would be not be much greater than it." True, the Persians still outnumbered the Greeks, but the unreliability of some of Persia's squadrons further reduced their numerical advantage.

Back at Artemisium and at Aphetae, prizes were awarded for valor else, too: Persia won the battle of Lade by diplomacy, not skill at sea. The main Greek contingent, which came from the island of Samos, agreed to desert, and that threw the battle to Persia. In other words, the Persian fleet had not proven itself to be supreme in battle.

Aware of all this, the Greeks at Artemisium were no doubt intrigued by Themistocles' promise of getting the Ionians and Carians to desert. They asked him how he would manage it. That, said Themistocles, was a secret for the moment. It would be revealed in good time. For now, let the details be left to him. Also, he asked for the authority to choose the moment when the fleet would make the prudent retreat homeward that was now obviously necessary.

Never docile, Themistocles' colleagues nonetheless agreed. Perhaps they were persuaded by his arguments, or perhaps they reasoned that he would make a convenient scapegoat should things go wrong. Or maybe the issue was decided by the distraction with which Themistocles tempted them: food.

He advised the generals to order the men to light watch fires and to slaughter the sheep and goats that the Euboean locals had incautiously driven nearby at day's end. Sheep-stealing in Greece is as old as the *Odyssey*, but the generals nonetheless felt the need to justify their act; if *they* hadn't grabbed the beasts, they reasoned, the Persians would have. Lamb and goat were a treat, compared to the usual fare of barley groats, salt fish, garlic, and onions. But then, many of the men had just had the hardest three days of their lives. Most of them had never before experienced hearing the roar of charging warships or seeing pale corpses slip beneath the waves.

That night, while meat crackled on wooden spits along the shore, the scene might have looked from a distance like one of those all-night festivals under the stars that the Greeks so loved. The constellations of the Bear and the Archer (as the Greeks referred to them; we call them the Big Dipper and Sagittarius) were low and prominent in the summer sky, and the shore was lit by thousands of fires. But close up, among the exhausted men, it was no scene of celebration. The word was out: the navy would be pulling out the next morning. Themistocles had chosen his moment. Then came the news from Thermopylae. The Persians had broken through the pass and slaughtered the Spartans, including the Spartan king.

in battle. Xerxes gave the honors to his Egyptian sailors for capturing five Greek ships, crews and all. That is, according to Herodotus: another tradition says that the Phoenicians of the city of Sidon took Persian honors for Artemisium. The five ships under Queen Artemisia of Halicarnassus also fought in the thick of battle. On the Greek side, Athens won the prize, and among the Athenians, the pride of place belonged to Cleinias son of Alcibiades, a wealthy aristocrat who provided two hundred sailors and his own trireme, all at his own expense. But there was little time for celebration. There was work to do: both sides had to collect their corpses and salvage what they could of their wrecks. The Athenians had suffered damage to fully half of their triremes.

But Themistocles was already looking ahead. He called together the Greek generals and told them that he had a plan. He thought that he might be able to detach the Ionians and the Carians from the enemy, and said that they were the best units in the Persian fleet. (The Phoenicians, for one, would not have agreed.)

Without a doubt, many Ionian Greeks and many Carians had reason to hate Persia. For example, they knew how Persia had treated the people of Miletus after the Ionian Revolt. Most of the men were killed, the women and children were made slaves, and those men who were captured alive were eventually resettled on the Persian Gulf.

Or take the islanders of Chios, whose experience at the naval battle of Lade in 494 B.C. was an epic in miniature. One hundred Chian ships took part in the fight. Although most of the Greek ships fled at the start, the Chians fought hard and captured a number of Persian ships. Finally, however, the badly outnumbered Chians lost most of their own ships, and the survivors fled for home.

But some of Chios's ships had been damaged, and the enemy ran them aground on the mainland. From there, the crews made their way on foot to the territory of Ephesus, a Greek city. By now it was dark. As it happened, the women of Ephesus were gathered outside the city to celebrate a festival. The men of Ephesus, terrified by the sudden appearance of a group of armed strangers, attacked the Chians and slaughtered them to the last man. Such was the tragic end of their struggle for freedom.

The Ionians remembered this, and they remembered something

The Greek navy had to leave Artemisium in self-defense. But they also had to leave in order to protect their wives and children at home farther south. Now that Thermopylae had fallen, the road to Athens was open. The main city-state between Thermopylae and Athens was Thebes, and Thebes had joined the Persians. The Persian king had sworn to destroy Athens, and now there was nothing to stop his army razing it to the ground. Sparta had promised to send an army to protect Athens, but after Thermopylae, it could not do so. The Athenian fleet had to hurry home to carry out the emergency plan prepared in advance.

Instead of waiting for the morning, the Greeks began to pull out that very night. After cremating their dead and manning their ships, they took care of one final detail before departure, something they dared not neglect because an oversight would have meant disaster. Every Greek, especially sailors, a group, then as now, famously super-stitious, knew that they must pray to the gods for a safe journey. It was a traditional ceremony that dates as far back as Homer. The Greeks said their prayers, sang a hymn, and poured a cup of wine from the stern of each ship as an offering to the deities. Then, finally, they left Artemisium.

Athens's resolution in its retreat is recalled by these lines, later inscribed on a white marble pillar near the temple at Artemisium:

With numerous tribes from Asia's region brought
The sons of Athens on these waters fought;
Erecting, after they had quelled the Mede,
To Artemis this record of the deed.

The poet Pindar put the meaning of Artemisium succinctly:

There the sons of Athens set
The stone that freedom stands on yet.

But the final word about Artemisium belongs to Themistocles. As the Greeks prepared to pull out, he ordered them to leave messages for the Persians who would shortly take over their camp. The task was entrusted to Athens's fastest ships, in the expectation that they could catch up to the rest of the fleet. On the rocks around the several springs at the site, Themistocles had them display placards and also paint messages to the tens of thousands of Greek sailors in Xerxes' navy. Not many of those men could read, which meant that the literate few would read the statements out loud, and the report would echo around the beach. According to Herodotus, the messages read as follows:

> *Men of Ionia, you are doing wrong by making war upon your fathers and enslaving Greece. The best thing that you can do is to join us; if you cannot do this, you might at least remain neutral, and ask the Carians to do the same. If you cannot do either of these things, but are held by a force so strong that you cannot step aside, then when we get down to cases and next meet in battle, fight badly on purpose, mindful that you are descended from our ancestors and that we inherited our hatred of the barbarian from you.*

Themistocles calculated that the messages would have one of two effects: they would either lead to desertions from the Persian fleet or make the Persians distrust their Greek sailors. It was, in short, wicked propaganda. No less could be expected of a man once called the subtle serpent of the Greeks.

CHAPTER TWO

≈

THERMOPYLAE

Stripped of its helmet, Leonidas's head is framed by its long hair.
The taut skin of the warrior's face, its color gone, stands out all
the more against a short and pointed beard. The dirt of battle is
probably still upon Leonidas, and there is a dark purple bruise on his
chin from the pooling of what little blood is left. Ragged bits of tissue
and bone hang from his severed neck, and flies and beetles have landed
on his skin. If the dead king's eyes could see, they might look all the
way to Athens, the road to which now lies open for Persia.

Leonidas son of Anaxandrides, king of Sparta, commander in chief of
the Greek resistance to Persia at Thermopylae, died in a heroic last stand.
After the battle, as Xerxes son of Darius, the Great King of Persia, toured
the battlefield, he came upon Leonidas's body and ordered the beheading
of the corpse and the impalement of the severed head on a pole. One of
those who no doubt saw Leonidas's severed head was the former king of
Sparta, Demaratus son of Ariston, now allied with the Persians.

Three kings were present at the aftermath of the battle of Thermopylae. One sat on the greatest throne in the world, the second was
deposed and exiled, and the third was dead. Yet the actions of the dead
man, as explained by the exile, almost turned the ruling monarch from
his appointed course and changed the entire history of the Persian
invasion of Greece. Leonidas almost kept the battle of Salamis from
ever happening.

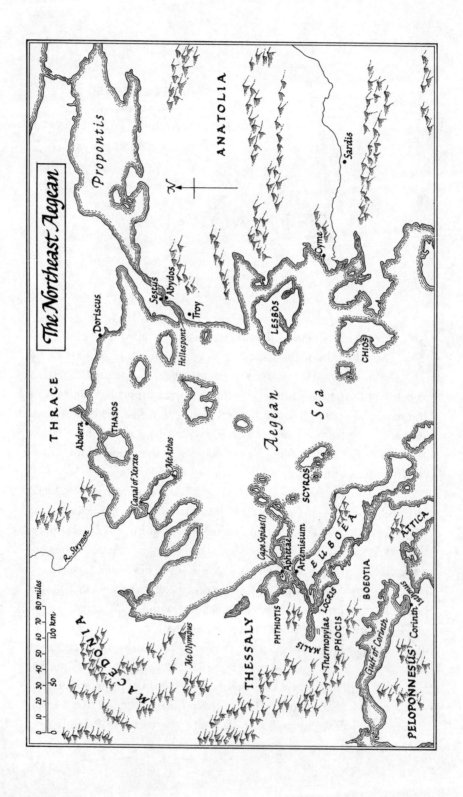

The Northeast Aegean

Thermopylae was the turning point. It raised the stakes of everything that would follow. Xerxes had learned how high the price of victory would be, if Persia could pay it at all.

A humiliation for the Persians, Thermopylae had been Leonidas's
finest hour. He held off the Persians for three days. Fewer than eight
thousand Greeks, spearheaded by an elite unit of three hundred Spartans, gave a savage beating to a Persian army that outnumbered them
by a ratio of perhaps twenty to one. Men willing to die for the glory of
the Great King came up against the most efficient killing machine in
history.

On one side had stood the Spartan soldier. With his bronze helmet,
breastplate, and greaves, each Spartan seemed to be sheathed in metal.
There was bronze, too, in the plating of his shield, which was large, cir-
cular, and convex in shape. A crimson-colored, sleeveless wool tunic
extended from shoulders to midthigh. The braids of his long hair ran
out from under his helmet, while a horsehair plume swayed above it.
The long hair, a Spartan trademark, was meant to look fearsome. Each
Spartan was barefoot, itself a symbol of toughness, and carried a short
iron sword and a long pike. The latter, which was his main weapon, was
an ash-wood spear, about nine feet long, with an iron spearhead and a
bronze butt-spike. Arranged in close order in the phalanx, shields
interlocking, the Spartans thrust at the enemy with their pikes.

On the other side there had stood the Persian and Median
infantrymen, soldiers of the two leading peoples of Iran. By comparison with the Spartans, they looked as if they were dressed for the
parade ground rather than the battlefield. Each Iranian wore a brightly
colored, sleeved, knee-length tunic, under which an iron-scaled breastplate protected the torso, but he had neither helmet nor greaves. He
wore a felt hat or a turban on his head, while his lower body was covered either by a long draped robe or a pair of trousers. He wore gold
jewelry, even into battle. His feet were protected by shoes. His shield
was smaller than a Greek's and made of wicker rather than of wood and
bronze plating. The Persian spear was much shorter than the Greek
pike, which put the Iranians at a disadvantage against an enemy with a
longer reach. Nor could the dagger carried by an Iranian outreach the
Spartan sword. Unlike the Greek infantryman, the typical Iranian soldier carried a quiver full of cane arrows with bronze or iron points and

a bow with its ends shaped like animal heads. Yet Persian arrows could do little damage against a wall of Greek shields or a rapid charge by bronze-covered infantrymen. No wonder that a Spartan at Thermopylae is said to have quipped that he did not mind if the Persians' barrage of arrows was so thick that it blocked out the sun, since he preferred to fight in the shade.

But equipment was only part of the story. Thermopylae was a triumph of Greek military science over Persian blundering. Leonidas chose his terrain wisely and his tactics logically. He reasoned that in the narrows of Thermopylae—at one point, only fifty feet wide—a small number of men could hold off the Persians. Wave after wave of Persians could attack, but each would break on the long spears and the rugged training of the Greek infantrymen.

The Spartans had the only full-time army in Greece. Their training exceeded anything that the Great King's men—or the other Greeks—had undergone. With the exception of the kings, every Spartan citizen was schooled in a rigid, military education called, simply, "The Upbringing." Only trained and hardened Spartans could have carried out a maneuver like this at Thermopylae: turning and retreating in an orderly way and then, once they had tricked the Persians into charging them with a roar, changing course in an instantaneous wheel and crushing the enemy.

For two days the slaughter continued. Then, on the third day, the Persians outflanked the Greeks by taking a path over the mountains. Once again as in the past, Greek treason saved the Persians. At Thermopylae, the Greek traitor was a native of the region, Ephialtes son of Eurydemus of Trachis. In exchange for money, he guided Xerxes' elite soldiers over the steep, narrow, and hard-to-follow mountain track.

Alerted by scouts to the Persians' movement, Leonidas dismissed most of the allied troops before the enemy could close off the far end of the pass. About a thousand other Greeks remained with the Spartans. Leonidas's strategy is unclear. Perhaps he planned to have his men guard the rear and then escape at the last moment but in the end failed to do so, or perhaps he planned all along for them to stand and fight to the death. In any case, when the Persians attacked, the Greeks first fought with their spears, and when their spears were all broken, they used their swords. When their swords were gone, they went after the

Persians with hands and teeth. When Leonidas finally fell, the Greeks drove the enemy off four times before recovering his body. Before the Greeks were at last overwhelmed by Persian spears and arrows, they killed two of Xerxes' half brothers, Abrocomes and Hyperanthes.

Xerxes' men cleared the pass in the end, but the image of Leonidas's head loomed over it. In the pitiless Greek light of high summer it was a reminder of Persian weakness. Since the Persians normally took pride in treating their enemies with respect, they would not have insulted the body of a fallen foe like Leonidas unless he had enraged them by the force of his resistance. Leonidas's head was a reminder that the butcher's bill for killing four thousand Greeks (the others escaped) was twenty thousand Persians. Any more such victories and the Persians were ruined.

The Great King had hoped to win the war in central Greece. His army and navy would overwhelm the Greeks through Persian numbers and Greek defections. But the navy was defeated by a combination of Greek boldness, Persian strategic errors, and the very size of the fleet, which rendered it too big to find a harbor in a storm. The Persian army fared better, but only at a steep cost. Xerxes' war was not going according to plan.

The Great King of Persia had crossed the Hellespont into Europe with his army three months before, in May. For almost the whole time since, Xerxes' expedition had been less a war than a gigantic picnic. City after city had feted him and his men at its own expense.

Xerxes had marched his army through the northern regions of Greece in Thrace and Macedonia and past Mount Olympus into Thessaly. He marched them into central Greece, through Phthia, the legendary homeland of Achilles, and into Malis, where myth had Heracles spend his last years. Meanwhile, the Persian fleet sailed nearby, along the coast. The army stopped at the pass of Thermopylae, which it found blocked by the Greeks. The navy stopped about fifty miles to the north, at Aphetae, opposite the Greek fleet at Artemisium.

And then the war came. Xerxes should have relished the moment, because he had spent four years preparing for it. But he could not have foreseen the week in August that he had just endured. During that terrible week, his navy had not only failed in its plan to destroy the Greek fleet, but it had lost two hundred ships in a storm off the island of

Euboea and perhaps seventy more in battle. Add the loss of four hundred ships in another storm off Cape Sepias on the Greek mainland the week before, and the Persian fleet was reduced to about half its original size. Meanwhile, at Thermopylae, Xerxes' army had been pummeled by a paltry force of Greek infantrymen—and before his very eyes. He had to concede that when it came to soldiers he had "many people but few men." Or so Herodotus says, but kings do not give up illusions easily.

That the Great King led the invasion of Greece in person was no surprise. Xerxes might have put on airs like a pharaoh, but he was a Persian and Persians made war. He advertised heroism in his very name: Xerxes is Greek for the Persian *Khsha-yar-shan,* the king's throne name, which means "ruler of heroes." Tall and handsome, Xerxes looked like a king. And he followed in the footsteps of Cyrus the Great, founder in 550 B.C. of the Achaemenid Empire (named for Achaemenes, the semilegendary founder of Cyrus's clan). Every king since Cyrus had led an invasion, and every king had conquered new territory.

Xerxes struck a chord in the Persian soul when he declared in an inscription: "I am skilled both in hands and in feet. A horseman, I am a good horseman. A bowman, I am a good bowman, both on foot and on horseback. A spearman, I am a good spearman, both on foot and on horseback."

At Thermopylae, Xerxes had stayed close enough to the fighting to inspire the men but far enough away to limit his danger. Surrounded by royal guards, he sat on a high-backed throne, where he is said to have jumped to his feet three times in horror at the mauling inflicted on his troops. Not that Xerxes' position was risk free. The Greeks claimed afterward to have sent raiders into the Persian camp at night who penetrated even the royal tent before they were repelled. The story is so improbable that it might even be true. In any case, it highlights the risks that real leaders take.

The road to Thermopylae had started in eastern Anatolia a year before. There in 481 B.C., Xerxes had mustered the troops from Iran and the eastern provinces and begun the long march westward. They reached Sardis in the fall and after wintering there, left in April 480 B.C. But preparations for the war—the immense organization of men and arms, ships and supplies, the building of bridges and the carving of canals—had already been going on for three years. Indeed, the war had been on the horizon even before November 486 B.C., when Xerxes succeeded to the throne of his father, Darius. At the time of his death, the sixty-five-year-old Darius had been gearing up for an invasion of Greece in order to avenge Persia's defeat at Marathon in 490 B.C. The new king, probably thirty two years old, would have to decide both whether to fight and what kind of war to wage.

Xerxes ruled what was, without exaggeration, the greatest empire in the history of the world to that date. His domain extended from what is today Pakistan in the east, westward through central and western Asia to Macedonia in the north, and across the Sinai Peninsula to Egypt in the south. It took roughly four thousand miles of roads to travel from one end of the empire to the other. The empire covered nearly 3 million square miles and contained perhaps as many as 20 million people, which makes it about as big as the continental United States of America. Yet with an estimated total world population in 500 B.C. of only about 100 million, Xerxes' empire held perhaps one-fifth of the people on the planet.

The immense majesty of the Persian peace brought order and prosperity to a huge range of peoples and cultures. Outstanding administrators and builders, the Persians built roads and palaces, inns and even parks—known in Greek as *paradeisoi,* from which comes our word *paradise.* They established provincial governments and codified the law. They created the world's first large-scale coinage, which proved convenient for collecting the tribute (taxes) that they imposed on the various provinces.

Xerxes was born to this stupendous heritage probably in 518 B.C. He was both the son of Darius and, through his mother, Atossa, the grandson of Cyrus the Great. To be an heir of someone like Darius was a blessing and a curse. Darius was a self-made man who took power in a coup d'état: he went on to become a mighty conqueror, a brilliant administrator, a religious visionary, and an architectural genius. In fact, Darius was one of the greatest kings in the long history of the Near East. Darius had ruled as Great King for thirty-six years when he died.

The Persians set great store on the impression made by their king and did not leave matters to chance. Royal infants were fussed over by eunuchs, while adult kings were tended by hairdressers, makeup artists, and perfumers—the latter following the king even on military campaigns. Monarchs kept their looks by coating themselves with an ointment consisting of ground-up sunflower seeds mixed with saffron, palm wine, and fat from one of the rare lions to be found in Persian territory. The king always had a mustache and long beard; should nature fail him, toupees and false beards and mustaches were all available. In order to maintain his dignity, in public the king never spat, blew his nose, or turned to look behind him.

On formal occasions, Xerxes probably dressed like one of his successors, who wore a long purple robe, "interwoven with white at the center, and his gold-embroidered cloak bore a gilded motif of hawks attacking each other with their beaks." Other descriptions mention gold-embroidered files of lions on the royal robe. The king's sword, its scabbard encrusted with precious stones, was slung from his gilded belt. He wore a royal diadem encircled by a white-flecked blue ribbon.

Yet it was easier to look like a king than to be one. Xerxes faced the formidable task of confirming himself a worthy son of Darius. Few things could better earn Xerxes respect than avenging his father against the Greeks. "This is indeed my capability: that my body is strong. As a fighter of battles I am a good fighter of battles." So Xerxes proclaimed in an inscription. But he would have to prove it.

And he would have to wait. Egypt rose in revolt in the last months of Darius's life and it fell to Xerxes to suppress the uprising. In 485 B.C., Xerxes went in person to Egypt to lead an army against the rebels. This, his first campaign, was a decisive victory, and by January 484, Egypt was once again a loyal Persian province. There was trouble in Babylon, too, around the same time (the precise year is unclear), but it was easily crushed by troops under a general sent by Xerxes. In 484, with Egypt back in the fold, the Great King returned to the question of Greece. And a complex question the Greek war was. There was pressure on Xerxes from many sides to launch an invasion, yet there were good reasons to hold back.

The leading hawk at court that year was Xerxes' cousin Mardonius, the son of Gobryas and Darius's sister. The leading dove was Xerxes' uncle, Artabanus son of Hystaspes, a full brother of Darius. Each man spoke from experience. Uncle Artabanus had advised Darius back in 513 B.C. not to invade Scythia (roughly, today's Ukraine), and he had been right: the invasion proved to be a disaster. Artabanus had served as a commander in Scythia. Cousin Mardonius knew Greece, having led an abortive armada there in 492 B.C., two years before Marathon; it was destroyed by a storm in the northern Aegean. In the aftermath, Darius fired Mardonius from his command.

An ambitious man, Mardonius sought in 484 B.C. both to reverse his earlier disappointment and to win the power waiting for the first Persian governor of Greece. Most of the other courtiers shared his hard-line position. Not even the king's eunuchs were neutral: one of them once brought Xerxes some figs from Athens for dessert, in order to remind the king of the expedition that he was supposed to lead.

Artabanus and Mardonius each advanced powerful arguments. One man emphasized opportunity, the other, danger. One maintained the prejudice that ignorant Greeks knew nothing other than to send their armies brutally to death. The other cited Greece's win at Marathon. One grasped the chance to crush a rising power, the other fretted about a Greek counterattack.

Xerxes hesitated. He was a young and still relatively new king who depended on his advisers, and they were split. The Great King had so many demands on his time that it was difficult for him to be a strategist. However full his calendar, for example, he had to remember the annual festival in which he—alone in the court—danced and got drunk. He had to plant trees in the royal parks by his own hand—no doubt a symbol of fertility and prosperity. He had to know whom to honor with a seat on his right and whom on his left, who should receive a gift of a silver armchair and who a parasol bordered with precious stones, and he had to know whose good deed needed to be recorded by his secretary and whose deed could be forgotten.

Yet after hesitating about Greece, Xerxes needed first to make a decision and then to enforce it with a sledgehammer. He needed to be the rock against Mardonius's ambition and Artabanus's pessimism, the lightning that could galvanize the sluggish apparatus of the Persian state. Instead, Xerxes responded with finesse. He behaved more like a politician than a commander.

Xerxes dared not abandon his father's war against Greece, but he dared not make war over the public opposition of Artabanus. To solve the problem, Xerxes referred to a dream. The ancients believed that dreams contained messages from the gods. Xerxes' dream threatened ruin unless he went forward with the invasion. Artabanus backed down; in fact, he said he had the same dream himself. Like many shrewd politicians in history, Xerxes used revelation to impose consensus.

And so in 484 B.C. the decision was made to invade Greece. But the Great King and his advisers still had to hammer out the war's strategy and tactics. And they had to do so in the heat of the smithy rather than in the leisure of the seminar room.

Like politics, war is the art of the possible. Not even the Great King had the luxury of choosing military strategy in a vacuum. Xerxes had to take many things into account. The king and his advisers had to engage in a net assessment of the strengths and weaknesses of Greece and Persia. They had to factor in the constraints of Persian domestic politics. And before anything else, they had to define the mission's goals.

According to Herodotus, Xerxes told the leading Persians that he planned to burn Athens, but that would be only the beginning. His army would conquer the Peloponnese as well. In the end, they would "make the land of Persia border only on the sky that belongs to Zeus himself"; they would "make all lands into one land." No doubt Xerxes did say something like this, as it sounds like the official Persian ideology of universal kingship. But that doesn't mean that he believed it. He might have promised world conquest, but he aimed at conquering Greece.

This was an ambitious but measured goal, since much of northern and central Greece already was in his hands. Darius had added Thrace and various Aegean islands to the empire and made Macedonia an ally. Xerxes had allies in Thessaly who eagerly supported his invasion plans. So Persia's writ practically ran to a spot less than 200 miles from Athens, and Sparta lay only 135 miles beyond that. A Persian horseman could cover the distance in a few days.

Yet those three hundred miles might prove the longest distance in the world if defended by the Greek army and navy. Persia had unrivaled wealth in money and manpower; unparalleled ability in engineering and logistics; superiority in both projectiles and cavalry; superb ships, harbors, and seafaring allies; and diplomatic and psychological capabilities of such sophistication that only a state able to muster the resources of the world's oldest civilization could have unleashed them. But

Greece had better infantry and better seamanship than Persia as well as far shorter supply lines and superior knowledge of the terrain.

It would have made sense for Persia to respond with the force multiplier of cunning and innovative tactics. A raid on Athens's unfortified harbor, for example, or a cavalry raid in central Greece that could destroy crops might bring friendly traitors to power in Athens. Persia could win the war at little cost.

Generations earlier, under Cyrus the Great, Persia had excelled at just such unconventional warfare. Now, however, it was deemed beneath the dignity of the King of Kings. The commanders of the world's greatest empire, who ruled from a ceremonial capital that sat on a 350-acre terrace at the royal city of Persepolis, liked to think big. And so, Persia resorted to the least efficient and most expensive force multiplier: numbers.

Domestic politics may have played a role in this choice. Xerxes' own men, no less than the enemy, needed to be impressed. What is more, they wanted jobs. "I give much to loyal men," Xerxes had carved in stone—and he meant it. A big army offered more ways for the Great King to reward loyalty than a small strike force would have.

The high command of the Persian army that invaded Greece, to take a case in point, was a family affair. No fewer than ten of Xerxes' brothers and half brothers served as officers, as did at least two sons of Darius's brothers, two sons of Darius's sisters, one son-in-law of Darius, Xerxes' father-in-law, and at least two other members of the extended Achaemenid clan.

So it would be an attack in massive numbers, both by land and sea. After crossing the Hellespont, Persia's armada amounted to 1,207 triremes in June. By mid-August, about a week before Artemisium, the Persians had added another 120 warships from allies in northern Greece, for a total of 1,327 triremes. The Greeks could not come close to matching that colossal sum. The figure of 1,207 comes from Herodotus and Aeschylus; it has often been questioned, but it does not have to be. It dovetails with the large number of ships at Lade in 494 B.C. and with Persia's emphasis on logistics and supply in 480 B.C. Herodotus says that the triremes were followed by three thousand merchant vessels large and small, carrying food, supplies, and perhaps spare rowers.

But the grand fleet faced big problems. The units of this multinational navy varied greatly in quality and would be hard to turn into a single fighting force. Some of Persia's naval allies, especially the Ionians, were of dubious loyalty. Besides, so large a fleet would have trouble finding harbors.

On land, Persia boasted magnificent cavalry, amazing archers, and supremacy in siegecraft. The ten thousand elite infantrymen whom Herodotus calls the Immortals (perhaps a mistranslation of the Persian for the Followers) were superbly trained. Unfortunately, they could not match the cohesion or heavy armor of the best Greek infantrymen. As for the cavalry, the mountainous countryside of Greece offers few opportunities for horse charges. And once the Greeks made the hard decision not to defend their cities, Persia's sappers and rampart builders were of little worth.

The one sure thing about the number of soldiers who marched under Xerxes is that it was very large. At a muster of the army at Doriscus in Thrace in June, the infantry consisted of forty-seven different ethnic units from all over the empire. They wore everything from bronze armor to leopard skins, and they were armed with weapons ranging from spears and swords to arrows tipped with sharpened stones and to wooden clubs with iron studs. The cavalry consisted of ten different ethnic units and even included a corps of camels.

No camels and few men ever saw any fighting, which fell almost entirely to Iranian troops, that is, Persians and their near neighbors. Most of the men were there only to show the flag and to keep their necks from the vengeance of the king's executioner, who was sure to descend on slackers. In truth, what Xerxes held at Doriscus was less a military review than the biggest pep rally in history.

Herodotus says that 1.7 million infantrymen and 80,000 cavalrymen mustered at Doriscus. But these figures go far beyond what ancient conditions allowed, and modern scholars have rightly whittled them down. The likeliest estimate for Xerxes' army counts about 75,000 animals and about 200,000 men overall—150,000 combatants and 50,000 officials, slaves, eunuchs, concubines, family members, and other hangers-on.

To turn from numbers to tactics, the Persians did not appreciate unconventional warfare, but they understood diplomacy and psychology. They knew that the Greeks did well in war only when united, so

Persia's job was to divide them. Persia had managed that before: both at Lade in 494 B.C. and earlier, in Cyprus in 497, Persian commanders talked key Greek leaders into turning traitor and then crushed the rest. The same tactic almost worked again at Marathon in 490 B.C. Thanks to turncoats within the city's gates, the Persians nearly took Athens in spite of defeat on the battlefield.

In short, the key to Persian victory against Greece was treason. Xerxes understood this in 480 B.C. and tried to bribe or threaten most of the Greek city-states into surrendering. It was an easy job, since few Greeks were prepared to resist.

The intriguing possibility exists that Xerxes' diplomats went even farther afield. The other major invasion of 480 B.C. was Carthage's attack on the Greek cities of Sicily. Carthage, the great naval and military power located in North Africa, was originally a colony of Phoenicia, in turn Persia's ally. Carthage's invasion occupied the Greek city-states of Sicily and kept them from sending help to their brethren in Greece. So Xerxes had incentive to help Carthage, but later reports of Persian-Carthaginian cooperation in 480 B.C. may merely be a guess.

What is certain is that Persia deployed the tools of psychological warfare in its buildup to invasion—and deployed those tools massively. The Persians mixed sweet talk with intimidation. For instance, they ostentatiously set up huge deposits of food for the troops at selected points on the invasion route in Thrace and Macedonia. The river Strymon in Macedonia was bridged near its mouth. In addition, Xerxes had thousands of his men undertake a gigantic engineering project in northern Greece: they dug a canal across a narrow isthmus—1.2 miles wide—on the peninsula of Mount Athos and built protective stone breakwaters at either end. It took three years to complete this project, which would allow the navy to avoid the stormy and dangerous southern tip of the Mount Athos peninsula.

Recent archaeological excavations on the peninsula have found traces of Xerxes' canal. The absence of any building structures, harbor installations, or marine organisms in the sediment all point to one conclusion: the canal was abandoned as soon as the ships passed through. The excavators wrote that the evidence "suggests that Xerxes built the canal as much for prestige and a show of strength as for its purely functional role."

Almost the same could be said for Xerxes' bridges across the Hellespont. The Hellespont is a narrow ribbon of water, about thirty-eight miles long, separating Anatolia from the continent of Europe. Xerxes decided to bridge the waterway near its southwestern end, near the city of Abydos, where the Hellespont is only about one mile wide. Teams of Egyptian and Phoenician engineers were put in charge of the project.

It is exhausting merely to read Herodotus's account of the building process. On each of two bridges nearly three hundred warships (a mixture of penteconters and triremes) were anchored after having been lashed together by cables—white flax for the Phoenicians and papyrus for the Egyptians. A gap was left at two points for small boats to pass through. Walkways were laid on each bridge: these were covered by soil and fenced on either side, to keep the animals from looking down and getting frightened. Cables were attached to the land and wound tight on wooden windlasses. And all of this happened on the second try: the engineers had nearly completed two bridges when a storm blew up and destroyed them.

After the first bridges were destroyed, Xerxes ordered the beheading of the bridge builders and the punishment of the recalcitrant waters: the Hellespont would receive three hundred lashes, a pair of fetters, and possibly even a branding with hot irons. Herodotus ridicules all this as the height of barbarian arrogance. Yet the men who were executed might have been guilty of criminal negligence, and the lashing of the Hellespont was no doubt a religious ritual.

The real point of the bridges in the first place is open to discussion. Artabanus feared them as a target of the Greeks, who might cut them as the Scythians nearly had cut Darius's bridge over the Danube. Nor did Persian logistics require the bridges, as their forces could have been ferried across the Hellespont. In that case, however, the public would have been deprived of the spectacle of the Persian army crossing the bridges. Herodotus reports on the ceremony on the day that the expedition began.

At dawn, the men burned perfumed spices on the bridges and covered the roadways with myrtle branches. At sunrise, Xerxes poured an offering of wine from a golden cup into the Hellespont and asked for the sun god's assistance. Then he threw the cup, a golden bowl, and a

Persian sword into the water. The crossing took seven days and seven nights, and only the unstinting use of whips kept things moving. In that time, 200,000 men and 75,000 animals could well have crossed.

Most commanders like to keep their army's size and strength secret, but not Xerxes. On the contrary, when his men found Athenian spies in Anatolia, Xerxes released them and had them sent back home. Likewise, when his triremes captured a squadron of merchant ships carrying grain, bound for Greece, Xerxes did not impound them. Quipping that they were carrying grain for his men to eat when they got to Athens, he let the ships pass. Xerxes didn't want to surprise the enemy; he wanted to overwhelm the enemy with information.

And it looks as if Xerxes gave the same message to his own allies, if a report in a Roman-era collection of stratagems may be trusted:

> *When Xerxes was campaigning against Greece he brought together many nations by dispersing agents to say that Greece's leading men had agreed to betray their country. Since it looked less like a battle than a profit-making expedition, many of the barbarians became his allies voluntarily.*

Numbers, psychology, and politicking all combined in April 480 B.C. when the Great King's army marched out of Sardis in procession. The support services, the pack animals, and a mass of non-Persian troops came first. Then, after a gap, came 1,000 elite cavalrymen and 1,000 elite spearmen, Persians all. Next came the holy chariot, drawn by a team of ten Nisaean horses, from a region in Iran famous for its horses. It was followed by Xerxes himself in his royal chariot, also drawn by Nisaeans. Then marched two more elite groups of cavalrymen and spearmen, each of 1,000 Persians, followed by 10,000 Persian infantry and 10,000 Persian horse. After another gap, the rest of the army followed, all mixed together. They marched one and all between the two sides of the corpse of the unfortunate son of Pythius.

Pythius the Lydian was a local lord who had welcomed Xerxes and his forces to Anatolia in 481 B.C. Pythius offered to feed them all lavishly, at enormous cost to himself, and moreover to contribute most of his fortune to Xerxes' war chest—and Pythius's wealth nearly rivaled the king's. Xerxes responded chivalrously: not only did he refuse the old man's offer, but he actually increased the lord's wealth with a gift from the royal treasury. More important, he made Pythius what Herodotus calls his hereditary friend— perhaps *bandaka* is to be understood by this. The Great King's *bandaka* were his dependents or, literally, "those who wear the belt (*banda*) of vassalage."

Poor Pythius let it all go to his head. A few months afterward, at Sardis in the spring of 480 B.C., he asked Xerxes for a favor. Pythius had sent his five sons to Xerxes' army. He had experienced second thoughts and, in order to ensure an heir, begged Xerxes to release his eldest— and favorite—son from service.

Xerxes was furious; such defeatism on the part of the Great King's *bandaka* had to be punished. In return for the earlier generosity, Xerxes would spare four of his sons, but the king ordered his servants "to find the eldest son of Pythius and to cut him in half, and having done so, to place one half on the right side of the road and the other half on the left side, and to order the army to march between them."

And so, at this signal of his ferocity, Xerxes unleashed the grandest military force that had ever marched and sailed. The bridges across the Hellespont, the gigantic magnitude of forces, the canal cut through the Mount Athos peninsula, the huge dumps of food along the anticipated route—these were all tools of psychological as well as physical warfare. By dividing their enemies and by terrifying them with displays of force, Persia would soften them up. The Great King's massive number of soldiers and ships would take care of the rest.

And that, in fact, was the flaw in the plan: the rest. If the Greeks declined to play the role of terrified natives before what amounted to Persia's gunboats, then the Persian invasion might come crashing into walls of bronze and wood. The intriguing question is whether Xerxes was aware of the risk that he was taking.

Herodotus describes a remarkable conversation at the Hellespont in the spring of 480 B.C. between a skeptical Artabanus and a confident Xerxes. Artabanus had earlier reminded Xerxes of the famous defeats of his dynasty: Cyrus's loss to the Massagetae of Kazakhstan in 530 B.C., at the cost of his life; Cambyses' failed campaign against the Ethiopians in 524, Darius's Scythian expedition in 513, and Darius's disappointment at Marathon in 490. The land and the sea were both Persia's enemies, Artabanus supposedly said. The sea had no harbor big enough to shelter Xerxes' fleet in case of storm. The land would beckon the army onward, but the further they went, the more precarious would be their supply lifeline. Artabanus also doubted the reliability of the Ionians in Persia's fleet: no small qualm, since the Ionians were, with the Phoenicians, the best divisions in the Persian navy.

Xerxes dismissed these objections, according to Herodotus. And he sent Artabanus back to Persia to protect Xerxes' "household and tyrannical rule" as sole guardian of the royal scepter. Xerxes demonstrated his political skill by deftly disposing of a defeatist while also showing him respect. But the king also took Artabanus's words to heart. He called a meeting of the leading Persians and warned them to steel themselves in order not to shame their glorious heritage. The Greeks were brave men, he said, and the Persians would have to be braver if they were to prevail.

At Abydos in about May 480 B.C., before his men crossed the Hellespont, Xerxes ordered a marble throne, which was now placed on a hillside. From there, the king had a panoramic view of the plains and beaches filled with his soldiers and the Hellespont crowded with his ships. He ordered a trireme race; his wish was carried out immediately; the winners were the Phoenician ships of the city of Sidon. Xerxes rejoiced at the splendor of his forces and then he did a strange thing: the Great King began to cry.

Herodotus reports the reason for Xerxes' tears. It had suddenly occurred to the king that in a century, he writes, not one of the men he saw would still be alive. So brief is our time on earth. But perhaps there was another reason for his tears. Maybe he had reflected on the huge risks that lay ahead for his magnificent army and navy, and maybe that was what made Xerxes weep.

The Great King might have remembered those tears after Thermopylae. Perhaps he had to fight them back in a conversation after the battle with one of the most striking of his advisers: Demaratus, the exiled king of Sparta.

Demaratus had not seen Sparta in seven years. He was a middle-aged man who might have yearned for his lost throne, but Demaratus is unlikely to have harbored illusions about Sparta's willingness to take back a traitor. But because he was a Spartan and, as he believed, a descendant of Heracles himself, he might not have cared. Demaratus

was a man who relished vengeance. And, as Herodotus points out, whoever took on Demaratus came to a bad end.

The Spartans had the greatest infantrymen in the ancient Mediterranean. Demaratus knew it, but it had taken Thermopylae to convince
the Persians. Xerxes could no longer deny what his men were up
against. Nor could he take lightly the advice of his resident Spartan.

In Herodotus, Demaratus plays the role of the wise exile who tells
the king a hard truth at his own life's risk. Demaratus warns Xerxes
that the Greeks will fight; that the Spartans will fight hardest; and that
the Great King, therefore, had better scrap his strategy and come up
with a new war plan. It is a good story, flattering to Demaratus, and
many scholars doubt it. They suggest that Herodotus picked up the tale
from one of Demaratus's sons and passed it on.

But the historian was no pushover. He may well have interviewed
Demaratus's descendants, but he was not about to buy snake oil from
them. Rather than going into rapture over Demaratus's straight talk,
Herodotus reveals the Spartan as a swindler. It took an exile like the
historian to expose the confidence job of a sacked king and fugitive
turncoat like Demaratus.

Demaratus was as unsentimental a veteran of political infighting
as Sparta's stubborn society had ever produced. His reported comments
at the Persian court, that he feared flattery more than insult and bribery
more than rejection, have the sour flavor of personal knowledge. On a
likely reconstruction, Demaratus reigned in Sparta for over twenty
years, from ca. 515 to ca. 491 B.C. After a very hard-fought power struggle, Demaratus was deposed, fell afoul of the new king, and eventually
fled Sparta. He made his way to the man known as the friend of the
friendless: the Great King.

It was about 487 B.C. and Persia had already become a haven for
losers in Greece's power battles. Darius welcomed Demaratus in the
grand manner, making Demaratus his *bandaka*, and a favored one at
that. Darius knew that Demaratus was an invaluable source of information and potentially an ally, if restored to his throne.

But Demaratus's qualifications as military adviser were mixed. On
the one hand, as a former king, Demaratus knew Spartan politics and
had commanded the army. On the other hand, there is no evidence that
he ever had gone into battle, except for a late and questionable report

that he led an army against the walls of Argos—when they were defended by the city's women! The men, it seems, had been slaughtered in battle by a Spartan force led by a rival of Demaratus. Headed by the Argive poet Telesilla, the Argive women are supposed to have circled the walls and defeated Demaratus and his men.

As far as is known, therefore, Demaratus was no great warrior. Nor did his advice to Xerxes attest to military genius. Herodotus records three conversations during the Persian invasion of Greece between the Great King and the Spartan exile: one at Doriscus and two at Thermopylae.

They must have made an odd pair, the King of Kings in his purple robes and gold jewelry and the austere Spartan, raised in a country whose citizens slept on straw pallets and allowed their sons only one cloak a year. Nor did Xerxes have to rough it on the road. The royal tent was a veritable palace in miniature. To judge from later copies, the tent stood about fifty feet high and was about twenty-five hundred feet in circumference. It boasted embroidered hangings lavishly decorated with animal themes as well as precious metals everywhere. Gourmet meals were served on gold and silver tables for diners on beautifully draped gold and silver couches. There were even golden bridles and a bronze manger for the horses.

At Doriscus, Demaratus warned Xerxes that no matter how greatly they were outnumbered, the Spartans would fight. And the Spartans, he pointed out, were great warriors. They would obey the command of their law and fight to the death.

At Thermopylae, Demaratus appeared on the scene to decipher a strange report brought back from the Greek camp by a Persian spy. The spy had caught the Spartans outdoors drawn up in lines, but they practiced maneuvers that left him baffled. While some of the Spartans exercised naked, others combed their hair. Xerxes, too, found this behavior odd, but Demaratus explained that the Spartans were in the habit of grooming their hair before risking their lives. What the scout had seen, therefore, was a deadly sign of Spartan ferocity.

After the battle at Thermopylae, Xerxes summoned Demaratus again. The Spartan had correctly predicted Sparta's tough stand, so Xerxes asked Demaratus for information and advice. How many more Spartans were there? And how might Persia defeat them?

Demaratus might have been thrilled at these questions because they opened the door for revenge on Sparta. He told Xerxes that Sparta had eight thousand soldiers, all as good as the men who had fought at Thermopylae. In order to beat them, he advised the Great King to change his strategy. Xerxes should force the Greeks to divide their armies by sending a force to attack Sparta's home territory and thereby compel the Spartan army to return home. Meanwhile, the main Persian forces could defeat the rest of the Greeks.

Demaratus had a plan all ready: send three hundred triremes—almost half of the remaining Persian fleet—to Cythera, an island off the south coast of the Peloponnese. Using Cythera as a base, the Persians could raid Spartan territory and perhaps raise a revolt of Sparta's enserfed agricultural laborers, the Helots. These workers, always eager to rebel against the lords who mistreated them, represented Sparta's Achilles' heel.

"If you spring from this island," Demaratus said, "you will frighten the Spartans. And with a foreign war in their own land, they will no longer be fearsome and even if the rest of Greece is under siege they will not come to the aid with their infantry. When the rest of Greece is enslaved, only a weak Sparta will be left."

If Xerxes had followed Demaratus's advice, the Great King would never have risked his entire navy in a single battle. After his losses of ships and men to the wind and Greece's gains at Artemisium, Xerxes could hardly have been eager to take a chance like that. And if he could keep his navy intact, Xerxes might win the war. But Demaratus had outlined a bad strategy. Had the Persians followed it, they would not have faced a do-or-die naval battle: they would have faced *two* die-or-die naval battles.

The Persian fleet of about 650 triremes still outnumbered the Greeks, who could not muster more than about 350. But the Greeks had the advantages of home waters, short supply lines, and maritime expertise. If Persia divided its fleet, then the Greeks would equal its numbers and could attack the Persians at will and in two stages. The Persians would have risked losing everything.

Xerxes' brother Achaemenes, commander of the fleet, was present at the conference, and he seethed at Demaratus's proposal. After pointing out its strategic weakness, he accused Demaratus of treason and jealousy, which he said was typically Greek.

Xerxes offered a courtly defense of his *bandaka* while conceding Achaemenes' point about the prevalence of jealousy. But Demaratus was Xerxes' guest, and Achaemenes would have to keep his hands off the Spartan. Still, the Great King accepted Achaemenes' policy advice. The fleet would remain united. There would be no expedition to Cythera.

This was a key moment in the war. The Persian high command considered an alternative strategy but rejected it. Like most military decisions, the choice was made not on military grounds alone but in the heat and dust of the political arena.

In his three dialogues with Xerxes, Demaratus displayed the single-mindedness of a delusional man. His Spartans were ten feet tall. Before Thermopylae, he made the Spartans into supermen. After the battle, he had them represent the sole obstacle to a Persian victory in Greece. Never mind the Athenians and their navy: focus on the Spartans and win the war. This was less the advice of a strategist than the obsession of an avenger.

Sparta's infantrymen did pose a threat to Xerxes' troops. But Xerxes' best strategy against Sparta was to destroy the Greek navy. After doing so, Persia could move its soldiers by sea and land them anywhere in Greece at will. Persia could crack the Greek alliance and pick off its enemies one by one. So Xerxes kept the fleet undivided and headed for Athens. Everything would depend on his making the right decisions there, of course, but without a united fleet, he would not have even the chance.

One Spartan king had died trying to stop Persia's march southward, and another had put his life on the line in an endeavor to deflect it. Leonidas would be remembered as a Greek hero, Demaratus as a traitor, but neither succeeded in keeping Xerxes from his determined course. Whether it was the will of the gods or the stubbornness of the Great King, the Persians would not be denied their appointment in Athens.

One day after his men had finally broken through at Thermopylae and Artemisium, Xerxes gave the order. The mighty force began to march, sail, and row its way south. All eyes now turned toward Athens.

CHAPTER THREE

~~

ATHENS

Though tall and long-limbed, he has put on weight. He is smooth-skinned and beardless and has a full head of hair, which he wears twisted into tight curls. He is a grown man but retains the high-pitched voice of a boy. And he is present, along with the generals, politicians, priests, ambassadors, bodyguards, secretaries, attendants, chefs, dressers, flatterers, mistresses, and illegitimate children who make up Xerxes' retinue, as the Great King enters Athens.

Like the other dignitaries of the Persian court, he is dressed in a long, flowing robe decorated with embroidery. Since he stands high in Xerxes' eyes, his cloak may well be a royal gift, dyed a kingly purple or scarlet. His outfit is completed by a cloth hat and a pair of sandals and a great deal of gold jewelry: armbands, anklets, a torque, and—one last touch—a pair of earrings, probably elaborate, perhaps a combination of gold and faience beads. He is perfumed, of course.

His name is Hermotimus and he is a eunuch. This description of his appearance is an educated guess, based on ancient evidence. But much else about Hermotimus is certain. Castrated as a boy, he had been sent as a gift for Xerxes to Susa, the winter capital of the Persian Kings. He had served the Great King so well that Hermotimus was now first among the royal eunuchs. Eunuchs had a reputation for intrigue, but apparently they made up for it by their industriousness and attention to detail. Because eunuchs had no children of their own, the Persian kings prized them for their loyalty. Eunuchs inspired special trust in Persia as managers, watchdogs, and gatekeepers in the royal palaces, especially in the harem, where they served the royal women and children.

It was probably around September 20 when Hermotimus entered Athens, about three weeks after the battle of Thermopylae. The distance between Thermopylae and Athens, by the shortest possible route on ancient roads, was just over 140 miles. The Persians no doubt wanted to pursue their enemy hotly and rapidly. But the best that they could do was to send an advance force ahead, probably consisting of cavalry and elite troops. The bulk of Xerxes' big and heterogeneous army moved only very slowly, perhaps at a rate of about ten miles a day, including one day's halt every seven to rest the animals. Further slowing the army was the need to conquer Phocis and Boeotia before reaching Attica.

Xerxes' full army probably took over two weeks to reach Athens. Assuming it took a few days to regroup after Thermopylae, the army might have begun its march south around September 1 and reached

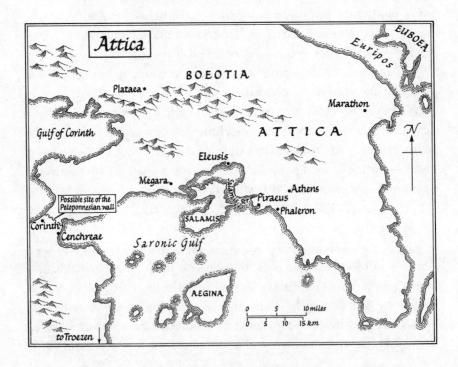

Athens by about September 20. The Persian advance guard presumably covered the distance at a much more rapid pace.

Herodotus suggests that the Persian fleet reached Athens's main harbor, which was at Phaleron Bay, only nine days after the final battles at Artemisium and Thermopylae. He implies, furthermore, that the Persian army had reached Athens before the fleet. Assuming that the army, in this case, refers to the advance guard, then the first Persian land forces reached Athens around September 5, while the fleet reached Phaleron around September 7. The bulk of the Persian forces were far behind.

Along with Xerxes and his men, Hermotimus had proceeded south from Thermopylae into the mountainous regions of Doris and Phocis. They had as guides Greeks from Thessaly, pro-Persian sorts who hated their neighbors in Phocis more than they did any foreign invader. Led by these men, the Persians wound their way through the upland valleys of rocky Phocis, plundering and burning property, including a temple of Apollo. Most of the inhabitants had taken to the hills for safety, but a few unlucky souls fell into Persian hands. The women were gang-raped so violently that they died. The region of Doris, a friend of both Thessaly and Persia, was spared.

On the border of the region of Boeotia, Xerxes divided the army into two divisions. The smaller of the two headed westward for the oracle of Apollo at Delphi, the wealthiest and most prestigious shrine in the Greek world. The larger division, which was headed by Xerxes, drove south in carts through Boeotia toward Athens. Delphi was awash in gold and silver gifts from the faithful, including a refined-gold statue of a lion that allegedly weighed 570 pounds. Xerxes was said to be eager to bring home such trophies, but the fabulous treasures eluded him. A violent thunderstorm on the outskirts of Delphi struck the army with lightning and sent rocks crashing down from Mount Parnassus, which panicked the superstitious men into turning back.

The Boeotian towns of Plataea and Thespiae were not as lucky. They alone of the city-states of the Boeotian plain had supported the Greek cause. The other cities, led by Thebes, had joined the Persians. The Greeks had a verb for this; "to Medize," after the Medes, a separate Iranian people from the Persians but close enough for the Greeks: Greeks were always vague about the facts of those whom they called barbarians.

Being a military people, the Boeotians knew how a soldier itches for loot when he sees a city gleaming in the sun, and they did not want to run the risk of tempting the Persian army. So, for good measure, when they Medized, they hosted Macedonian ambassadors, men who had been sent by Xerxes' trusted friend, the Macedonian king Alexander (an ancestor of Alexander the Great). Having no such protectors, Thespiae saw its territory ravaged, and Plataea was burned. The inhabitants of both places had already taken refuge in the Peloponnese.

Xerxes' army next marched over the mountain pass into Athenian territory. What Hermotimus thought, as the wagon, on which he no doubt traveled, crested the hills and offered him his first glimpse of the territory of Athens, can only be guessed. But we would not be surprised if his mind turned to punishment. Xerxes was about to discipline the Athenians for having burned Sardis and for having humiliated his royal father's men at Marathon, to say nothing of having broken their promise of submission. Hermotimus knew, as few others did, that justice requires paying people back in their own coin. Herodotus says, in fact, that no one ever did a better job of getting even than did Hermotimus.

Hermotimus came from Pedasa, a city in Caria, located just a few miles from Halicarnassus, Herodotus's hometown. Pedasa was inhabited by the Leleges, a non-Greek people of whom little is known today. One striking detail is the legend that in times of trouble, the priestess of Athena in Pedasa grew a beard, perhaps a symbol of even the women's willingness to fight for the defense of their land.

Tough, warlike, and dug into their well-fortified cities, the Pedasians held out against Persia's initial conquest in 546 B.C. and fought fiercely when they joined the Ionian Revolt in 499 B.C. Maybe it was then, when Persia suppressed the rebellion, or maybe it was in the course of some unrecorded pirate raid, that young Hermotimus was captured and enslaved. It happened that he was an especially good-looking boy, and he came from a region, Caria, that was known for its supply of good-looking boys.

Xerxes brought Hermotimus along to Greece in 480 B.C. The king trusted the eunuch enough that, upon their eventual return to Anatolia, he made Hermotimus the secondary guardian of certain of the king's illegitimate sons, who had been present during the expedition. Queen Artemisia of Halicarnassus was in charge of getting the boys home safely. It was not unusual for members of the royal household to accompany the king on campaign. Among Xerxes' illegitimate sons in Greece was presumably Tithraustes, who, fourteen years later, in 466, commanded a large Persian navy against the Greeks at the battle of the Eurymedon River in Anatolia. At Athens in 480, he would have to be satisfied with observing.

The plain of Attica, as the territory of the city-state of Athens is called, stretches out below the mountains. Most of Attica is made up of farmland and forests; the urban space of Athens in 480 B.C. was tiny, a distance that would take an hour's walk from end to end. In the clear blue light of September, the Persians' advance guard could make out the columns of the temples on the Athenian Acropolis, the center of the city of Athens. The sound of the wind blowing through the trees might stir them to picture the soft, city beds that were about to replace the pine needles on which they had earlier bivouacked.

The water of the Saronic Gulf and the distant mountains of the Peloponnese serve as a backdrop. Well within the Persians' view and much closer at hand is the island of Salamis, which is separated only by a narrow channel from the mainland of Athens. As the Persians crested the mountains of Attica, they might have imagined that total victory lay in their grasp. The main obstacle consisted of some three hundred triremes, the Greek fleet that had regrouped in Salamis harbor after the battle at Artemisium. The Persian navy had sailed down the west coast of Euboea, looting as it went. The Persians had a Greek pilot to guide them through the twisting waterway, one Salganeus of Boeotia. But they were so dismayed at the narrowness of the Euripos strait that they had him executed on the grounds of misleading them—unfairly, since this was indeed the best route.

The Persian fleet finally rounded the tip of Attica at Cape Sunium, and now it was moored at Phaleron, about three miles south of the Acropolis. Meanwhile, about forty miles southwest of Athens, a Greek army hurried to build a wall at the narrow Isthmus of Corinth in order to block the Persians by land. But all that might seem far away on the morning when the Great King's men would head for Athens and revenge.

Athens is only three miles from the sea, but it does not feel like a port. Rather, the ancient city's hills—the hills of the Muses, the

Nymphs, the Areopagus, and of course, the Acropolis—remind a visitor of the mountains in whose foothills Athens sits. Indeed, the city is enfolded by mountains: to the southeast, Mount Hymettus; to the northeast, Mount Pentele; to the northwest, Mount Parnes; and to the southwest, Mount Aigaleon. Only due south does Athens open to the sea. There, at the shore three miles away, a traveler enters a different world, one of the light and air of the Greek islands.

Athens might have reminded Hermotimus of the city of his birth. Ancient Pedasa has been tentatively identified with the site known today as Gökçeler Castle, a few miles northwest of the ancient site of Halicarnassus. Gökçeler Castle sits high in the hills of the Bodrum peninsula, set in a classic Aegean mountain landscape. Its acropolis is a steep, defensible hill. The imposing line of the fortification walls, with their massive, well-worked stones, is still visible, despite the wild growth of trees and bushes. It was good land for grazing sheep and goats, good land for terracing for olive cultivation, good land for bird hunting. Quiet in the hills, Pedasa seems a world away from the sea, although the water, only a few miles away, is visible in the distance, at least from the top of the citadel.

Back in Athens, Hermotimus might have shepherded the royal princes on a tour of the city, or what was left of it. He might have cited the signs of Persian pillage as proof that revenge is sweet. And Hermotimus could have cited his own experience as a case in point.

Just a few months earlier, while at Sardis in the winter of 481–480 B.C., the eunuch had made a side trip to the Greek coastal city of Atarneus. There, he happened to run into a Greek from the island of Chios named Panionius. He was the very man who, years earlier, had castrated Hermotimus. Indeed, Panionius castrated good-looking boys as a profession. Now was the moment of Hermotimus's revenge. He lied to Panionius, claiming that he had no hard feelings, since Panionius's knife had cut a path to wealth and power at the Persian court. Indeed, Hermotimus invited Panionius to share his success by moving from Chios to Atarneus—Panionius and his entire family.

Panionius fell for the ploy and moved his family, at which point Hermotimus struck. He revealed his true anger at having been castrated. Panionius, said Hermotimus, had made him "a nothing." Now Hermotimus unveiled his plan for revenge. Hermotimus forced Panionius to castrate his four sons, and then he made the boys do likewise to their father. There is a hint in Herodotus that it was more than tit-for-tat; that while Hermotimus lost only his testicles, Panionius and his sons each was left with only a hole for urination. This savage act of reprisal suggests the sort of bloody justice—if not the precise punishment—that Xerxes had in mind for the Athenians.

At the end of the sixth year of his reign, and four months after he had crossed the Hellespont, the Great King finally rode into Athens. The Persians no doubt planned their usual penalty for rebels and recalcitrants. Athenian men would be put to the sword, women would be raped, children rounded up. Human dragnets would be launched; long lines of men would scour the countryside and haul in prisoners. Then tens of thousands of Athenian survivors of Persia's vengeance would be marched or rowed off eastward, far from the Aegean, to places on the Persian Gulf or in the mountains of Central Asia, in order to serve the glory of the Great King. There they would fret over future generations and their precarious ability to pass on ever dimmer memories of Athens to their young.

It was all a familiar pattern by now, from the bloodshed to the uprooting to the lamentations. It was the fate, after the failure of the Ionian Revolt in 494 B.C., of such islands as Chios and Lesbos and of the cities of Eretria and Miletus and, many years earlier, of other cities in the ancient Near East. But it never happened in Athens, because when the Persians arrived, there was almost no one there. Nearly the entire territory of Attica, the one-thousand-square-mile area that was roughly equal in size to the American state of Rhode Island or the British county of Hampshire, had been stripped of its people. From the mountains of Marathon to the lowlands of Eleusis, from the silver mines of Laurium to the harbor of Piraeus, Attica was nearly empty.

It was not easy to evacuate a Greek city-state. One other city had tried to do so with mixed results. Rather than submit to Persia, in 540 B.C. the people of Phocaea in Ionia voted to move lock, stock, and barrel. But there was enough resistance that they had to drop a lump of iron into the sea and all swear not to return to Phocaea until it floated again—that is, never. They also put a curse on anyone who stayed behind. Even so, more than half of the population of the city broke their oath, braved the curse, and sailed back home to become Persian subjects. The remainder eventually resettled in Italy, after many troubles.

Athenians in 480 B.C. faced similar temptations and greater problems. Phocaea was a small place; Athens was one of the largest city-states in the Greek world. There were probably about 150,000 men, women, and children in Attica in 480 B.C. And most of them would leave.

They would go to three destinations. Women and children were meant to head across the Saronic Gulf to Troezen, a city-state on the east coast of the Peloponnese, but some also went to the Saronic Gulf island of Aegina. Aegina and Troezen are each about a day's sail from Athens. Athenian men of fighting age—in this emergency, possibly ages eighteen through fifty-nine—headed for Salamis; that island was, it seems, the preferred destination also for the elderly and for whatever household goods could be transported. Salamis lies off the coast of Attica, only about a mile away.

Like Aegina and Troezen, Salamis is accessible by sea. So far as is known, Athens was evacuated entirely by ship. The veterans of Artemisium had no time to rest before going back to sea, ferrying their countrymen to safety. As for the evacuees, anecdotes survive of tearful dockside leave-takings.

Troezen was a logical choice for Athenian relocation. Troezen had long-standing connections to Athens. Myth made Troezen the maternal home of Theseus, Athens's legendary hero-king. The island of Aegina was not as obvious a destination, since until Xerxes' invasion, it had been Athens's archenemy. But Aegina had closed ranks with the anti-Persian Greeks, and perhaps now, in 480 B.C., the island wished to make amends for its past. The welcome given to Athenian evacuees was a good start.

Salamis was the key to Athens's strategy. Unlike Troezen and Aegina, Salamis was Athenian territory. Originally independent, Salamis had a strategic location, skirting both Attica and the neighboring city-state of Megara, which made it much fought over by its neighbors on the mainland before finally being conquered by Athens not long after 600 B.C. In time, Athenian families settled on the island. A few years before 480 B.C. one of Salamis's most famous sons was born: the Athenian tragedian Euripides.

The view from the Athenian Acropolis makes the strategic value of

Salamis clear. The narrow straits separating Salamis from the mainland lie due west of the Acropolis. The rugged outline of the island rises beyond a sliver of water. Standing on the Acropolis, a person feels almost as if he could grab hold of the island. By evacuating to Salamis, the Athenians found a base within sight of home.

Although the Athenian relocation had already begun before August 480 B.C., it accelerated with the news of the fall of Thermopylae. The Peloponnesians had promised that if they had to retreat from the pass, they would make a stand in Boeotia. Under no circumstance would they leave Athens to find its own way. Yet the Peloponnesians had reneged. Their armies were forming a defensive line at the Isthmus of Corinth, gateway to the Peloponnese, that is, about forty miles to the southwest of Athens. The allies had deserted Athens. The Athenians had to settle for a Peloponnesian agreement that, after Artemisium, the Greek fleet would regroup at Salamis rather than at a harbor at the Isthmus. But the Peloponnesians, who were itching to get back closer to home, did not promise to actually fight a battle at Salamis. Since that was precisely what the Athenians wanted to do, and since Athens had the leverage of the largest fleet in Greece, disagreement lay ahead.

Alone and abandoned on land, the Athenians decided to evacuate their homeland and make a stand at Salamis. This was no hasty or eleventh-hour plan. It had been decided on before the Athenian fleet went north to Artemisium, perhaps nearly a year earlier. And it had been approved by the Athenian assembly, where six thousand or more men met, debated, and voted on the plan of action, which was passed as a decree. "It was resolved by the Council and the Assembly of the People": so every decree of the Athenians began. As the assembly took the heavy step of voting for mass departure, the rarest of things may have descended on that rowdiest of parliaments: silence.

The Athenian people had voted for their own exile. But behind the strategy was one man. Themistocles was the leader whose name was recorded on the official record and the politician who would be blamed if everything failed in the end.

A document inscribed on stone, known as the Themistocles Decree for the name of the man who moved its passage, confirms Herodotus's report while adding several important details. Dating from ca. 300 B.C., the inscription may indeed be based on the original document passed by the Athenian assembly. The Themistocles Decree shows that the evacuation of Athens began well before the battle of Artemisium, in August 480 B.C. It also demonstrates how carefully the people of Athens were thinking ahead.

They made use of Salamis in more ways than one. For example, all the politicians who had been ostracized were recalled in the interests of national unity, but since some of them had been ostracized because of pro-Persian sentiments, they were kept at arm's length on the island of Salamis.

Nor was religion neglected. Before the departure of the fleet, for instance, the authorities were to sacrifice to Zeus All-Powerful, to Athena of Victory, and to Poseidon the Securer: that is, to the king of the gods, to the patroness of the city, and to the god of the sea. Power, victory, and security were the themes of the hour.

The decree's mobilization of military manpower is even more striking. Not only Athenian citizens but resident aliens were called up. Careful provision was made to combine seasoned rowers with landlubber infantrymen in each of the two hundred ships in the Athenian fleet. The names of each ship's crew were posted on boards for all to see.

Each name betokened Themistocles' political acumen. Xerxes had made his vendetta against Athens into a campaign of conquest, but Themistocles then turned it into a people's war. This was both his malice and his genius, because evacuation incited the Athenians and left the Persians unfulfilled, which set the stage for a bloody battle.

Now Athenians turned to the gods, and the god whom the people wanted most to hear from was Apollo. They consulted his prestigious oracle (literally, "mouthpiece") at Delphi, but its response was not encouraging. Just when the Athenians sounded out the oracle is not known, but it was probably in late 481 or early 480 B.C.

The Greeks firmly believed that the gods offered signs of the future, if only men know how to read them. The pseudoscience of divination, therefore, was vital to Greek religion. Its branches included the interpretation of dreams, observation of birds, sacrifice, chance omens such as sneezing, and consultation with representatives of the gods at oracular shrines. Of the last, none was more prestigious than Delphi, where the god spoke through a priestess in a trance. Delphi's prestige rested not only on piety and self-promotion, but also on the solid record of good advice that the oracle had amassed over the years. That, in turn, reflects the thick network of communications that Delphi maintained. The oracle's advice was based often enough on fact to be worthy of attention.

Aristonice, priestess of Apollo at Delphi, told the Athenians not even to consider resisting Persia: "O wretches," she asked, "why are you sitting?" Her advice: "Flee to the ends of the earth, leave your homes and the heights of your city," because "miserable things are on the way." Seeing that Apollo's customers were, to put it mildly, unsatisfied with this response, one of the authorities at Delphi told the Athenians to try again. This time they should approach the priestess as suppliants, holding laurel branches. It was no doubt understood that they would eventually have to repay Apollo's patience with a more substantial gift.

This time the priestess held out a little more hope. She said that although everything else in Athens would be captured by the enemy,

> Far-seeing Zeus grants to thrice-born Athena a wooden wall,
> The only place not to be sacked, it will help you and your children.
> Do not wait for the great host coming from the continent,
> Cavalry and foot soldiers; turn your back and withdraw from the foe.
> Eventually you will stand opposite them.
> O divine Salamis, you will destroy the sons of women
> Either at seedtime or at harvesttime.

Certainly the gods move in mysterious ways, but it is hard not to conclude from so detailed a response that the priests of Apollo had done their homework about the policy options under consideration in Athens. The oracle offered something for everyone, as a heated discussion back in Athens demonstrated.

Nearly everyone wanted to fight; the question was how. Some Athenians, particularly in the older generation, took "wooden wall" to mean a wooden palisade with which the Acropolis should be defended. But others said that "wooden walls" meant wooden ships, i.e., the Athenian fleet. All effort should focus on readying for battle the new navy begun in 493 B.C. But their opponents raised an objection: Salamis.

If Apollo had meant to encourage Athenians to fight at sea, he would not have referred to destruction at Salamis; on the contrary, he was warning them to avoid Salamis. So said the fretful, and they were

led by the oracle collectors. These men, professional divines who ped-
dled books of predictions, had a significant following in Athens. They
were defeatists; rather than resist Xerxes, they wanted Athenians to
emigrate as the Phocaeans had. But Themistocles outwitted them.

Far from discouraging the Athenians, the god was steering them
toward "divine Salamis," said Themistocles. Surely Apollo would have
referred to "wretched Salamis" if he had meant to dissuade Athens from
the sea. The "sons of women" who would be destroyed must mean the
Persians, he said. Note, too, that the oracle predicted a battle there
either in spring (harvesttime in Athens) or fall (when the grain is sown
in Athens). In war, as in all else, timing is everything; this particular, as
will become clear later, is highly significant.

No politician wins without allies. No ally is more valuable than an
ex-enemy, especially a famous enemy. In Cimon son of Miltiades, that is
precisely what Themistocles got. Miltiades was the victor of Marathon
in 490 B.C. and no friend of Themistocles. After Miltiades' death from
gangrene in 489 B.C. his mantle passed to his young son. In late 481 or
early 480 Cimon might have led the charge against Themistocles but
instead did just the opposite, and in the most public way possible.

At the height of the debate over the oracle, Cimon led a public procession. He was an aristocrat and a member of what amounted to one of
the most exclusive clubs in Athens, the cavalry. You could always tell a
cavalryman in Athens by his long hair and his dandy's clothes, an odd
combination of Spartan toughness and Ionian conspicuous consump-
tion. Tall and curly-haired, Cimon stood at the front of his procession
of fellow horsemen. They marched from the edge of the city through
the streets toward the Acropolis. There, in Athens's holiest shrine, the
temple of Athena Polias, Cimon dedicated his horse's bridle to the goddess. Then he took one of the shields hanging on the temple wall, said a
prayer to Athena, and marched down to the sea.

In a grand gesture of political theater, the uncrowned king of
Athens's conservatives gave his public blessing to the radicals. What
Cimon said, in effect, was that the national emergency had abolished
the difference between aristocratic knights and the lower classes who
manned the rowers' benches. For the duration of the Persian Wars, all
Athenians would be seamen. Cimon had proclaimed, in effect, a sacred
union. It was a gesture of statesmanship of such daring that it would be

tempting to see Themistocles behind it somehow, if not for the knowledge that he was not the only clever patriot in Athens. Cimon deserves
credit for sacrificing party for country.

Themistocles won the debate over strategy. Herodotus reports
that the Athenians voted to await the barbarian invasion of Greece with
their entire supply of manpower deployed on ships. As agreed by the
Hellenic League at its meeting at the Isthmus, the other Greek allies
would defend the country by land. They would try to stop the Persians
in the north, but if that failed, the Athenians resolved to evacuate Attica
and fight at Salamis. The pious were mollified by a resolution to leave
the city in the care of its patron god, Athena.

Nothing so became the land of the Athenians as the manner of
their leaving it. In light of the common criticism of democracy as soft
and submissive, it is worth appraising the price that democratic Athens
was willing to pay for freedom. The Athenian assembly voted not only
to send its young men out to battle but to uproot its elderly, its women,
and its children. And the march of the population of Athens aboard
refugee ships—the population of a city so ancient that its name is older
than the Greek language itself—the willing steps of a people who did
not know if they would go home again, might have been as stunning a
sight as the seven days' procession of Xerxes' army across the bridges
of the Hellespont.

Later generations would revere the decision for exile and inscribe
and reinscribe it in stone. They celebrated its daring, and they were right.
While most Greeks surrendered, while their Peloponnesian allies tried to
abandon them, the Athenians thought it a high honor to resist Persia.
Rather than flee Greece, says Herodotus, "they stayed behind and waited
courageously for the enemy to invade their land." The day they passed a
motion to evacuate Athens, the Athenians decided that not only their soldiers and rowers stood on the watchtowers of history, they all did.

On a likely reconstruction, the Athenians decided to carry out the
evacuation in two stages. The date of the decree may be as late as June
480 B.C. Athenian women, children, and old men probably left first,
while the young men stayed behind to man the fleet.

The final evacuation began only when the men returned from
Artemisium, about September 1. The Athenian fleet put in at its harbor
at Phaleron about three days after leaving Artemisium, a distance of

about 214 nautical miles. The Persian fleet had remained in northern Euboea for six days after the battle, in order to repair ships, receive reinforcements from the Greek islands, and see the battlefield at Thermopylae. That meant that the Athenians had less than a week to carry out the bulk of their mass departure. To be sure, neither the Persian navy nor the Persian army's advance guard, which reached Attica about September 5, could scour all Attica, which meant there was still time to escape until the full Persian forces arrived around September 20. But the first sight of Persians in Attica no doubt lit a fire under Athenian stragglers.

The evacuation turned out to be more spontaneous and slapdash than the Athenian assembly had planned. But Law and Order were Spartan goddesses; the Athenians worshipped Freedom. Athenians were famously individualistic and suspicious of authority, and no doubt many had ignored the earlier mandate to leave. Others may have first left but then, when the Persians failed to appear, returned to Athens. So the exodus of September 480 B.C. included women and children, people who, in principle, should have already left for Troezen. Some now went to Troezen, some to Aegina, and the rest to Salamis.

Yet even with the news from Artemisium and Thermopylae, it was still not easy to convince the Athenians to leave home. Help came from Athens's council of former chief magistrates, the Areopagus, named for the hill near the Acropolis on which it met. The Areopagus voted every sailor a maintenance allowance of eight drachmas, about enough money to buy food for three weeks. The money probably came from the state treasury. Classical Greek navies carried only the most minimal supplies. Sailors were expected to buy food at local markets, which made an allowance essential for most men.

Themistocles was a member of the Areopagus, but an alternate story denies his ability to convince that council to assign state funds to the fleet. Instead, the money depended on a scheme of his. In the confusion of departure, someone stole the gold Gorgon head of the statue of Athena on the Acropolis. On the excuse of looking for this priceless relic, Themistocles managed to get people's luggage ransacked. He confiscated all the money he found and used it to pay the men. We do not know which story is the truth, nor do we know if the Gorgon head was ever found.

It may be that the city of Troezen encouraged the evacuation as well. At least in later years, Troezenians claimed that they passed a law to support Athenian refugees at public expense. Each Athenian family relocated to Troezen was voted a modest daily subsidy; their children were allowed to pick fruit from any trees they wanted; and teachers were hired for them as well.

An added fillip for departure came from the Acropolis. The ancients believed that when a city faced destruction, its patron deity left first. The patron of Athens was the goddess Athena, who revealed herself in many ways, one of which was supposedly as a great snake that lived in a temple on the Acropolis. No one had ever seen the snake except, allegedly, the temple staff, who claimed to have proof of its existence. Once a month the priestess of Athena the Guardian of the City left out a honey cake and, somehow or other, it disappeared. The snake, it was thought, must have eaten it. This month, however, the impossible happened: the honey cake was left untouched. The priestess drew the conclusion that Athena had abandoned the city. She concluded that the Persians would destroy Athens, and she informed the Athenian people.

Behind the priestess, it was whispered, stood the serpent of the speaker's platform, Themistocles. The story of the snake and the honey cake, they said, was just a comedy of his devising. Themistocles allegedly convinced the priestess to concoct the tale of the rejected honey cake in order to manipulate public opinion. If Themistocles did indeed negotiate with the priestess, she was probably no pushover. A mature woman from a prominent family, she managed the most important cult in the city. She served for life and lived on the Acropolis. She was surely as savvy politically as she was pious.

One way or another, the priestess informed the city of Athena's flight, but not every last Athenian followed. In the countryside, where most Athenians lived, what looked like safe hiding places tempted those who could not bear to leave. The Persians caught them and sent five hundred Athenian prisoners across the Aegean Sea to the island of Samos. How many Athenians they murdered in Attica is not recorded.

It was the supreme emergency in the history of the nation. Democracy in Athens lasted 250 years, and most of that time Athens was a naval power, yet this was one of only two occasions when every single available man was drafted for service aboard ship; the other occasion came later at the low point of the Peloponnesian War. Little in the long history of government by the people tested democracy like this moment.

If it worked, the evacuation of Athens would be celebrated as one of the supreme strategic retreats in the history of war. If it failed, it would be lamented in exile.

Few of Athens's blue bloods wished to risk capture by Xerxes. Among their ranks in the evacuees was a teenager named Pericles, son of the aristocrat Xanthippus son of Ariphron of the deme of Cholargos. One day Pericles would be the first man in Athens. In 480 B.C., however, for the second time in his fourteen years, Pericles and his family, including his brother and sister, were going into exile. In 484 B.C., Xanthippus had been ostracized and the family left Athens, possibly for the northern Peloponnesian city of Sicyon, where they had relatives. That had been a private drama, but in 480, all Athens shared Pericles' experience of upheaval.

Anecdotes of the departure abounded. One story, for example, said that Xanthippus's dog was so devoted that he swam after his master's trireme across the mile-wide straits of Salamis, reached the other shore, and immediately died of exhaustion. A spot in Salamis known centuries later as the Dog's Tomb was said to mark his grave.

The departure of a Greek warrior was ordinarily marked by a ceremony. Typically, the woman of the house would use a small pitcher to pour a libation, an offering of wine to the gods, in the hope of a safe return. But who made the libation when the whole family departed, as most Athenian families did in September 480 B.C.? Whoever presided, perhaps the words echoed these sentiments of the Greek poet Theognis of Megara:

> *May Zeus who dwells in the sky ever hold his right hand over this city*
> *to keep off harm, and may the other blessed immortals do likewise, and*
> *may Apollo make straight our tongue and mind.*
> *. . . after offering libations satisfying to*
> *the gods let us drink, . . .*
> *fearing not the Median war.*

The Athenian refugees carried what little they could into exile. The rest they left behind, everything from clay tableware, lamps, and loom weights to glass bowls, coins, and jewelry buried in the backyard, and bronze objects of every kind—pots, bowls, ladles, tripods, weights decorated with dolphins. The wealthiest left family graves marked by statues, including images of horsemen and athletes, immigrants and infantrymen, lions and boars, sphinxes, wreaths, and flowers. They left behind records of past mourning, like the epitaph for one Anaxilas of Naxos, who died around 510 B.C., leaving behind a family "fraught with grief, sorrow, and lamentation." They left behind tombs containing gold rings, earrings, and necklaces; iron swords and spearheads; ceramic toys; knucklebones; and painted pottery of every shape and size, decorated variously with scenes of gods and heroes, lovers and conquerors, roosters and sphinxes, athletes and warriors, weavers, satyrs, and dolphins.

As the Persians made their progress through a largely empty Attica, they looted whatever they could and demolished whatever seemed worth the trouble of destruction. The vengeance that had been denied at Marathon was finally at hand.

What did the Persians think of the Athenians as they smashed their vases? Did they stop to look at the painted scenes? Did they notice that the images of drinking, playing, and praying were far outnumbered by those of fighting? Did they consider the meaning of all those pictures of warriors spearing, stabbing, and pummeling each other to death and then fighting over the corpses—having of course first stripped the enemy dead of their arms?

What did the Persians think of the Athenians as they overturned their statues? Did they notice, for instance, a bronze statue of Apollo holding a bow? This tall, strong, lean, and powerful figure is more street fighter than god of light. What did they make of Artemis with her quiver or Athena in her bronze helmet and breastplate of goatskin and snakes?

Did it occur to the Persians that they had taken on a nation of killers? Or did they simply dismiss the Greeks as braggart savages? No doubt the latter, since soldiers rarely imagine their own death. Whatever they found in deserted Attica, the Persians probably preferred focusing on the kind of scene illustrated by an Iranian cylinder seal of the period. This object, made of the semiprecious stone chalcedony, would be rolled across a wet clay stamp on a document to yield an image of Persia triumphant. It showed the Great King spearing a fallen Greek foot soldier.

When the Persians reached the city of Athens they found it empty. Athenians were not in evidence except on the Acropolis. The men there were not many in number, but they were diverse. A group amounting to, at a guess, several hundred consisted of treasurers of the temple of Athena, who were all wealthy men; men too poor or too physically infirm to support themselves on Salamis; and, finally, those who simply refused to believe that the "wooden wall" meant ships and not a wooden palisade on the Acropolis itself. They put up a better fight than might have been expected.

The Athenian Acropolis is a natural fortress, its slopes sheer and precipitous. Oblong in shape, it stands about 512 feet high and covers a space of about 1,000 by 500 feet—about three times as long and three times as wide as an American football field. The defenders barricaded the Acropolis with doors and wooden beams, which they presumably took from the temples. In all likelihood, they built the barricade on the stone gateway to the Acropolis.

The Persians, meanwhile, based themselves on the nearby Areopagus, or Hill of Ares, a rocky summit that rises to a height of about 375 feet across a narrow valley from the west end of the Acropolis. From there, Persian archers shot flaming arrows up into the wooden enclosure that the Athenians had built. Tied to each arrow was a strip of hemp or some other plant fiber that had been dipped in flammable liquid, such as pine resin, and which was ignited as it was shot.

Beforehand, the Persians had called on Athenian exiles that they had in tow and sent them over to the Acropolis to talk sense to the defenders. The exiles were heirs of the former tyrant Hippias, last seen in Athens in 490 B.C. at the battle of Marathon. The wardens of the Acropolis were unimpressed. They responded to the exiles' offer by rolling stones down on the Persians who attempted to climb the Acropolis.

For what Herodotus calls "a long time"—perhaps several days—the Persians were stymied. Then they found a way up via a trail in the cleft of the rock on the northwestern part of the Acropolis, a way so steep that it had been left unguarded. When the defenders saw the Persians reach the top, some of them committed suicide by leaping off the hill. The others took refuge in the temple of the goddess. Murder in a sanctuary was a great crime under Greek law. And yet, says Herodotus, as soon as the Persians reached the top of the Acropolis, they made straight for the temple and "they opened the gates and murdered the suppliants." There were no survivors.

Athens's unknown warriors could not have looked less gallant: men too poor to own armor or too duty-bound to join the fleet at Salamis or too frail to move without a walking stick. Yet like the Spartan soldiers at Thermopylae, these Athenians defended Greek soil to the death. So far as is known, no monument was ever erected to them, but as Pericles said not long afterward, brave men have the whole earth as their sepulcher.

After slaughtering the Athenians, the Persians looted the treasures of the temples and then set fire to the whole hill. The wooden beams of its stone buildings blazed, leaving fire-stained wrecks.

The Persians had destroyed the Acropolis but not the Acropolis known to us. The Athenian Acropolis whose ruins are famous today is largely the product of the generation after the Persian Wars. The Acropolis's best-known building, the Temple of Athena Parthenos, the Virgin Goddess Athena—the Parthenon—was completed in 432 B.C.

The Athenian Acropolis of 480 B.C. was not the icon of Western art that it would later become. Its art and architecture were exuberant, experimental, even grotesque—anything but serene. The old temples of the Acropolis were full of statues of lions and sea monsters, of Gorgons and gaily painted snakes, of men with trim black beards, of long-tressed women in long pleated gowns, of youths with hair teased into snail-shell-style curls.

The bric-a-brac of the cluttered space of the old Acropolis reflected centuries of accretion rather than a single classical program. For the Athenians to rebuild the Acropolis, as they did, beginning in the 440s B.C., they had first to clear away the old buildings and statues. The fires set by Xerxes' men in 480 B.C. proved, therefore, to be an act of creative destruction, although it did not seem that way to the Greeks at the time.

On the contrary, it might have seemed like the end of the world. The Persians had destroyed the sum total of a people's religious faith. Everything that the Athenians had accumulated over the centuries, patiently and piously, had been ruined in an afternoon. To the ancient Greeks, what the Persians did amounted to a crime against the gods. Fighting the barbarians afterward was no longer an act merely of self-defense; it was an act of piety.

Xerxes now controlled Athens. He sent a horseman hurrying back to Susa to bring the good news to Artabanus, who was the Great King's uncle, his regent, and the arch-dove of the preexpedition debates. Xerxes had reason to welcome the congratulations that his men now surely showered upon him. Hermotimus was no doubt among them.

Back in Persia, in the Palace of Darius at Persepolis, carved into a doorjamb, stands a sculpture in relief of a beardless attendant. Well-dressed, carefully groomed, and good-looking, he is usually thought to be a eunuch. In his right hand, he carries a perfume bottle, a round-bottomed, tubular flask closed with a stopper. He holds a towel draped over his left hand. He strides ahead, as if to bring the objects to the Great King.

So we might imagine Hermotimus, after the fall of the Acropolis, waiting on Xerxes. As a high-ranking eunuch, Hermotimus would have brought the ruler honeyed words instead of cosmetics and cloths, but the principle was the same: devotion. Hermotimus would not have wanted to miss an opportunity to flatter the Great King.

But the eunuch, a connoisseur of vengeance, would probably have turned a skeptical eye on the flames over Athens. The Greek fleet still sat in the Salamis channel, within sight of the Persian victors on the Acropolis. Hermotimus would want nothing less than to see the enemy's ships smashed.

The Greeks had not surrendered. Athens was occupied, Athens was burning, but the Athenians were unbowed. The sack of the Acropolis no doubt struck terror in some Athenian hearts, but for the most part it seems only to have increased their appetite for battle.

In fact, the Greeks' greatest enemy at this point was not Persia but themselves. The arguments swung this way and that during the course of violent disagreements at Greek naval headquarters. The Greeks had abandoned Athens, but their navy now lay barely a mile away. The fleet had docked at Salamis, in the harbor across the channel from the mainland that now lay in enemy hands. On that fleet now depended the future of Greece.

CHAPTER FOUR

~~

SALAMIS

He is dressed in a long, coarse, woolen garment wrapped tightly around his body. Draped over his shoulders, the crimson-colored cloak extends to his ankles. Carefully braided strands of his long hair run down both his chest and back. His bronze helmet is crowned with a transverse crest as a mark of his high rank. He carries a wooden staff as a sign of office. He is barefoot.

His face, or what is visible of it under the helmet, has the lean look of a lifetime of rugged training. If his eyes betray any expression, it is probably the dispassion that the Spartans considered to be almost always appropriate, except when they were mourning the death of a family member in battle, in which case they were supposed to smile from pride. The Spartans were a paradoxical people, and in Eurybiades son of Eurycleides, their ironies reached a peak. This description of him is an educated guess, but the burdens that he bore were all real.

He was the commander in chief of the Greek navy, and on Salamis on September 23, it was his job to hammer out a common strategy among his squabbling allies. In Salamis the goats were grazing and the Greeks were butting heads. The role of conciliator did not come easily to a Spartan, but neither did the role of admiral. The Spartans were a nation of infantrymen. Sparta's navy was small and unimportant, a mere concession to the geographical accident that Spartan territory

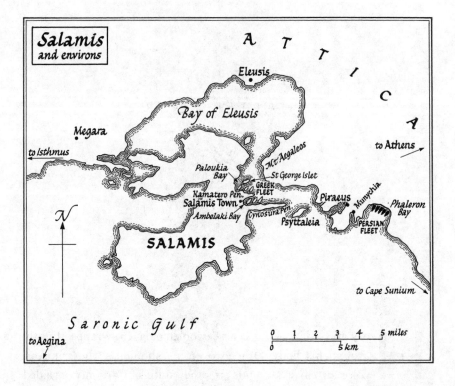

extended to the sea. Yet as *navarch*, "admiral," Eurybiades exercised power that would have been denied to him on land. Only a king could command a Spartan army on land, and Eurybiades was a commoner.

Eurybiades was an ambitious man but a feeble manager. As far as we can tell, he had neither strong opinions nor deep insight. He was not about to whip the bickering Greeks on Salamis into shape. But he was a patriot and had the one touch of greatness of knowing when to yield to a better man.

The war had swollen the size of Salamis's population. In peacetime there were perhaps 5,000 to 10,000 inhabitants on the island; suddenly, another 100,000 to 150,000 people had arrived. That included the personnel of more than three hundred triremes of the Greek fleet as well as a large portion of Athens's civilian refugees. And at times it might have seemed as if every last Greek on Salamis was at odds with all the others. The locals were no doubt tired of the newcomers even as the less scrupulous tried to squeeze a few extra coins out of them. The rowers complained about their captains. The captains complained about their commanders. The commanders of each city-state's contingent complained about the other city-states' contingents. Everyone appeared to have his own strategy and was ready to defend it to the death. Meanwhile, the Greeks looked across the straits at the empty countryside of Attica and waited for the barbarians. For two weeks Persia's forces had been lumbering in, from the first fast horsemen to the last camp followers.

"Pounded by the sea," as Sophocles calls Salamis, and short on arable land, the ancient island, like its modern counterpart, is likely to have housed fishermen in nearly every cove. Each morning in the predawn hours when the water was at its calmest, and so least likely to disturb their nets, they headed out to sea. But even if every fisherman on Salamis had doubled his catch, the islanders still could not have fed all the immigrants. The Athenians no doubt ferried over grain and other supplies to the island, but there was a limit to the amount they could have provided. Nor was it practical for them to carry over freshwater, which is usually at a premium in Greece.

The refugees had reason to be frightened, the sailors had reason to be vigilant, and everyone had a right to be tired. The civilians had been uprooted; the naval personnel had been rowing and fighting for more than three weeks. During that time the seamen had also had to repair ships, cremate the dead, practice maneuvers, and mount a major evacuation. And, with all the to-ing and fro-ing, most of them had traveled five hundred miles and more. Yet the biggest battle still lay before them.

This was Salamis at the beginning of the fourth week of September of 480 B.C., a harbor turned into a safe haven and a backwater turned into a naval base. That the Greek fleet was at Salamis at all was itself the result of a Themistoclean ruse. After Artemisium, when the Athenians learned that there would be no infantry stand in Boeotia, they asked their allies to stop at Salamis on their way back home to Aegina, the Peloponnese, or the island of Ceos. The Athenians needed to evacuate their people from Attica. Afterward it would be convenient for them to meet the allies at Salamis to plot the fleet's next move. The allies agreed. Meanwhile, reinforcement ships, which had not been at Artemisium, had gathered at Pogon, near Troezen, on the western side of the Saronic Gulf. They made for Salamis as well.

Salamis was simply a meeting point. No ally had agreed to fight a battle there. On the contrary, the obvious move might have seemed to move the fleet to a harbor at the Isthmus of Corinth. The Greek alliance's army was making its stand there, and surely it made sense to have the navy nearby.

At the very end of August the Spartans received news of the disaster at Thermopylae. The full moon of August 19 had marked the end of the Olympic Games as well as of the Carnea, a Spartan festival. During the festival religious scruples added to the arguments of Spartan doves against mobilizing in any large number. Now that they had satisfied the gods and Thermopylae had fallen, the Spartans immediately called their army out in full force and marched to the Isthmus. Here, joined by troops from Corinth and from a dozen or so other Peloponnesian city-states, they blocked the main road and began building a wall across the narrow Isthmus, at its narrowest less than five miles wide. They worked night and day on the project, using stone, bricks, timbers, and sand baskets.

Corinth had an excellent harbor on the Saronic Gulf not far from the wall, at a place called Cenchreae. It is understandable if Corinthians and other Peloponnesians preferred to fight there rather than at Salamis.

Yet the fleet was at Salamis and any movement would have seemed like a retreat. Themistocles, who wanted to fight at Salamis, knew that, just as he knew that Athens's approximately two hundred triremes made up more than half of the Greek navy. Athens had a great deal of clout.

Salamis is an island of modest dimensions. It is about thirty six square miles in area, making it about twenty-five times smaller than Attica. It is an island of low hills, whose highest point is a mountain in the south rising 1,325 feet.

Salamis is a horseshoe-shaped island, containing about sixty-four miles of coastline, with its hollow side facing west. Nestled along the western coast of Attica, Salamis stretches as far west as Megara, the city-state whose territory lay between Athens and Corinth. On the coast opposite Salamis to the north, between Megara and the city of Athens, lies the Athenian town of Eleusis. The sea widens into a gulf here. Eleusis was sacred to Demeter, goddess of agriculture, and home of the

Eleusinian Mysteries, an annual ritual offering hope of life after death.

In the northeast corner of Salamis is the long and narrow Cynosura peninsula. In Greek, Cynosura means "dog's tail." Cynosura juts into the sea, pointing like a dagger northeastward toward Piraeus and the city of Athens beyond. Just northeast of Cynosura lies the islet of Psytalleia; together the islet and the peninsula all but block off the eastern end of the Salamis straits from the Saronic Gulf. Traveling westward in the straits, about three miles to the west of Psyttaleia one reaches another islet, known today as St. George. Between the two islets, on the northeast side of Salamis and opposite the Athenian mainland, lies the harbor of the ancient city of Salamis.

This harbor, today known as Ambelaki Bay, is an excellent natural anchorage. About one-quarter mile wide at its mouth, it is always calm. The Kamateró peninsula rises to the north, protecting the harbor from the north wind, while south of the harbor the Cynosura peninsula offers shelter from both the south wind and the waves of the Saronic Gulf.

We may imagine that in 480 B.C. part of the Greek fleet was based in Ambelaki Bay. As the site of the classical city, Ambelaki Bay would have been outfitted with a quay for docking ships. But the fleet was large enough that its ships would have spilled over to the next bay northward, Paloukia Bay. Sheltered from the winds by the Kamateró peninsula and by St. George, Paloukia Bay is lined with sandy beaches, ideal for mooring triremes.

Mythology made Salamis home to King Ajax, son of Telamon, a stalwart of the Greek army at Troy. A huge man, Ajax was known as the "bulwark." As a hero, Ajax represented the triumph of brawn over brains, that is, the opposite of his archenemy, the wily Odysseus. Though based on Ajax's island, the Greeks would have to emulate Odysseus if they were to defeat Persia. And they would have to match their words with deeds.

Some of the evacuees were no doubt billeted in Salamis's homes and public buildings, but there could hardly have been room for very many. The captains might have stayed aboard their ships, perhaps in makeshift cabins, but a trireme was too cramped to sleep more than about half of its crew. Many if not most of the newcomers to Salamis would have camped out.

Conditions could hardly have been luxurious. In normal times, it was considered scandalous for a captain to give his oarsmen time off to get washed in the public baths, just the sort of thing to make them too soft for battle. In the emergency of 480 B.C., there was no time for such extravagance, and if there was a bathhouse in Salamis, it could not have fit even a fraction of the men crowded onto the island.

The rowers would have to bathe in the sea or go dirty. But if the Athenians had planned ahead properly, they were probably not hungry. Since Athens's leaders had expected to use Salamis as a base, they are likely to have stored big supplies of food there for the Greek fleet.

Twenty-two Greek cities were represented at Salamis, for a total of more than three hundred ships. Six states from the Peloponnese provided vessels: Sparta, Corinth, Sicyon, Epidaurus, Troezen, and Hermione. In central Greece, Athens and Megara contributed ships, while Ambracia and Leucas represented northwestern Greece. From the islands there were ships from the city-states of Chalcis, Eretria, and Styra in Euboea, Aegina in the Saronic Gulf, and from the Cyclades, Ceos, Naxos, Cythnos, Seriphos, Siphnos, and Melos. Croton in Italy was the only western Greek city to take part. It sent one trireme, but its crew may all have resided in Greece: political refugees, they were eager to find a patron to help them return home and overthrow their enemies.

Most of these states provided only a tiny number of ships. Leucas, for instance, sent only three triremes; Cythnos sent only a trireme and a penteconter; while Melos, Siphnos and Seriphos sent only penteconters—two from Melos, one each from Siphnos and Seriphos. With its defection at Artemisium, Lemnos provided one trireme. These numbers speak eloquently of financial and demographic poverty and of loyalty to the Greek cause. Plataea, which had sent men to Artemisium to help fill the rowers' benches of Athens's triremes, was not represented at Salamis. After Artemisium, the Plataeans had hurried home to convey their families and property to safety.

Several of these states were in the process of being swamped by the Persian tide. Plataea, Chalcis, Eretria, and Styra had fallen. Athens was in the process of evacuation, and once the Persians reached Athens, nothing stopped them from overrunning Megara, the next city-state to the west. Troezen was crowded with Athenian refugees. Except for

Seriphos, Siphnos, and Melos, the other Cycladic ships came from states that had submitted to Persia. The commanders disobeyed orders and joined the Greeks.

Still, the allies might have been disappointed at their inability to attract more ships to Salamis. There was one prominent no-show. The Corcyreans had promised ambassadors of the Hellenic League to fight for Greece and against slavery. The western Greek island of Corcyra (modern Corfu) had even launched sixty triremes, a fleet second only to Athens's in size. But the Corcyreans sent the ships only as far as Cape Taenarum in the southern Peloponnese in order not to anger Xerxes— the eventual winner of the war, they were sure. To the Greeks they pleaded the excuse of the Etesian winds, the powerful nor'easter that sometimes blows in the fall and stops navigation cold.

Then there was Sicily. Its leading Greek city-state was Syracuse, ruled in 480 B.C. by a tyrant named Gelon. The Hellenic League had asked Gelon for help against Persia. He promised a huge number of ships and men but named too high a price: supreme command. Both the Spartan and Athenian ambassadors who went to see him refused. Besides, Gelon had a war with Carthage on his hands. In the end, Gelon sent only a representative to Delphi, carrying a treasure to give as a gift to Xerxes, should the Great King prevail.

The three biggest contingents at Salamis were from Aegina, with 30 ships, Corinth, with 50 ships, and Athens, with 180 ships, about half of the triremes in the Greek fleet; Sparta contributed only 16 ships.

The Greeks had 368 ships at Salamis, as a reasonable reading of the tricky evidence concludes. To take only fifth century B.C. sources: the playwright Aeschylus says that the Greek numbers at Salamis "amounted to thirty tens of ships, and another ten elite ships"; the historian Thucydides reports a claim that the Greeks had 400 ships of which two-thirds (i.e., 267) were Athenian. Aeschylus's figures are imprecise and poetic; Thucydides' are imprecise and attributed to a bragging speaker fifty years after the battle. Herodotus's numbers are better, if problematic.

Herodotus says that the Greeks had 378 ships, of which 180 were Athenian. He also adds that two ships defected to the Greeks from the Persians, bringing the number of ships to an even 380. Unfortunately, when Herodotus cites the ship numbers city-state by city-state, the figures add up to only 366 ships. Herodotus also specifies that the Greek fleet at Salamis was larger than the Greek fleet at Artemisium, which eventually numbered 333 ships. Assuming that Herodotus's city-by-city figures are more accurate than his total, it would seem that the Greeks had 368 ships (366 plus the two defectors) on the day of the battle of Salamis.

Sparta had been made commander of the allied fleet, probably at the meeting at Corinth in the autumn of 481 B.C. when the Hellenic League had been formed. The natural commander of the fleet would have been an Athenian, presumably Themistocles, but the other Greeks resented Athens's new naval power and feared Athenian muscle flexing. They insisted on a Spartan commander or they would dissolve the fleet. The Athenians yielded, and the Spartan government named Eurybiades.

Two city-states probably led the charge against the appointment of an Athenian as commander: Aegina and Corinth. Aegina is an island in the Saronic Gulf, south of Salamis, about thirty-three square miles in size. Located about seventeen miles from Athens, Aegina and its conical mountain (about 1,750 feet high) are clearly visible from the Acropolis. Like many neighbors in ancient Greece, Athens and Aegina were long-time rivals. In later years, Pericles expressed Athens's habitual contempt for its neighbor by describing Aegina as "the eyesore of Piraeus," referring to Athens's main port after 479 B.C. Eyesores, of course, need to be rubbed out, and under Pericles, Athens smashed Aegina's power once and for all. In 480, however, the rivalry was still burning.

Though small, Aegina before the days of Themistocles was a greater naval power than Athens. The Aeginetans were a maritime people who took the turtle as the symbol on their coins. For two decades before 480 B.C, Aegina and Athens waged a very violent war. In 490, on the eve of the Persian landing at Marathon, only Spartan intervention prevented Aegina from joining in the attack on Athens. The two states laid down their differences in 481 at the conference establishing the Hellenic League; no doubt Athens's sprint ahead in the arms race, by deciding in 483 to build a two-hundred-ship navy, encouraged Aegina to think peace.

Corinth smarted from less nasty wounds. Traditional rivals, Athens and Corinth had avoided all-out war. But Themistocles hardly endeared Athens to Corinth when he arbitrated a dispute between Corinth and Corcyra in the latter's favor. Corcyra was a naval power and a former colony of Corinth that had little love for its mother city. Looking even farther westward, Themistocles also strengthened Athens's connections with the Greek city-states in Italy and Sicily.

None of this Athenian interest in the west could have pleased Corinth, which had long had maritime connections there. By modern roads Corinth and Athens are fifty-five miles apart. Ancient Corinth was a wealthy city, grown rich on the oil of the olive trees that grew well in its fertile soil, on maritime trade, and on prostitution. Long the home of a tyranny that was famous for its vices, Corinth in 480 B.C. was now an oligarchy that preferred to sell vice to others. Corinthians were jealous and suspicious of an Athens that had once been a backwater but that had outstripped Corinth first as a trading center and now, recently, as a naval power.

The Corinthian admiral in 480 B.C. was Adimantus son of Ocytus. Corinth was an ally of Sparta, but Corinth loved its luxuries, and Adimantus was no doubt better dressed than Eurybiades. For that matter, he was probably better dressed than Themistocles. Unlike Athenians, Corinth's oligarchs had no need to look like men of the people. We may imagine Adimantus in an elegant cloak of woven linen, cream-colored with a dark purple edging. His bronze breastplate no doubt featured incised musculature. His helmet, also bronze and made out of a single sheet of metal, was surely of the Corinthian style: close-fitting and custom-made, with a nosepiece and eyeholes. The helmet's lower edge might have been decorated with a delicate, incised, spiral border. The helmet would give in to a blow without cracking, while padding underneath cushioned the impact. Adimantus may have worn a roll of cloth under his greaves to avoid chafing. His shield may have been emblazoned with an image of Pegasus, the winged horse that was a symbol of Corinth.

Between the return of their fleet from Artemisium and the arrival of the Persians, the Athenians had only five or six days to complete their evacuation. We do not know if the allied ships at Salamis helped the Athenians evacuate Athens or if they stood and waited. No doubt a steady stream of eleventh-hour transfers of people, property, and supplies across the narrow channel from Attica to Salamis was still flowing when the first hoofbeats of the enemy horses were heard. At any rate, even before the enemy had appeared, Eurybiades called the generals of the allied states to a council of war at Salamis. The date was about September 23.

A navy whose main admirals cordially hated each other. A naval commander in chief who came from a country famous for its inattention to ships. A naval base teeming with refugees whom it could not feed for long. A set of allies who were itching to leave the war zone. It was of this unpromising material that the Greeks had to forge a strategy for victory.

Since there were twenty separate commanders at Salamis, they needed a sizable space for their deliberation. Presumably, they met either in a public building or in a large private house. Every Greek city had its *agora*, the open space in the center of town that combined marketplace and political forum. The agora was usually bordered on one or more sides by a *stoa*, or covered portico, offering shelter from sun, wind, and rain.

We might imagine the generals at Salamis meeting in a covered portico of the agora, perhaps within sight of the statue there of the great Athenian statesman Solon, shown in the act of addressing the people, with his arm modestly tucked inside his cloak. Perhaps they even met in the Temple of Ajax, a shrine to the great hero.

It is an open question whether the Greeks would have made good use of leisure time for discussion had it been available. The Greeks were so famous for talk and argument that some doubted their capacity for action. Cyrus the Great of Persia, for example, had once dismissed the Spartan army by saying that Greeks were men who set aside a place in the center of town where they could swear oaths and cheat each other, referring to the agora.

The Greeks in council at Salamis would have the chance to prove Cyrus wrong, but they would have to move quickly. However long it took the full Persian force to get from Thermopylae to Athens, once they arrived, they seemed to fly.

Eurybiades opened the meeting by asking for recommendations for strategy. Which of the lands that they controlled should be the base for future naval operations against the enemy? He explicitly excluded Attica, since the Greeks were not defending it. So bald a statement of the facts might have stung Themistocles. True, Eurybiades did not exclude Salamis as a base, but he did not favor it, either.

A variety of opinions was heard, but the most common theme was that the fleet should move westward to the Isthmus of Corinth. Perhaps Themistocles argued that Salamis was no farther from the Isthmus, about twenty-five miles, than Artemisium had been from Thermopylae, a distance of forty miles. And all things considered, the Greeks had done very well at Artemisium. If Themistocles spoke in this vein, he might have been shocked at the response.

Herodotus reports the majority viewpoint among the speakers at the council, and apparently the Peloponnesians predominated among those who spoke. They made it clear that their concern was less the suitability of Salamis as a base for victory than as a getaway point after defeat. If the Greek fleet was beaten at the Isthmus, the Peloponnesian sailors had only to get ashore and they could walk home, if need be. If the Greek fleet was beaten at Salamis, however, the survivors would be blockaded on an island.

In short, the Peloponnesian admirals were defeatists. Their gloom could have only deepened when an Athenian messenger interrupted the council with the news that the Persians were in Attica and had set everything on fire. Worse, they had taken the Acropolis. This latter information, delivered in person, might have been confirmed by signal relay. The smoke of the buildings would have been visible from the hills of Salamis, and word of it could have been sent down to the city by a prearranged signal, perhaps a flashing of shields.

The result was chaos. Herodotus describes it as a *thorubos*, a loud, confused noise or confusion more generally. Some of the commanders made a quick exit. They rushed to their ships and ordered the sails hoisted for departure. The rest of the generals stayed at the meeting and passed a motion to fight the Persians at the Isthmus. In either case, the result was the same: Salamis, the last shred of independent Athenian territory, was to be abandoned. The Greeks had panicked, and Xerxes could not have asked for a better result if he had planned it.

The commanders left the conference and returned to their ships. By now it was nighttime, hardly the ordinary hour to board. But the

Greeks had a great deal to do if they were to be ready to leave for the Isthmus at dawn—and certainly they were eager to leave as soon as possible. Gear and supplies had to be loaded, equipment had to be tested, and there were always repairs to be made to wooden boats, especially boats as fragile as the trireme. Oars break, ropes snap, sails tear, leather oar-hole covers leak, seats split, and so on. In the fourth century B.C., an Athenian trireme carried a set of thirty spare oars, which is a sign of how common shattered oars were. Normally repairs would all have been made in the sunlight, and no doubt much had been done after Artemisium, but any time spent helping the Athenians evacuate would have taken time from repairing the ships. Now the men would have to make do with the flickering light of portable clay oil lamps.

Themistocles, too, returned to his trireme, which was probably moored in Paloukia Bay. We may imagine that, for the moment, he felt depressed. Even heroes have dark moods when their plans fail, and he surely had given considerable thought to the strategy of fighting at Salamis. At that moment, Mnesiphilus came aboard ship in search of Themistocles. Mnesiphilus was an Athenian politician, apparently an older man and fellow demesman whom Themistocles had looked up to as a young man. Now, Themistocles was the more prominent of the two. But Mnesiphilus was not shy and didn't fear controversy, as shown by surviving evidence of Athenian attempts to have him ostracized (he sidestepped them, as far as is known). As soon as he found out from Themistocles what had happened at the council to cause the hubbub along the shore, Mnesiphilus gave his advice.

Mnesiphilus told Themistocles bluntly that he had to get Eurybiades to change his mind and to reopen the strategic debate. No doubt Themistocles already knew this, but he needed to hear it from someone else. And Mnesiphilus went further. If the fleet left Salamis, he said, it would give up the act of fighting for a single Greek fatherland. Once the ships left Salamis, every city-state's unit would look after its own interests and go home. Neither Eurybiades nor anyone else would be able to reunite them. It was an astute argument. It drove a wedge between Eurybiades and the other commanders by playing on Sparta's smugness. Sure as Eurybiades was of his city's superior virtue, he would be willing to suspect the worst of others.

In short, Mnesiphilus had made an argument worthy of Themistocles. It was all the impetus Themistocles needed. He did not say a word, although he was thrilled with Mnesiphilus's reasoning. Instead, Themistocles simply left and immediately headed towards Eurybiades' flagship. We may imagine him hurrying over the hill between Paloukia Bay and Ambelaki Bay, where the Spartan fleet was probably moored, perhaps drawn up at the quay. When Themistocles reached the Spartan's trireme, he called for Eurybiades, saying that he wished to speak to him about a matter of common interest. The message was relayed by an aide to the commander in chief, who replied that Themistocles could come on board if he wished. The Athenian, we may imagine, climbed up a wooden ladder and joined Eurybiades on deck. There he sat down beside Eurybiades. They probably sat in the stern, perhaps under a canvas awning, perhaps on folding stools or sitting cross-legged directly on the wood of the deck. They probably spoke by the light of clay oil lamps.

At first glance, Themistocles and Eurybiades made an odd pair. The Athenian typified a society that was brash and free, while Eurybiades' country was famously slow and sober. Yet Athens and Sparta were both great powers and both enemies of Persia, while Eurybiades and Themistocles were both patriots. Although he lacked a Spartan's long hair, Themistocles' bulldog face conveyed a Spartan toughness. And while Themistocles had a quicksilver style, Eurybiades was a pragmatist.

"Of all the men we know," said an Athenian years later, the Spartans "are most conspicuous in considering what is agreeable honorable, and what is expedient just." Eurybiades no doubt found it disagreeable to reconvene the council of war, but it would be even more disagreeable to show up at the Isthmus without a united fleet. That would merely confirm his countrymen's prejudice against sea power. How much better it would be for Eurybiades to have a naval victory to bring home to the Spartans. Eurybiades had learned at Artemisium how much that victory depended on listening to the advice of Themistocles.

Then there was Thermopylae. Rather than give an inch to the enemy, Leonidas had sacrificed his men's lives and his own. As a Spartan, Eurybiades might cringe at the symbolism of surrender that would come with a withdrawal from Salamis.

In his meeting with Eurybiades, Themistocles repeated Mnesiphilus's argument without identifying the source. By taking credit for it, Themistocles both glorified himself and avoided the danger that Eurybiades might dismiss a line of reasoning that came from a mere underling. Themistocles then added several arguments of his own. It is not known what he said, but Themistocles must have been able to mix threats and flattery in the right proportion. Eurybiades agreed to reconvene the commanders.

It was probably not unusual for a war council to meet at night, because commanders had their hands full during the day, especially in late September, when daylight hours are rapidly decreasing. It was extraordinary, however, for a council to reconsider a plan that had just been decided. Before anyone could raise a point of order, even before Eurybiades could explain why he had called the council back into session, Themistocles began addressing his colleagues. Then, too, Themistocles was in a state of excitement.

Adimantus, the Corinthian commander, broke in. "At the games, Themistocles, those who start before the signal are beaten with the judge's stick." It was a clever insult, at the same time poking fun and threatening violence.

"Yes," Themistocles replied in his defense, "and those who are left behind do not win the victor's wreath."

What followed was an epic contest between the Athenian and the Corinthian. Aegina could have matched Corinth's disdain for Athens, but it would not support a retreat to the Isthmus, since that would leave Aegina behind Persian lines. So it came down to a battle between two speakers. Herodotus, who knew from Homer the impact of describing a clash of egos, no doubt heightens the tension in his narrative, but even a matter-of-fact account would reveal the drama of the occasion.

As a Spartan, Eurybiades was no stranger to the clash of egos in public. He had seen men compete with every weapon in the Greek rhetorical tool kit: honor, shame, humiliation, wit, pain, threats, and, just beneath a surface of civility, violence—violence that was all the more dangerous because it was controlled.

But in Sparta speeches were mercifully short and sharp: laconic, as the favored form of discourse was called, after Laconia, the geographical name for Sparta's territory. By comparison, other Greek speakers must have seemed like windbags. There is a report that during this meeting a frustrated Eurybiades lifted up his walking stick and threatened to strike Themistocles.

"Strike but listen," Themistocles said. The Spartan no doubt appreciated the pithy response; in any case, he lowered his stick and let the man speak.

Having brushed off Adimantus with relative gentleness, Themistocles directed his arguments toward Eurybiades. Here in council he said nothing about the danger of the fleet breaking up if it left Salamis, because that would have amounted to accusing his colleagues of treason to their face—a mortal insult. Instead, he emphasized the relative advantages of fighting at Salamis.

At the Isthmus, said Themistocles, they would have to fight a naval battle "on the wide open sea." That would hurt the Greeks, because they would be surrounded by the lighter, faster, and more numerous Persian triremes. Even if the Greeks won an engagement, the Persians would come back and whittle down Greek numbers. By contrast, Themistocles continued, his plan set the stage for a naval battle in the narrows, where the Persians could not deploy their full numerical strength.

"Fighting a naval battle in the narrows is good for us, and in the open sea it is good for them" is how he put it in a nutshell. He reminded the generals of the Athenian women and children on Salamis, thereby playing on their emotions. And he insisted that the Persians would not advance to the Peloponnese unless the Greek fleet enticed them there. Finally, Themistocles recalled the oracle that had promised victory at Salamis—no doubt without alluding to the debate in Athens over just what the oracle meant. He closed by reminding his colleagues that the gods help those who help themselves.

Themistocles' point about the need for heavier ships to fight in the narrows was no small matter. If Athens had purposely built its new triremes to be heavy, then it needed to fight in narrow spaces where there was no room to be outmaneuvered by lighter and faster ships and, preferably, to fight in a moderate wind, which tosses around light ships while barely moving heavy ships. Hence, Themistocles' insistence on fighting at Salamis. The Salamis straits were narrow and, as will become clear presently, had favorable winds.

Events would prove Themistocles a prophet about a naval battle in the narrows. And he was right about the sea off the Isthmus: it offered nothing like the closed space of the Salamis straits. But Themistocles was wrong about the Persian advance to the Peloponnese, because Persia was ready to head there without any encouragement from the Greeks on Salamis.

Adimantus had the right to be proud of Corinth's record of fighting for the Greek cause. Since Xerxes had no quarrel with Corinth, the Corinthians might have decided to Medize. Instead, their men fought in every major battle of the war while their women prayed to the gods not to bring the boys home but to let their warriors prevail.

But Adimantus missed the chance to rebut Themistocles' faulty reasoning. Instead, he insulted him. Adimantus told Themistocles to be silent because he had no fatherland. Then the Corinthian turned to Eurybiades and insisted that Themistocles be denied a vote because he was now a man without a country. Let Themistocles get himself a city before he gave any more advice.

Themistocles now either was furious or pretended to be. He snapped at an Eretrian commander who tried to rebut him, "What are *you* doing making an argument about war? You people are like squids: all shell and no guts." Themistocles was referring both to anatomy and numismatics: the squid has both a tough beak and a dagger-shaped internal shell, while Eretria used a symbol of an octopus (closely related to a squid) on its coins.

Adimantus had unintentionally stirred up sympathy for the Athenian by his crude remarks. Themistocles turned the emotion into fear. After abusing both Adimantus and Corinth, he reminded his colleagues that with two hundred triremes fully manned, Athens had a better city than anyone else in the council. In fact, no city in Greece could defend itself against an Athenian attack.

Then he turned to Eurybiades. "If you stay here," Themistocles said,

> you will be a man of courage and honor. If not, you will destroy Greece. For the ships carry the whole weight of the war for us. Mark my words. If you don't do what I advise, we will put our families aboard ships and convey them to Siris in Italy, which has been ours from of old, and the oracles say that we are bound to establish a colony there.

Themistocles had thrown down his last card. He had threatened to lead Athens into what might be called the Phocaean option: to leave Greece and relocate in southern Italy. Herodotus believes that it was the credibility of this threat that changed Eurybiades' mind. The Spartan knew that without Athens's ships, the Greeks could not stand up to the Persian fleet. So Eurybiades gave in.

Apparently Eurybiades had the power to overturn the vote of the council, for that is what he now did. He decided that they would stay at Salamis and fight it out by sea. "They had jousted with words over Salamis," says Herodotus, and now Eurybiades told the commanders to prepare to fight with their ships. They obeyed, but without the enthusiasm that would have followed had they voted in favor of the decision. The only vote on record called for a retreat to the Isthmus, and it remained to be seen if the other Greeks would continue to abide by their commander in chief's decree.

It was now dawn somewhere around September 24. Herodotus implies that the council had lasted all night long or at least most of it. There would have been little time for any commander to sleep. The night of drama was followed by a final, daylight shock. About an hour after dawn, at sunrise, an earthquake was felt by land and sea. The Greeks took this as a sign from heaven. The commanders voted to pray to the gods and to call upon the sons—that is, the descendants— of the hero Aeacus to fight at their side. In Greek mythology, those descendants included Ajax and his father, Telamon: it was presumably at the Temple of Ajax in Salamis Town that the Greeks prayed. Unfortunately, the other sons as well as Aeacus himself were represented by temple statues in Aegina, which was about fifteen miles away. The Greeks immediately sent a ship there to bring the statues to their camp.

So the battle of Salamis, the accidental battle, the battle that almost never happened, the battle for Greece to which many of the Greeks had to be brought against their will—the battle was now set to take place. That is, so said the Hellenic League, or at least some of it. The Persians, however, had yet to weigh in. Everything now depended on what they decided to do.

THE TRAP

CHAPTER FIVE

≈

PHALERON

She sits wrapped in a flowing linen tunic that is dyed purple. Her skin is perfumed with iris oil. Her cheeks are rouged with vermilion, and her eyebrows are dyed black. Her hair is swept back and gathered into a high, elaborate twist held with purple ribbons.

Her ears, neck, wrists, and fingers sparkle with gold jewels. She wears exquisite earrings, a necklace with intricately decorated teardrop pendants, and two bracelets with antelope figures at the open ends. She wears three rings: a gold ring with an agate seal incised with an image of a woman's head; a gold ring carved with a delicate floral pattern; and a gold and chalcedony ring with a figure of a Persian soldier leaning on his spear. There is a hint of the soldier, too, in the way she carries herself, as if to evoke the bronze and iron that are outlawed here in council with the Great King. In battle, when she wears a breastplate and helmet and carries a dagger and sickle, she looks like a goddess armed.

She is a woman who, we may imagine, knows and loves men and wants to have power over them. She has long ago resigned herself to her frailty and her intelligence. A lifetime of practice has taught her to hide her shrewdness behind flattery and charm. Poetry is in her blood and passion in her nature. Her brother Pigres writes epic verse in Greek, and later ages told a story about her leaping to her death when rejected by a lover, but only after first having attacked him in his sleep and scratched his eyes out. She combines the cunning of Athena and the seductiveness of Aphrodite. And behind both sits the ambition of Hera, queen of Olympus.

In any group of men, we may imagine, she is drawn to the most powerful. When she looks at a man of authority, her eyes shine with a reflection of his glory. She speaks to him in phrases that repeat his own words, only made young and beautiful again. She sings about him in the harmonies of the Muses, and when the song is done, she has what she wants. And grand as her ambition is, it is never overweening.

When dealing with a lesser man, as we know, she prefers force, especially if he dares to challenge her. Tough and courageous, she has a reputation for holding grudges and a penchant for settling them with the sword—wielded, of course, on her behalf, by a man.

Although she wants to see Persia victorious, her primary goal is to strengthen the standing of her city in the eyes of her sovereign, Xerxes. If she can achieve that goal by helping him to victory over Greece, then so much the better, but if it would serve her purposes better to console him in defeat, then she would not hesitate to make him stumble.

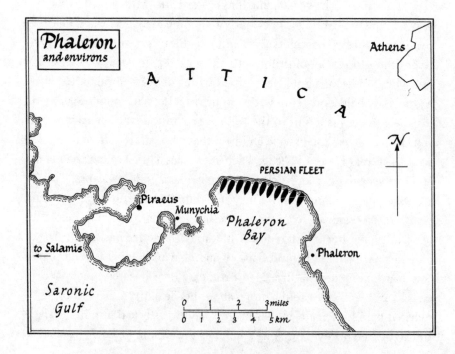

Of all the Great King's sailors, there is no one like her. She commands a contingent of ships from Halicarnassus and other cities in Caria, a region in southwestern Anatolia. She is queen of Halicarnassus: her name is Artemisia.

Ruling queens were not unheard of in the ancient Near East, but fighting queens were exceptional. There were 150,000 men in the Persian fleet at Phaleron, and Artemisia was the only woman. She was rare not only in Persia; she is one of the few female naval commanders in all history.

And Artemisia was no armchair warrior. "I did not lack for courage in the naval battles off the island of Euboea nor was there anything mediocre about my deeds there." So Artemisia introduced herself at Phaleron. Herodotus was smitten: "I must especially marvel," he wrote, "that a woman was campaigning against Greece."

This day, around September 24, 480 B.C., was a day to test Artemisia's cunning. For today she would have to face the Great King in a naval council, alone before all the other commanders.

Xerxes the Great King, the King of Kings, "the king"—to quote his inscriptions—"of every country and every language, the king of the entire earth, the son of King Darius, the Achaemenid, a Persian, son of a Persian," did not ordinarily go down to the seashore to visit a naval encampment. Nor did the self-styled "only king to give orders to all other kings" usually take counsel with the minor monarchs who ruled the corners of his realm, much less with the squadron commanders of his fleet. And yet around September 24, Xerxes did just that.

The day after he sacked the Acropolis, Xerxes traveled the distance of about three miles from Athens to Phaleron Bay. His purpose was to visit his fleet in person and to hold a council of war. He would not have taken the political risk of letting so much light into the mystery of his majesty unless he had a very good reason. And he did. But that will become evident presently. First, consider the gathering that greeted him.

Once Xerxes sat down, the despots of the various peoples in the fleet as well as the squadron commanders took their seats. They sat in order of the rank that Xerxes had assigned them, beginning with two Phoenician kings, his favorite naval allies. After the Phoenicians came kings, princes, and commanders from three continents: Cypriots and Egyptians, Macedonians and Cilicians, Ionians and Dorians, Lycians and Aegean islanders. There were four commanders of the fleet, all Persians, including two of Xerxes' brothers. The scene resembled a sculpted frieze from the walls of one of the great Persian palaces: the assorted princelings of the various provinces, arrayed in native garb and adoring gaze, all come to render service. And one queen.

Artemisia ruled the Carian city of Halicarnassus as well as the nearby islands of Cos, Calymnos, and Nisyros. She had inherited her throne from her late husband—his name is unknown—who had ruled under the overlordship of the Persian emperor. The Carians had sent seventy ships to the Hellespont; we do not know how many vessels still survived at Phaleron. Although Artemisia commanded only five ships, she was second only to the Phoenicians for her fame in the Persian navy.

Artemisia was old enough to have a son in his twenties. She could have sent him on the expedition of 480 B.C. and stayed home, but she chose to fight. She had, says Herodotus, a "man's will." Considering the young age of marriage for most women in the ancient world, Artemisia might have been in her late thirties in 480 B.C. Artemisia's subjects were a mixture of Greeks and Carians, as was Artemisia herself: her father, Lygdamis, was Carian; her mother, whose name is unknown, came from the Greek island of Crete. The name Artemisia is Greek and a common name, derived from Artemis, goddess of the hunt. Caria also included a people named Leleges, whose origins are obscure, as well as men with Persian names, perhaps colonists.

The city of Halicarnassus has a magnificent natural harbor, its main entrance protected by an offshore island. Rising on a hillside, the city looks like a natural amphitheater. Imagine Artemisia going up and down the steep hill, borne on a litter. From the acropolis she could clearly see the outline of the island of Cos in the distance, a powerful, long, low ragged ridge.

Halicarnassus might have been settled by the warlike Dorians, and it might have boasted an excellent military harbor, but the city did not feel martial. The heat, the humidity, the sparkling water, the soft greens of the plants, the chirping birds, the lizards, all contributed to a sultry feeling. Ancient Halicarnassus was lush, rich, happy, snug in the embrace of the sea and mountains with nothing but the isles of Greece and the blue Aegean on the horizon.

Artemisia's subjects made good sailors and soldiers: legend says that they had sent ships to King Minos of Crete instead of tax, and in historical times they served as mercenaries under the pharaohs of Egypt. Although Halicarnassus's contingent in 480 B.C. consisted of only five ships, they were rated highly by Xerxes—or so says Herodotus, a native son of Halicarnassus, although an opponent of Artemisia's dynasty.

It took considerable political skill to rule Caria's mixture of peoples, to say nothing of maintaining loyalty to the Persian overlord. Halicarnassus was a multicultural city on the borderland between Greeks and barbarians. Long after Athens had declared artistic independence of the Near East and invented the European idiom, Halicarnassus still lay under the imprint of Near Eastern artistic norms. At Halicarnassus, the maritime highway to Greece began, but so did the land highway to Persia. In Halicarnassus you heard the hoofbeats of Central Asia, but you breathed the sea air of the Mediterranean.

Think of Artemisia aboard her flagship, seated on deck in the stern, protected by a canvas awning, the lone woman on a boat bristling with armed men. She was probably shorter than most of her shipmates but perhaps not by much, since aristocrats were better fed than ordinary folk. Artemisia was every inch a commander. Only a tough and assertive woman could have sat where she did. When challenged, she did not retreat. At the muster of Persian warships at the Hellespont in May, for example, she had not shrunk from a quarrel with another ship captain from Caria, Damasithymus son of Candaules, king of the city of Calynda, located southeast of Halicarnassus. Venom, it was rumored, still remained in their relationship.

To judge not only from 480 B.C. but from its subsequent history, Halicarnassus was much more comfortable with rule by a woman than mainland Greece ever was. Fourth century B.C. Halicarnassus saw the powerful queens Artemisia II and Ada. Statues of queens were erected alongside statues of their husbands, both at Halicarnassus and at the international shrine of Delphi.

If the men of Halicarnassus might allow a woman to lead them, the Persians would not necessarily follow suit. To be sure, Persian society did not impose as many restrictions on women as did Greek and especially Athenian society. And yet Persia was no paradise of equality. Mothers, for example, received special food rations for new-borns, but those who had boys got twice as much as those who had girls. Herodotus reports that Persian men proved themselves on the battlefield by fighting well and in the bedroom by fathering many sons.

For the Persians, therefore, a woman commander ran against the grain. But even so, Artemisia commanded a squadron. It is a tribute to her influence with Xerxes but to something else as well: it is a tribute to her propaganda value. By including her in their navy, the Persians sent a message: even a woman could fight the effeminate Greeks. The Athenians were duly insulted. "They were rather indignant to have a woman go to war against Athens," says Herodotus. They ordered their captains to take Artemisia alive, with a reward offered of one thousand drachmas (three years' wages for a workman). Seventy years after the Persian invasion, Artemisia still served as a symbol of the uppity woman in Aristophanes' comic masterpiece *Lysistrata*. And a statue of Artemisia earned a place in a kind of rogues' gallery of Persian enemies that Sparta erected after the Persian Wars.

So Xerxes is likely to have appreciated the symbolism of Artemisia's presence at Phaleron. According to Herodotus, he should also have valued her counsel, since it was the best advice that he got from his subordinates. But good counsel was not Xerxes' primary objective at Phaleron. The meeting there was less a strategy session than a rally. The decision to fight at sea had already been made, and Xerxes simply wanted to seal it with his own presence.

His toadies would have congratulated him on the outcome of the battle of Artemisium. After all, the Athenian fleet had limped home from the engagement with half of its ships damaged. The Great King was not to be deceived, however. In his judgment, his men had fought badly at Artemisium. And he knew the reason why: they had suffered from his absence. If the king had shown himself at Artemisium, his men would have fought their best. His charisma would have inspired them, his rewards would have encouraged them, and his punishments would have terrified them.

Xerxes understood an essential point about the Persian army and navy: each was an organization in which there was little incentive to get the job done unless you could cut a fine figure in front of the boss.

Hence his determination to be there at Salamis and, for that matter, at Phaleron. At both places he meant to demonstrate his personal involvement in the war at sea. Not that he would board a trireme in battle: the Great King was too precious to risk at sea. Rather, he would observe from shore, where most of the action would be visible.

At Phaleron, Xerxes wanted advice less than acquiescence. Unlike the Greeks in council about five miles away in Salamis, the Persian commanders at Phaleron did not receive encouragement to speak freely. In fact they were not permitted to speak to Xerxes at all. Each of them was canvassed by the emperor's cousin and chief military adviser, Mardonius son of Gobryas, who then reported their opinions to the emperor.

Phaleron Bay is an excellent natural harbor, ringed by sandy beaches. It forms a semicircle, sheltered from the winds between the low hill of Munychia (282 feet) to the northwest and the narrow plain that reaches the foothills of the ten-mile-long Hymettus ridge to the southeast; its peak, Mount Hymettus, rises to a height of 3,370 feet. At the southeastern end of Phaleron Bay's half circle lay Phaleron Town, a small maritime community, protruding into the sea at a gentle cape. On a late September day Phaleron Bay's turquoise water would sparkle under a blue sky that, in early autumn, is often dappled with clouds. A breeze commonly blows off the sea.

The hill of Munychia, sacred to Artemis, made a fine fortress offering a wide view of land and sea. The Athenian tyrant Hippias was in the process of fortifying Munychia when he was forced into exile in 510 B.C. No doubt in 480 B.C. the Persians posted a garrison on Munychia. Hymettus was famous for its sweet, pale-colored thyme honey and for its blue-tinged marble. Zeus was worshipped on the mountain.

The Persian fleet had been based at Phaleron for about two weeks. Groups of ships were probably hauled up onto the beach in turn, pulled by manpower on ropes onto greased timbers. On shore the ships were repaired or allowed to dry; otherwise, they were moored just offshore, the stern barely hanging over the beach. The men no doubt camped out near the ships.

The whole sweep of the shoreline was surely filled with ships and sailors. On a plausible reconstruction, based on the later battle order, the Phoenicians held the western end of the shore, the Egyptians were in the center, while the Ionians and Carians moored their ships in the east.

During the weeks at Phaleron the men repaired triremes. Every ship or at least every squadron would have carried a set of tools. We get a taste of the instruments at hand from a surviving wooden toolbox from a Byzantine ship: its contents included hammers, chisels, gouges, punches, drill bits, files, knives, an ax, a saw, an awl, adzes, and a spike. Besides taking care of the ships, the men treated their own wounds, mourned their missing comrades, practiced maneuvers, nursed grudges born of failure at Artemisium, scouted the sea-lanes and the enemy's preparations, rummaged for loot, thought about home, complained about the food, taught each other a few words of their language, bet over cockfights, took turns with the women camp followers or made do with boys, gossiped and boasted and worried and prayed to their respective gods. Then, the day before, they cheered at the sight of the flames of vengeance shooting up from the Athenian Acropolis.

The night before the Great King's council at Phaleron, there had been a smell of burnt temples and angry gods in the air—enough, perhaps, to alarm the superstitious, never in short supply aboard ship—when they heard the nocturnal cry of Athena's owls. That morning, they woke to an earthquake, which might have further aroused pious concerns. The god-fearing might have been relieved to learn that Xerxes had ordered that very morning that the Athenian exiles in his army go up to the Acropolis and make their peace with the local gods. The Achaemenids had not acquired a multiethnic empire by waging holy war.

The council at Phaleron no doubt began with a prayer. Afterward, Mardonius made the rounds from commander to commander, beginning with the king of Sidon. Every man said what he knew Xerxes wanted to hear: it was time for a naval battle. The fleet was ready; the men were eager. It was time to crush the Greeks at Salamis and win the war. Only one person offered different advice: Artemisia. Perhaps only a woman would have been allowed to speak her mind without incensing the others.

In any case, she advised Xerxes not to fight. And she did not mince words: "Spare the ships. Don't make war at sea. Their men are as superior to ours on sea as men are superior to women." She reminded

Xerxes that he had already accomplished his main goal, which was to conquer Athens.

No doubt Xerxes knew that that was not quite correct: yes, he had aimed to take Athens, but his main goal was, rather, to conquer all Greece, and the Peloponnese still remained free. Furthermore, the Athenians and their fleet had escaped him. Tacitly conceding these points, Artemisia recommended a land attack on the Greek army at the Isthmus. She was sure that meanwhile the Greek fleet would leave Salamis and scatter to its separate cities. The Greeks on Salamis were divided, and besides, she had heard that grain was in short supply there.

If the Persians forced a naval battle at Salamis, Artemisia said, she feared not only defeat at sea but the ruin of the land army as well. Finally, she made no bones about her colleagues. She told Xerxes: "Good men have bad slaves and bad men have good slaves; since you are the best man of all, you have bad slaves indeed." Artemisia named names: the Egyptians, Cypriots, Cilicians, and Pamphylians were all worthless.

It must have taken courage for Artemisia to speak so bluntly, and certainly some will doubt Herodotus's veracity. But he insists that he knows these were tough words and that Artemisia's friends feared that they would cost the queen her life, because Xerxes would take them as an insult. With typical Greek realism, Herodotus also reports the pleasure that Artemisia's enemies took in her remarks, because they resented her prominence in Xerxes' eyes and assumed that she was now finished. In fact, Xerxes said that he esteemed her more than ever for her excellent words, but nonetheless he rejected her advice. He would fight at sea.

Artemisia, we may imagine, had too much self-confidence to have feared for her life. Nor is she likely to have been surprised by her failure to persuade the Great King. She understood politics well enough to know that Xerxes had already made up his mind before coming to Phaleron. But she may have already been looking to the postwar world. If, as she expected, Persia would be defeated in the straits of Salamis, then her standing in the Great King's eyes would have risen greatly. It was a risk worthy of a queen.

Xerxes probably did not take the time at Phaleron to think through Artemisia's recommendations. If he had, he would have found that her advice was good but incomplete. Persia had a third choice besides fighting at Salamis or waiting at Phaleron, and that was a joint land-sea offensive at the Isthmus.

The Isthmus of Corinth is a rugged, mountainous region that narrows to a width of about five miles. The Greeks could have blocked off the few roads and funneled Persian attackers onto mountain tracks and into gullies. But the Greeks did not have enough time to build high and solid walls. Even though they worked night and day, they would have had to settle for wooden palisades and walls of haphazardly piled stones. With a determined push, the Persians could overrun or even knock down the defenses here and there.

To be sure, the fight at the Isthmus would be bitter. But the Persians could virtually double the odds in their favor if they ferried troops by sea and landed them in the Greek rear, thereby surrounding the enemy. It might be another Thermopylae.

In order to carry out encirclement, the Persians would have to move their fleet from Athens to the Isthmus. A good harbor was available at Cenchreae, a Corinthian port on the Saronic Gulf and close to the wall. But landing at Cenchreae would not be easy, since the shore would almost certainly be lined with Greek troops.

Besides, the Greek fleet might see the Persians sail from Phaleron and then leave Salamis and follow the Persians to Cenchreae. Neither side would risk battle on the open sea, where survivors could not swim to safety; trireme navies always preferred to fight within sight of shore. But once the Persians drew close to Cenchreae, if the Greeks attacked, then the Persians would have to fight off a coastline held by the enemy, ready to capture or kill any Persian who managed to swim to shore.

In short, it would be risky for Persia to move its fleet to Cenchreae, which may explain why Artemisia never mentioned the possibility. But without the fleet, the Persians would face nearly as hard a fight at the Isthmus as at Thermopylae. They would have to face eight thousand Spartans instead of three hundred. Xerxes could hardly have relished the prospect.

The alternative was to break the Greek fleet at Salamis. And that meant either waiting for Greek treason or collapse, or fighting a battle. No doubt the Persians were already looking hard for potential Greek traitors. Because they could attack any fleet that tried to resupply

Salamis, they held the island effectively under siege. But time was not on Persia's side.

In late September in Athens, there is about twelve hours of daylight. The days are shorter than in summer, and the stars have shifted in the night sky. Here and there one even sees a fallen leaf. On the hills as evening falls, a stiff breeze often blows. Some nights, the breeze turns into a cold wind. Camped out under the foreign skies of Athens, many a Persian might have thought of the change of seasons. It was fall, and winter would follow.

The sailing season in the ancient Mediterranean was short, especially for triremes. As fragile as they were fast, triremes risked ruin in rough waters. They preferred to sail only between May and October, and preferably, only in the summer months. In late September, it was just about time for the Persian fleet to return to their various home ports.

And they had to eat. Attica had been stripped of every food item the Athenians could take, though no doubt there was still something for the hungry: fruit on the trees, water in the springs and cisterns, and birds and rabbits in the fields. Yet most of the Persians' supplies had to be brought to Attica. Land transportation was slow and expensive, so the supply highway had to go by sea. Since triremes were too light to carry cargo, the Persians brought food on a flotilla of provision boats. These consisted both of Greek *akata*, which were medium-sized, pointed-hull vessels rowed by a crew of thirty to fifty men, and Phoenician *gauloi*, which were larger and rounded-hull sailing ships. Some Persian provision vessels had been lost in the storms of August but not all, and new ones may have arrived in convoy with the trireme reinforcements that came from Greece.

One expert modern estimate concludes that the Persians needed a minimum of eighty-four supply ships shuttling back and forth between Attica and the supply depots in Macedonia in order to feed their army and navy at Phaleron. Not even the Great King's seasoned bureaucrats would have found it easy to provide such logistical support, but they might have been able to pull it off. Maybe the secret was cutting a corner here and covering up a shortfall there. The upshot is that the oarsmen at Phaleron might have been hungry, too hungry to pull hard in battle. But that is speculation.

The Persians could not wait at Phaleron forever. No doubt they considered landing troops on Salamis and advancing on the Greek ships. There are good harbors on the west coast of the island, and it is a short march overland eastward to the Greek positions. But the Greeks surely guarded every landing ground with armed men. Another possibility was to build a bridge across the mile-wide Salamis channel and march the men across, the way Persia had bridged the Hellespont. But the twenty-four-foot depth of the Salamis channel would have rendered this a difficult undertaking even with control at sea. As long as the Greek navy was at large, it would take a naval battle in order to protect the builders, which brought the Persians back to the need to fight at sea.

That, in turn, increased the pressure on Persia's diplomats to find a Greek traitor, and on Persia's recruiters and agents to find more men and ships. Between the storms and unrepaired losses, the Persian fleet on the day after Artemisium had declined from a total of 1,327 triremes to about 650, about half its original size. Tens of thousands of men had been lost in storms and battle as well. In the three weeks since then, reinforcements had arrived from mainland Greece and the islands. "The farther the Persian went into Greece, the more the nations that followed him," writes Herodotus.

Impressed by what he had learned of the size of these reinforcements, Herodotus went out on a limb. "In my opinion, at any rate, the Persians were not less in number when they invaded Athens both by land and in their ships than they were when they had reached Sepias and Thermopylae." Few scholars are inclined to agree with him. Herodotus himself had commented on the storm that wrecked two hundred Persian ships off Euboea that "it was all done by the god so that the Greek force would be saved and the Persian force would be not much greater than it." It does not look as if that verdict was reversed in less than a month and from regions not known for large navies.

Central Greece was populous but neither it nor the Cycladic Islands were in a position to provide the Persians with many ships, let alone hundreds and hundreds. The Persian fleet is unlikely to have commanded more than seven hundred triremes at Salamis. When Herodotus speaks of massive reinforcements, either he is referring only to manpower and not ships or he is simply wrong.

No doubt the Persians had taken their new recruits out to sea at

Phaleron and given them the chance to row or serve on deck as marines. But the Persians would have noticed that every one of their reinforcements was Greek and so not entirely trustworthy. There was also reason to distrust some and perhaps all of the allies accused by Artemisia. The Cypriots had joined the Ionian Revolt of 499 B.C. The Egyptians, too, had revolted from Persia and more recently—in 486. At Artemisium the Egyptians might have won the prize for valor from Xerxes, but perhaps that was more of a goodwill token on his part than a reward for services rendered. The Cilician squadron had been defeated by the Athenians on the second day at Artemisium. We know nothing of the Pamphylians (originally thirty ships), but they were a people of Greek descent and hence of questionable loyalty.

Disloyalty, a drop in the number of ships, possible supply problems, and dangerous terrain: there were so many reasons for Xerxes to avoid a battle at sea. But Xerxes might have reasoned that at Artemisium the enemy had enjoyed the advantage of surprise; at Salamis the Persians would not underrate the foe a second time. He might also have reckoned on momentum. Spurred by their success at the Acropolis, his soldiers would bear down on the dispirited Greeks, whose panic the day before might have been reported to him by spies.

Xerxes may have come to the conclusion that heaven had suddenly dropped victory into his lap. The first of two enemy capital cities had fallen. The Greek army and navy remained intact, but they were in disarray. The enemy army was improvising a hasty defense; the enemy fleet was divided and on the verge of panic. A short, sharp move by Persia might be enough to push the Greeks over the edge. The invading force that had already taken Athens might end the season yet at Sparta.

And so, the navies would fight at Salamis. That master of manipulation, the Great King, had decided to tie his fate to an image. He had been taught the power of images from childhood on. The avenger, rising over the straits of Salamis on his throne, looming against a backdrop of honorable smoke from justly ruined temples, would spur his ships to success. The struggle might be severe, but in the end the Persians would win, just as they had at Thermopylae. Who knew? His agents might even find a convenient traitor soon. Not for Xerxes the return home with his hands half empty.

No sooner had the king spoken than the order was given to launch the ships. This had been expected: fleets do not spring into action at a moment's notice, at least not successful fleets. Besides, Xerxes had already prepared to take up a position on land at the edge of the battle. As the order was passed from squadron commander to captain to crew, tens of thousands of men lined up, climbed wooden ladders at the water's edge, and boarded their ships.

Artemisia's response to Xerxes' verdict is not recorded. She was a woman of valor, but she was no Antigone: she was willing to speak truth to power but not to engage in civil disobedience. When the ships rowed out of Phaleron Bay, Artemisia and her men were among them.

The Persians made for the straits of Salamis, the entrance to which lies about four miles to the northwest of Phaleron Bay. There, they divided themselves into lines and squadrons unmolested by the enemy. Presumably they took up their formations just outside the entrance to the Salamis channel, spread over a five-mile-wide waterway between Salamis and the mainland. The Persians hoped to draw the Greeks out of the narrow straits, but the enemy never appeared. As the light of day gave out, the order was given for the Persians to return to Phaleron. On September 24, the sun sets at Athens at 7:19 P.M., so we may imagine the Persians beginning their retreat around 6:00 P.M.

The Persian commanders were probably not surprised that the Greeks had not accepted a challenge to fight in unfavorable waters. But that was perhaps not the whole story. The Persians might also have been making the first move in a game of psychological warfare. By lining up at the entrance to the Salamis straits, they demonstrated to the Greeks both their aggressive spirit and their renewed numbers. The Greeks on Salamis saw the full force of the fleet that faced them. Any hope that the Persian navy had been ruined in central Greece by storm and battle was now dashed at the sight of this shipshape and well-reinforced armada.

Nor was the navy the only weapon deployed by Persia. That night, when the Greek fleet had returned to Salamis, the Persian army began marching toward the Peloponnese. In the night sky, the sound of tens of thousands of men and horses tramping westward through Attica would have carried across the straits to the Greek camp. In fact, the Persians might have ordered their men to hug the shore, the more to frighten the enemy. With luck, the terror of the Persian advance might split the

Greeks at Salamis, forcing part of the fleet to hurry toward the Isthmus and the other part to fall into Persia's hands, either through defeat in battle or through treason.

The Persian fleet headed back to Phaleron, where it planned to moor overnight. The men probably took their regular evening meal and then prepared for what lay ahead the next day, when they would enter the straits and provoke the great battle that the commanders wanted, all of them except Artemisia. Then news arrived that changed everything.

CHAPTER SIX

≈≈

FROM SALAMIS TO
PHALERON

A man sits in a small wooden boat. It may be an Athenian dispatch boat, or perhaps it is one of the hundreds of fishing boats on Salamis. In order not to attract attention, only two men are rowing the vessel, as we may imagine. As they make their way in the dark past the barely visible hill of Munychia—lit by a small number of lamps—toward Phaleron Bay, the little crew feels every wave against the thin hull. And the sea outside the Salamis channel, unprotected by island or peninsula, is rougher than the waters inside the straits. Earlier that same evening, the mighty Persian fleet, about seven hundred triremes strong, had rowed these very waters, moving from Phaleron to the mouth of the Salamis straits and then reversing course. Now the tiny vessel is following in the Persians' wake. It is nighttime on about September 24.

The man is simply dressed, in a tunic and boots, perhaps with a cloak to protect him against the sea breeze and with a well-fastened hat. No doubt he is not carrying the gnarled stick usually held by someone in his position of responsibility over children. He is probably unarmed, so as to make his peaceful intentions clear.

If he looks worried, it is not just because his companions are rowing him in the dark, which is never without risk, or even merely because

109

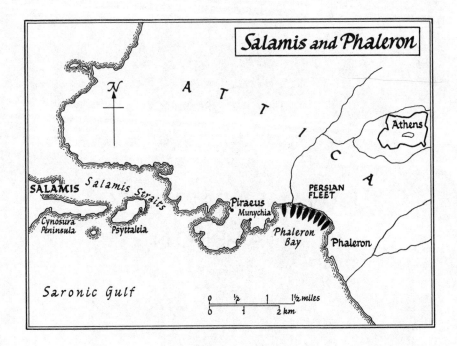

they are headed for the enemy encampment, always a perilous place to land. Rather, he is worried because he knows that he is carrying the weight of the war, because it is on his words that the fate of Greece depends. This is a huge burden for a man without a country or a family name or even his freedom.

In later years the rumors about him flew. He was a Persian, no, a eunuch; he was a prisoner of war, no, a slave; he carried out his mission at dawn, no, at night. Some scholars deny that his celebrated deed ever took place. In that case, his story hoodwinked not only Herodotus but the people of Thespiae as well. After the Persian Wars, the inhabitants of this small Boeotian city made Sicinnus—we call the man simply Sicinnus, for we know neither his father's name nor his country of origin—a citizen, and at Themistocles' suggestion. As if that wasn't boon enough, Themistocles also made Sicinnus a rich man.

We can be sure that Sicinnus was Greek. Greek cities, such as Thespiae, did not enfranchise Persians, nor did they enfranchise eunuchs, since one of a citizen's duties was to furnish the city with Greek children. His name may indicate that Sicinnus came from Phrygia, a district in northwestern Anatolia. Phrygia was famous for its cult of the Great Mother, a goddess to whom Themistocles, too, was devoted. Since Phrygia was under Persian rule, Sicinnus might have been familiar with Persian ways, and perhaps he even spoke Persian. As for his status, Sicinnus was indeed a slave, and it is plausible that he was once a prisoner of war as well, since many slaves owed their status to the misfortune of war. Themistocles must have freed him sometime after 480 B.C. before recommending Sicinnus for citizenship in Thespiae.

As a slave, Sicinnus played a hallowed role in a prosperous Greek household: he was *paidagogos* to Themistocles' sons. The *paidagogos* was both more and less than a modern pedagogue. He had to take the boys to school and home again each day, carrying their belongings, a lamp, and sometimes even a tired boy or two. He also had to supervise them in the streets and divert them from any of the various temptations offered by a booming town like Athens. The *paidagogos* did no formal teaching, but he bore a general responsibility for the boys' moral education. In short, a *paidagogos* had to be firm, alert, of good character, and, above all, trustworthy. No wonder Themistocles entrusted him with so important an assignment.

For the mission did take place. There is no reason to deny it except for its improbability, and that is a poor argument, since history is full of the improbable. Not just Herodotus, a Halicarnassian who wrote two generations after the events of 480 B.C., but Aeschylus, an Athenian who wrote in 472 B.C., confirms Sicinnus's deed. They differ about the details, but reports of secret missions often do conflict, and besides, Aeschylus and Herodotus wrote in different genres (respectively, tragic poetry and history), for different audiences, and for different purposes. Stark disagreements between the two should not surprise us.

But having asserted that Sicinnus's mission really did happen, we cannot understand its purpose or its results without looking back at the circumstances surrounding it. It began earlier that evening of September 24 on Salamis.

On the previous night, September 23, the showdown between Themistocles and Adimantus had ended up with Eurybiades' decision to keep the fleet at Salamis. But the Peloponnesian crews were not happy with the choice. The more they heard about the defensive works at the Isthmus, the more they wanted to abandon Salamis. On top of that, the afternoon of September 24 brought the entire Persian fleet to the entrance of the Salamis straits, offering battle. And after the enemy navy retreated to its base at Phaleron, the enemy army began marching along the Attic coast, westward toward the Isthmus.

As the day of September 24 wore on, the Peloponnesians began gathering in small groups and whispering. They kept their voices down but their dander up; they were simply amazed at the bad decision that Eurybiades had made. They were afraid of being stuck in Salamis on the verge of fighting a naval battle for Athens, and if they lost, they would be trapped, unable to defend their homeland. Perhaps they griped about how a fast-talking Athenian had pulled the wool over the eyes of a stalwart but simpleminded Spartan. Finally, the discontent broke out in public. Itching to join the stand at the Isthmus, "the men who were wasting their time in Salamis with all the ships were so terror-stricken that they no longer obeyed the commanders," as a later historian put it.

Eurybiades had lost control of his fleet. Perhaps another man might have done better, but he would not have found it easy. The Greeks rarely valued obedience above saying what was on their minds, not even now, when Greece itself was at stake.

By now, it was nighttime. Yet another assembly was called. The Peloponnesian commanders spoke at length and did not mince words. Athens, they said, was lost: it was, to use the traditional term, "land that had been captured by the spear." The thing to do was to leave Salamis at once and take their chances at the Isthmus. The Athenians, of course, disagreed. They, along with the Aeginetans and the Megarians, argued for staying and fighting at Salamis.

But it was no use. Or so Themistocles thought: he reached the conclusion that his policy would be rejected. Plutarch claims that the Greeks actually decided to withdraw that night, and went so far as to give orders for the voyage to their pilots. No doubt before that happened, Themistocles slipped out of the meeting discreetly and found Sicinnus. The ancient sources give the impression that the idea of Sicinnus's mission was a sudden burst of inspiration on Themistocles' part, born of desperation, but it seems more probable that the Athenian had planned things in advance. Themistocles was nothing if not perceptive, and he surely had noticed before how shallow support for his position was among the Peloponnesian crews.

Besides, Themistocles' stock in trade was to think the unthinkable. An upright soul might have soothed itself with the thought of Panhellenic unity, but Themistocles shunned illusion. Surely he had considered the possibility of a Peloponnesian sellout. It might have occurred to him that if he could not save Athens by straightforward words in open debate, he would have to resort to more devious methods. And in order to save Athens, there are few things that a man like Themistocles would have ruled out. He was certainly more than capable of forcing a battle at Salamis against the will of the majority of his fellow Greek naval commanders.

So he might well have planned Sicinnus's operation in advance. Among other reasons for this were the practical questions that needed to be solved. Sicinnus would have to be made ready to go on a secret mission, although he might not have been told what to say until the last minute. Trustworthy men would need to be found to row the boat. A launch site would have to be determined, and guards would have to be persuaded or bribed to turn a blind eye to an unauthorized departure. Themistocles had to do all of this and then return to the council meeting before anyone grew suspicious about his absence. Although it might all have been arranged at the last minute, advance preparation seems more probable.

But just what was Sicinnus's assignment? He was to deliver a message to the Persians. Three detailed descriptions of the message survive in the ancient sources. The earliest appears in Aeschylus's play of 472 B.C., *The Persians:*

> *A Greek man from the Athenian host*
> *Came and said the following to . . . Xerxes:*
> *When the darkness of night comes*
> *The Greeks will not remain, but will leap upon*
> *The rowing benches and by one way or another,*
> *Each by secret flight will save his life.*

Writing shortly after 430 B.C., Herodotus reports:

> *When he [Sicinnus] arrived with his boat he said the following to*
> *the generals of the barbarians: "The general of the Athenians sent me*

in secret from the other Greeks (because he happens to have the King's interests in mind and he wants you rather than them to have the upper hand) to say that the Greeks are terrified and plan to flee, and now is the best time of all for you to carry out the deed, so as not to let them run away. They are neither united nor will they resist you, but you will see them fight a naval battle amongst themselves, some taking your side and some not." And when he had declared these things, he departed and got away.

Finally, Plutarch, writing centuries later, about A.D. 100, writes:

He [Themistocles] sent him [Sicinnus] to Xerxes secretly, ordering him to say that Themistocles the general of the Athenians had chosen the King's side and is the first to announce to him that the Greeks are running away, and he urges him not to stand by and let them escape but, in a moment at which they are in disorder because they are sepa-rated from their infantry, to fall upon them and destroy their naval power. Xerxes received this as a message of goodwill and he was delighted. . . .

The three stories agree that a message was brought to the Persians from the Athenians, announcing that the Greek fleet was on the verge of fleeing from Salamis. They all go on to say that the Persians accepted the message as genuine and so launched their ships. But there are dis-agreements among the three versions. Herodotus and Plutarch refer to Sicinnus by name, but Aeschylus does not. Aeschylus and Plutarch say that Sicinnus spoke directly to Xerxes, but Herodotus gives what is surely the more likely version, that Sicinnus spoke to the Persian com-manders. The Great King rarely spoke directly to anyone, let alone to Greek slaves. Still, it is possible that Sicinnus was interrogated by a Persian in Xerxes' presence, as Arcadian deserters had been interro-gated after Thermopylae.

Herodotus says that Sicinnus arrived after the Persian fleet had returned to Phaleron, that is, at night. Aeschylus says that the mission took place before sunset, while Plutarch implies a nighttime mission without specifically saying so. As a tragedian, Aeschylus had a poetic license denied to the historian or biographer. He might well have placed a sunset between speech and deed to add drama. In any case, the night is a far likelier time for a secret and potentially traitorous mission than is the daytime.

Besides, another issue comes into play. Aeschylus was a patriot writing for an audience of thirty thousand Athenians. It was far more politic to depict an unnamed man in the light of day than to identify the moral guardian of Themistocles' sons and to show him sneaking around in the dark.

Patriotism might also explain another discrepancy among the three accounts. Herodotus and Plutarch are clear on the point that Themistocles promised Athenian treachery to the Persians. Aeschylus is silent about this matter. Yet it's no wonder, since treason was no doubt a sensitive subject in a mass Athenian audience at a drama festival only eight years after the event. The foreign slave who labeled Athenians as traitors to Greece was perhaps not entirely popular in Athens. It was, after all, in the city of Thespiae and not in Athens that Themistocles found a home for Sicinnus, and then only because the Thespians had lost many citizens during the war and were hungry for replacements.

And so a common story emerges: Themistocles sent his trusted slave Sicinnus on a secret and dangerous nighttime mission to Persian naval headquarters. Sicinnus announced the imminent departure of the Greek fleet and urged the Persians to mobilize at once to stop them. They did so, and launched their fleet at nighttime. Before the Greeks at Salamis knew what had hit them, the Persians managed to surround them. As a result, there would be no more talk of running away to the Isthmus. The Greeks would have to fight at Salamis or they would have to surrender. In other words, Themistocles got exactly what he had wanted.

Just how the Persians managed to surround the Greeks, and just what "surrounding" means in this context, are big questions that we will address in the next chapter. In the meantime, another question leaps out: why did the Persians believe Sicinnus? For that matter, why did they let him escape rather than hold him for questioning or even torture?

To answer these questions is to understand the genius of Themistocles and his ability to read the mind of his adversary. Themistocles knew how badly Persia wanted to hook a big Greek traitor. And so he sent the Persians Sicinnus.

Themistocles knew how the Persians had used traitors at Thermopylae in August and in the naval battles at Lade and off Cyprus about fifteen years earlier. If he had been able to interrogate the high-ranking Persian commanders captured at Artemisium, he might have learned just how important treason loomed in the Great King's mind.

The key to misinformation is telling people what they want to hear. Sicinnus did precisely this. Sicinnus did not tell the Persians to fight a naval battle at Salamis. He did not need to. When he arrived in their camp, the Persians had already decided to risk their fleet in the Salamis channel. Sicinnus did nothing more than to precipitate the timing.

He did nothing more than that, and yet, in so doing, Sicinnus did everything: at Salamis, the timing was all. Consider Sicinnus's—and Themistocles'—nimble touch. As if aware that it is easier to tell a big lie than a small one, Sicinnus fed the Persians a host of secret details that happened to be true. He told them that the Greek council at Salamis was in disarray, which was true. He told them that the Peloponnesians wanted to withdraw the fleet at once to the Isthmus, while the Athenians, Aeginetans, and Megarians wanted to keep the ships at Salamis, which was true. He told them that unless the Persian navy stopped them, the Greek ships would flee, which was also probably true.

The only lie that Sicinnus told was the big lie: that Themistocles was ready to join the Great King's side. Or was it a lie? Who can be sure that, if the Greek fleet left for the Isthmus, Themistocles would not have considered a deal with Xerxes? It would not have been easy to convince Athenians to bear doing business with their archenemy. But if they were abandoned by their Greek allies, would the Athenian refugees on Salamis not have been better off going home under Persian protection than taking their chances in Italy, the likely outcome of a doomed resistance at the Isthmus? Themistocles might have reasoned that, with Persian honor avenged at the Acropolis, the enemy might be ready to bargain. As practical men, the Persians would immediately see the advantage of allying with a man of action like Themistocles instead of with has-beens like the heirs of the former Athenian tyrant, Hippias.

To be precise, Sicinnus's lie consisted of saying that Themistocles' *preference* was joining the Persian cause. In truth, Themistocles preferred to achieve victory for Greece. He proposed to do so by forcing a naval battle immediately.

But let us not assume that Sicinnus was a good liar. He would not have had to be. Themistocles knew that the Persians might torture Sicinnus, and Themistocles would not want to risk his man cracking under the strain. Far better to lie to Sicinnus, to tell him simply that his master had decided to defect rather than tell the truth about the double game that he was playing. The deeper his belief in Themistocles' treason, the more convincing a messenger Sicinnus would make. It would have been just like Themistocles to hide the truth not only from the Persians and his fellow Greeks but also from his trusted servant. As long as Sicinnus was trustworthy, brave, and reasonably articulate, he could carry out his assignment. Who knows? Sicinnus might also have been pro-Persian, which would have made him all the more appealing a messenger in Themistocles' mind.

After hearing out Sicinnus, the Persians let him go. That was not standard procedure. Earlier, when a Greek defector from Arcadia in the central Peloponnese appeared in the Persian camp, he was kept tied and bound. Perhaps Sicinnus was peculiarly smooth, perhaps he was lucky, but it may be that the Persians let him go because they needed to, and they needed to because Themistocles had promised to surrender. The terms of the deal still had to be worked out.

That, after all, is the way things had happened at the battle of Lade. The Persians met with Samian traitors before the battle and arranged for the Samian contingent to turn tail at the outbreak of the engagement. As soon as the battle began, the Samians hoisted their sails and fled. At the sight, most of the other Greek warships promptly did the same, leaving in the lurch a few stout sailors, mostly from Chios.

We may speculate that Sicinnus offered, or the Persians asked, for a similar arrangement at Salamis. The Persians would approach the Greek fleet, and the Athenians would hoist their sails and start a stampede toward surrender. And that might be the reason why the Persians let Sicinnus go. He was the go-between, vital to confirm the terms of Themistocles' treason.

Surely, someone was skeptical. Certainly one of the Great King's advisers warned him against "the guile of the Greek man," as Aeschylus calls it. Surely the Athenian exiles and the Theban allies in Xerxes' entourage denounced the slave of Athens's chief democrat. The Persians were no strangers to cunning: the royal court thrived on intrigue. The many Greek princes and squadron commanders in the Persian fleet all knew the story of the Trojan horse, and how the Greeks had conquered a city by means of a false gift. And yet none of them managed to see through the stratagem of Athens's latter-day Odysseus. Or, having seen through it, they could not successfully persuade Xerxes.

In retrospect, his gullibility stands out. At the time, however, Sicinnus's tale might have seemed reasonable. Traitors and deserters were the common currency of war. In all likelihood, Sicinnus was not the first person to bring the Persians intelligence from Salamis. Artemisia, for instance, is likely to have received her information about the shortage of food on the island from just such a source.

Nor did the risk of trusting Sicinnus seem large. If the Greeks were indeed plotting to escape secretly that night, the Persians had an opportunity to stop them. If that intelligence proved false, then the Persians would intrude upon a divided and dispirited foe at dawn. The Greeks would either have to accept the Persian challenge to fight a battle or concede their own inferiority, thereby further encouraging defection to the Persian side.

Besides, it might have occurred to Xerxes that his ships would reap the benefit of surprise if they moved at once. The Greeks might have envisaged the Persians entering the straits but not at night and certainly not that night. That very evening the Greeks had seen the enemy mass its fleet outside the straits. There seemed little danger that he would come back that very night and this time come into the Salamis channel.

And there might have been one further argument for action: the weather. Clouds are common in Athens in late September. A cloudy night was the best and maybe the only thing that would allow the Persians to enter the straits secretly under the Greeks' very noses. With a moon lighting up a clear sky, it would have been difficult to hide the truth from the Greeks on Salamis. Few tacticians can resist the chance of surprising the enemy. So if the night of September 24 was in fact cloudy, an eager Persian commander might have seized on Sicinnus's story as a way to precipitate a cherished plan. And Xerxes agreed.

And so the order went out: the Persian fleet would not wait until

the morning to seek out the Greeks. Instead, they would launch immediately, in "the middle of the night," as Herodotus calls it. Precisely what
hour that was is unknown. But assuming that Sicinnus began his mission after sunset (7:19 P.M.) and needed about an hour to reach Phaleron,
and considering that it would take an hour or two for the Persians to
hear him out and evaluate his message, and considering that yet more
time would be needed to rouse the men and ready the ships, midnight is
probably the earliest hour that the Persian fleet got under way.

Xerxes must have made ready to ride from Phaleron to a spot over-
looking the Salamis straits, about six miles away. He hoped that before
the next day was over, his men would have destroyed the enemy fleet
and thereby all but guaranteed his conquest of the rest of Greece well
before winter.

It all seemed so reasonable. And yet what if the Greeks were in fact
not at loggerheads? What if they were keen for battle, full of whole-
hearted passion to sweep the Persians from the Salamis straits? In that
case, the Persians would have done the enemy the favor of fighting in
his chosen location, in the narrows.

But in Xerxes' defense, consider that it was most unlikely that the
Greeks would turn from disarray to sudden unity. Themistocles' trick,
however brilliant, was not enough to bring about that result. Themistocles was many things, but a unifier was not one of them. It would take
someone else to play that role. Amazingly, a potential candidate was at
hand.

It was one of the most celebrated reconciliations in the history of
the ancient world. Aristides, son of Lysimachus, and Themistocles were
the most bitter of political enemies. A veteran of the battle of Marathon
in 490 B.C., where he may have served on the Athenian board of generals, Aristides enjoyed a prominent political career. There was a personal
element in the rivalry between Themistocles and Aristides, which some
sources trace all the way back to the playground. Themistocles' nature,
writes Plutarch, was

> *quick, reckless, unscrupulous, and easily borne with haste into any
> undertaking, while Aristides' was founded upon a firm character,
> which was intent on justice and not inclined toward any falsehood,
> buffoonery, or trick even in a game.*

But principle was at stake as well. One tradition makes Aristides a fox who flirted with pro-Persian sentiment; another makes Aristides a patrician who crossed swords with the populist Themistocles. According to this tradition, Aristides played paragon to Themistocles' rogue. Certainly Aristides had a reputation for fairness, whence his nickname, Aristides the Just. Herodotus calls him "the best and most just man in Athens."

In fact, Aristides seems to have been a prig, as we may judge from the farmer who came to town to vote in favor of ostracizing Aristides. When asked what he had against Aristides, the man replied that he was simply tired of everyone calling him Aristides the Just. The man got his way: Aristides was ostracized in 483 B.C. Themistocles had come out on top.

Aristides was recalled with the other exiles before the Persian invasion. Anyone who feared that he would continue his feud with Themistocles need not have worried. Polyaenus, a Greek writer in the era of the Roman Empire, tells this dramatic story of the two men's reconciliation:

> *Aristides and Themistocles were the worst enemies of anyone in politics. But when the Persians attacked, they went outside the city to the same place, each lowered his right hand, intertwined their fingers, and said, "We put down our enmity here, until we finish the war against the Persian." When they said this they raised their hands, separated their fingers, and, as if they had buried something, they heaped up earth in the ritual pit, and they departed and spent the entire war in agreement. And the concord of the generals was particularly responsible for the victory over the barbarians.*

If it is true that the former exiles were confined to Salamis, then this scene, if it is genuine, would have to have taken place there. Whether this amazing ritual actually happened is unknown, but there is no doubt about the importance of the concord of the generals.

It bore its ripest fruit on the night of Sicinnus's mission on September 24. Sicinnus no doubt left the Persian camp excited and immensely relieved. We do not know when he managed to return to Salamis, but we do know that he was not the first man to bring Themistocles the news of his success. That honor goes to Aristides.

That very morning, after the earthquake had upset the men, Aristides had been sent, along with at least one other general, on a trireme to Aegina to hurry back with the cult statues of Aeacus and his sons. The mission speaks volumes about Aristides' status in the Greek camp. He was not sufficiently important to be indispensable to the preparations for battle or discussions in council, but he was just the man for an operation of religion and morale.

By the time Aristides returned from Aegina it was late at night. Apparently he arrived not with the cult statues but with the news that they were on the way. When he landed at Salamis, Aristides went straight to the council hall, stood outside, and called for Themistocles. When Themistocles emerged, Aristides informed him that he could tell his colleagues to forgo the debate about moving to the Isthmus. Relocation was no longer an option. As Aristides had seen with his own eyes, the Greeks were now surrounded by the Persian fleet. His journey from Aegina had taken him almost directly into the path of the Persians, as his ship passed the south coast of Salamis and rounded the Cynosura peninsula into the straits. Since the Persians had not left Phaleron before midnight, and since it would have taken considerable time for them to get their ships in position opposite the Greeks—and in the dark—the hour of Aristides' arrival at Salamis could hardly have been earlier than two or three in the morning. That, of course, was not the normal time for a trireme to travel, but Aristides' mission called for all possible speed.

"We are shut in by the enemy in a circle," Aristides said. He had barely made it past them with his boat and escaped pursuit. Now he advised Themistocles to return inside and deliver the news.

We need not imagine that Aristides meant the word circle literally. The Greeks used the word kuklos to mean not only circle but, among other things, the vault of heaven, the horizon, the Milky Way, a person's cheeks, an assembly place, a crowd of people standing around, and the annual cycle of the seasons. By kuklos, Aristides meant only that the Persians had surrounded the Greek fleet at either end of their mooring stations on the eastern coast of Salamis. He did not mean that the Persian fleet had surrounded the entire island. Plutarch makes clear how Aristides' words are to be understood:

> *The barbarian triremes were launched at night, and after they sur-rounded the strait in a circle, they occupied the islands.*

We might say, then, that the Persians had ringed the straits at either end.

Apparently Themistocles could hide neither his joy at the infor-mation nor his pride in his role as a manipulator. "You should know that the Medes are doing what they are on my initiative," he told Aristides. And the Greeks would soon be bent to Themistocles' will as well: he had forced them to fight at Salamis, like it or not. It must have been bliss for Themistocles to contemplate his power, but to lord it before the eyes and under the nose of his archenemy Aristides—that must have been very heaven.

But ever the strategist, Themistocles limited his crowing to Aris-tides. Far from taking credit before the other commanders, he told Aris-tides to deliver the news himself. "If I say it," Themistocles said, "it will look as if I am lying and they will not believe that the barbarians are really doing these things."

Inside the council hall, the Greek generals were "shoving each other with their words," as Herodotus puts it. They thought that the Persian fleet was safely ashore back at Phaleron, from where they had seen it depart the day before.

Aristides duly entered the meeting and delivered his news. "The entire camp of the Greeks is shut in by Xerxes' ships," he said. He advised them to get ready to defend themselves. And having made his shocking announcement, Aristides left.

A debate immediately broke out. Most of the commanders were so determined to leave Salamis that they refused to believe Aristides, in spite of his reputation for probity. But the matter was soon settled by another arrival, a man named Panaetius son of Sosimenes. He was the commander of a trireme from the small Aegean island of Tenos, one of the many islands that had sent ships to Xerxes after Artemisium and Thermopylae. Perhaps the Tenians had done so halfheartedly, or perhaps Panaetius had lost his enthusiasm for the Persian cause when the fleet entered the dan-gerous waters of the straits. In either case, he deserted to the Greeks.

It was a decisive defection. After Panaetius repeated what Aristides had said, the council conceded. The combined words of the most just man in Athens and of a treacherous islander who was not tarred with the brush of being Athenian had finally worked. The commanders acknowledged the truth of their reports, and so they prepared to fight a naval battle.

By now, it was three or four in the morning. This was not the usual hour to load seventy thousand men onto triremes and prepare them to row out to battle. But it would have to do.

≈

CHAPTER SEVEN

FROM PHALERON
TO SALAMIS

H e sits on the quarterdeck of his trireme, reclining on a purple
cushion and protected from the wind by a cloth canopy. The
ship slips almost silently past the dark coast. In the distance,
across the straits, he can make out the fires of the Greek fleet. Nearby,
the sound of the infantrymen, marching westward through Attica,
makes it hard for him to hear the ship at all. But when from time to time
he does make out the sound of the ship, all he hears is the oars sliding
through the water while, at rhythmic intervals, two stones are struck
together to keep time, making no more noise than the crunch of footsteps on a layer of shells. They might be a crew of workmen gone to
harvest mollusks for the factories of Phoenicia that make purple dye. In
fact, they are sailors, the best in the world, and in the predawn darkness
of September 25, they are off to win the war. They are the seamen of
Sidon, and he is their king, Tetramnestus son of Anysus—conceivably
the monarch known in Sidonian texts as Eshmunazar.

Tetramnestus wore a bronze helmet and a linen breastplate over a
linen tunic dyed purple. No doubt he carried a sword. He is likely to
have worn gold earrings, rings, and bracelets. On a gold chain around
his neck he might have worn a blue glass amulet as protection against
evil spirits.

The Persian fleet was on the move. Seven hundred ships strong, it was rowing, firmly but quietly, toward the straits of Salamis. Its mission was to encircle at either end the places where the enemy had moored. The Greeks were expected to attempt a breakout to the Isthmus that very night. The Persian navy's job was to stop them. They would shock the Greeks, check their movement, and then destroy that discouraged congeries of chatterboxes in a battle of annihilation—all of this with the help of a substantial squadron of Greek traitors.

It was a dangerous mission and difficult technically. Not only did the Persian warships have to infiltrate the Greek home waters of the Salamis straits, they had to do so on a dark and cloudy night, unaided by moonlight or stars, and they had to do so without being detected. For centuries the Phoenicians had been the sea dogs of the Mediterranean, and in the fifth century B.C., Sidon—"great Sidon," "the mother of Canaan," "the first-born of Canaan," as it was known—was the first city in Phoenicia. Situated on a promontory between the snow-covered

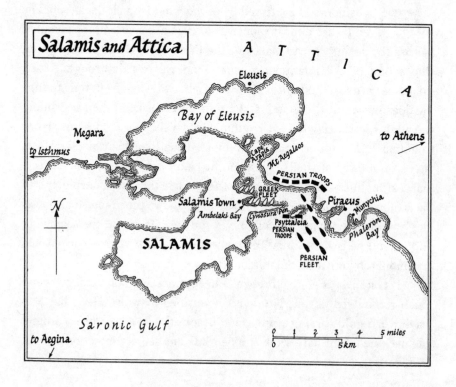

mountains of Lebanon and the limpid blue sea, Sidon exercised the "experience in naval deeds inherited from its ancestors." Who else but Sidonians could have led such an assignment for Persia?

Tetramnestus was Xerxes' favorite king and this was his moment. Before the next day's sunset, Tetramnestus planned to destroy the Greek navy, thereby handing his master swift and certain victory over all Greece. The king of Sidon was the most valued ally in Xerxes' navy. Even the image of a warship on the seal stones of the Royal Treasury of Persepolis was copied from a Sidonian coin.

No need for one of Xerxes' brothers—the admirals Achaemenes and Ariabignes—to lay down the law to the men of Sidon, or to those of Tyre or Aradus, their Phoenician comrades in arms. It was the untrustworthy Ionians and Egyptians whom the Persians had to keep their eyes on. Not politicians but military professionals, as the Persian commanders Megabazus and Prexaspes arguably were, were seconded to the Phoenician squadron, because the Great King could trust the Phoenicians. And none of the Phoenicians stood higher in Xerxes' eyes than the men of Sidon. Hadn't the Persians built a royal park—a paradise—outside Sidon? Hadn't they funded an enormous temple outside Sidon to the blessed Eshmun, the great healing god of Sidon, revered in all Phoenicia? Hadn't Sidon finally outstripped its longtime rival, Tyre? For Sidon, Persian rule had been a golden age. Now it was time to repay the Great King.

Alas, the war was not going as Tetramnestus might have wished. To be sure, it had begun splendidly. Sidon had won the boat race at the Hellespont in May, under the delighted eyes of Xerxes, who watched it from his white marble throne. The next month, at Doriscus in Thrace, His Majesty chose a Sidonian ship from which to review his fleet. The Phoenician contingent of ships was originally three hundred strong. Seated under a golden canopy, the Great King sailed along the single line of ships that was drawn up four hundred feet from shore with the prows turned shoreward and the marines on deck in full battle array. Xerxes asked questions about each ship, and his secretaries recorded every word. What a glorious day for Sidon that had been!

The Sidonians had next led the fleet through the Mount Athos canal and southward into central Greece. As the lead squadron, they probably hauled their ships onto the shore at Cape Sepias and so survived the storm intact. And then came the embarrassment at Artemi-sium. No doubt Tetramnestus insisted that his men had done their duty there; the others had lost the battle. If only the Great King had left that crowd of landlubbers at home. What good were Cilicians, Lycians, and Pamphylians as sailors? Some of the Cypriots were of Phoenician blood, and so knew the sea, but the wretched Egyptians and Ionians were traitors and not to be trusted.

Now, Sidon would have a second chance. How fitting for it to come at Salamis, since legend had it that the island was named for a Phoeni-cian trading post and the Phoenican word *sh-l-m*, "peace." At Salamis, the Greeks would learn their lesson.

How easily a Phoenician might discount Greek prowess at sea. The Phoenician city-states were older and longer civilized than the Greek. The Phoenicians were longtime masters of the trireme, but the Athen-ian trireme navy—the greatest squadron in the Greek fleet—was only three years old. As for Greek success at Artemisium, that might be dis-missed as beginner's luck.

Tetramnestus might have thought back to the scene, hours ago at Phaleron Bay, when it had begun—this last, decisive mission of the Great King's fleet. From its precise launching to its bravura sweep up the Saronic Gulf to its soundless parade past an ignorant enemy, the Persian navy had performed brilliantly. And yet, even so, now, as the dawn drew near, Tetramnestus might have found it hard to avoid an undercurrent of doubt.

The operation had begun at sunset on the day before, September 24. The men returned to Phaleron Bay from their show of force at the entrance to the Salamis straits. The crews came ashore sweating and agitated, men whose destiny had been delayed. We can imagine them climbing down onto the sandy beach, irritated or elated to be back there without having shed blood. Some men feared battle, but others wanted only "to cut the Greeks off in Salamis and make them pay for the battles of Artemisium."

After disembarking, the men ate their evening meal. Not only had they rowed a round trip of ten miles to the entrance to the Salamis straits and back, but when they reached the edge of Salamis they had sat at their oars, constantly rowing and backing, as their boats stood smartly at their stations, the more to frighten the Greeks with a show of discipline and order. This was no little work, although to keep things in perspective, it does not compare to the 120-plus-nautical-mile-per-day voyage that a trireme fleet was capable of making. Still, the rowers at Phaleron must have been hungry. The Persian officers and marines, who had not had to exert themselves as much as the oarsmen, were no doubt very well fed.

The rowers are likely to have had simpler fare, such as onions, salt fish, thyme, salt, and barley groats. Foraging parties might have gone out for seasonal fruit, such as figs and apples, while hunters might have bagged birds or rabbits. Fresh water was essential after the toil of rowing. The one thing that most everyone would have craved was wine, the standard drink from Greece to Persia, except for Egypt, where beer was the staple drink of the poor. Especially before going into battle, a little wine went a long way. Whether all these needs were met depended in large part on the ability of Persia's merchant ships to keep the supply lifeline going.

After eating and drinking, the men would have divided into groups. Ship's carpenters and their assistants would have checked for problems and made what repairs were needed—and on a boat, some repairs are always needed. Some men would have gossiped. Some would have played games like checkers or dice. Some might have sung. Others might have prayed, for everyone knew that the morning might bring the great naval battle that they had long awaited. And those who could have would have gone to sleep.

But any rest would have proven short. Before midnight, the order would have come to launch the fleet at once, that is, to move the bulk of the fleet. Before the general order for mobilization was given, a squadron had already been sent out on a special mission. We do not know which ships or how many were dispatched. Their assignment was to occupy Psyttaleia, an islet between Salamis and the mainland.

Psyttaleia greatly interested Persia's high command because of its strategic location. Specifically, it lay in the pathway of the coming naval battle. Once the fighting began, many men and shipwrecks would be carried there, as the Persians imagined, and whoever controlled Psyttaleia could help his own forces and kill the enemy's.

A look at the map shows that Psyttaleia lies at the entrance to the Salamis channel, and so at one end of rather than in the middle of what would be the battlefield. But it certainly did lie "in the pathway" of any Greek flight out of the straits, just as it lay between the eventual battlefield and the Persian base at Phaleron Bay. Furthermore, the more shoreline one controlled in a naval engagement, the better, precisely in order to save or kill shipwrecked men and to capture any damaged hulls that came ashore. The Persians already controlled the Attic coast and the Greeks the coast of Salamis; by taking Psyttaleia, the Persians created another shoreline stronghold. Note also that the southeast shore of Psyttaleia is far enough away from Salamis that, on a dark night, the Persians could land there undetected. All of this explains the priority of Psyttaleia in Persian plans.

But the main task back at Phaleron was to mobilize the bulk of the Persian fleet, well over 100,000 men (a total of about 150,000 minus the men sent to Psyttaleia). Simply moving that number would be an achievement. Moving them in a swift and orderly way was a marvel, especially when the men had already put in an afternoon's work. Yet that was just what the Persians now did.

When the order to launch the ships came, every rower had to file aboard and find his place. He probably carried a small amount of food and water with him, enough to get through the long night and day ahead but not so much as to weigh down the boat.

Every trireme was provided with two ladders at the stern, and the men could have boarded each ship in pairs. It probably took no more than fifteen minutes to man a ship. The boat would not have been filled haphazardly but, rather, by sections: for example, by center, bow, and stern. Every rower was probably assigned a regular seat on board. This would allow him to get used to the timing of the men around him and to adjust his stroke accordingly. After taking his seat, each rower had to make an equipment check. First he had to ensure that his cushion was tied firmly to the seat. Then he had to inspect his oarloop. An oar is a lever; on every stroke, it has to turn around a support or fulcrum. On a trireme, the oar pivoted on an upright, wooden peg called a tholepin. The oar was held in place by a leather strap, sewn into a loop, the oarloop. The oarloop held the oar tightly against the tholepin.

After constant use, the oarloops tended to stretch or crack. So each time the ship was launched, every rower had to examine his oarloop and readjust or even replace it as needed. The oarloops had to be greased from time to time with mutton tallow. Likewise rowers in the hold had to make sure that the leather oar port sleeves had remained watertight. These sleeves, too, had to be greased regularly.

Meanwhile, the marines and archers gathered up their equipment. They put on their helmets, picked up their spears from where they had stood them—butt-end down—in the ground, adjusted their arrow cases, and placed their daggers in their belts. They were the last men to board the ship. We may imagine that, as in the Greek navy, these deck soldiers received a pre-battle speech on land from their commanders. Or rather, perhaps, a set of speeches, for no one language would have satisfied the makeup of the Persian navy. Everyone in the fleet knew how much was at stake, including their heads. Whether or not Xerxes threatened to punish any commander who let the Greeks escape, as Aeschylus claims, his habit of executing those who failed him was well known.

Finally, before they launched the fleet, the men would have prayed. Libations would have been poured and, depending on a country's customs, sacrifices made. The men would have lifted their voices to the Phoenician deities Eshmun, Astarte, and Melqart; to Apollo, worshipped alike by Greeks, Carians, and Lycians; to the Egyptian gods Neith and Sekhmet; and to Ahura Mazda, the Persian Lord of Wisdom.

In terms of ethnic diversity, the Persian fleet at Phaleron was the second greatest assemblage of humanity in the history of the world to that date. Only the Persian army was greater. If one takes into account class as well as ethnicity, the Persian fleet was even more diverse than the army: in antiquity, rowers were poorer on average than infantrymen, and the personnel of the fleet ranged from penniless oarsmen to kings and one queen.

The Persian navy was, says Aeschylus poetically, "the wonderful flock of Asia rich in men." It included Egyptian "marines from the marshes, the skillful and innumerable rowers of ships," "the crowd of easy-living Lydians," "a long line of [Babylon's] golden, mixed crowd mounted on ships and relying on their archer spirit," and, of course, "the flower of the men of the Persian land." Aeschylus says that there were Bactrians, Cilicians, Lyrnaeans, Mysians, and Phoenicians. Herodotus does not mention all these peoples in connection with the Persian navy, and we might wonder whether the ships really did carry Babylonian archers and Bactrians, men roughly from modern Afghanistan. By the same token, Aeschylus is discreetly silent about the large presence in the Persian fleet of Greeks: from Anatolia, Cyprus, the Aegean islands, and even the Greek mainland itself.

Herodotus records the names of the most famous commanders in the fleet: besides Tetramnestus, they were two Phoenicians, King Matten son of Siromus from Tyre and Merbalus son of Agbalus from Aradus; a Cilician, the Syennesis, that is, the king, whose name we know only as the son of Oromedon; a Lycian, Cyberniscus son of Sycas; two Cypriots, Gorgus son of Chersis, king of the Cypriot city of Salamis (the name is a coincidence) and Timonax son of Timagoras; and three Carians, Pigres son of Hysseldomus, Damasithymus son of Candaules and king of the city of Calynda, and, of course, Artemisia, queen of Halicarnassus. Above them stood four Persian admirals: Achaemenes son of Darius and Atossa, Xerxes' full brother, commanded the Egyptians; Ariabignes son of Darius, Xerxes' half brother, commanded the Ionians and Carians; while Megabazus son of Megabates and Prexaspes son of Aspathines commanded the rest of the fleet.

The full complement of each ship was 230 men: 200 natives, including rowers and marines, plus a group of 30 men consisting of a mix of Iranian (either Persians or Medes) and Sacae marines and archers. In wartime, few units manage to maintain their notional strength, especially after the storms and battles suffered by the Persians. No doubt Xerxes' new recruits had narrowed the manpower gaps, but some of the triremes may well still have been undermanned.

With their contingents of forty marines and archers, the decks of Persian triremes bristled with fighting men. The marines of the Persian fleet were as colorful a lot as had ever sailed. Dressed in uniforms ranging from bronze or linen breastplates to woolen tunics and goatskin capes, and from bronze or plaited helmets to turbans, they carried a wide assortment of weapons. Their arms ran the gamut from javelins and swords to sickles and daggers to boarding pikes, long knives, and heavy axes.

The largest contingent of deck soldiers was the Iranian and Sacae marines and archers. As far as we know, they were armed like their infantrymen. The Persians and Medes were dressed in soft felt caps, embroidered tunics with sleeves, fish-scale iron breastplates, and trousers;

they carried wicker shields, quivers, bows and arrows, short spears, and daggers. The Sacae wore trousers and tall pointed hats; they carried bows and arrows, daggers, and battle-axes.

The Sacae had a reputation as formidable archers, and, by all accounts, they deserved it. The Greeks on deck would have their hands full defending themselves with their shields against the Sacae. If his ship was rammed, a Greek who swam to safety would be vulnerable to Sacae arrows.

Once the Persian ships were loaded, the men harangued, the prayers and libations made, the fleet was ready to depart. In all likelihood, the Phoenicians held the western end of the shore, the Egyptians were in the center, while the Ionians and Carians moored their ships in the east.

At a signal, the fleet began to depart. They left by squadron, forming up in line-ahead order. Aeschylus writes:

On the long ships, rank encouraged rank
And each one sailed in its appointed place.

Plausibly, the Phoenicians in the west went first, followed by the Egyptians in the center—unless they had already left to commandeer Psyttaleia—and finally the Greeks and Carians in the east. On each ship, rowers strained to get the vessel going from a standing start. It would have been efficient to have the top level of rowers get the boat moving and then have the two lower levels join in later. The rowers took short strokes at first, increasing them in length until the ship was well under way and gliding freely between strokes.

Around the shore of the bay, torches lit the scene. As squadron after squadron quit the shoreline and rowed in serried order westward toward the open sea, as warship after warship disappeared in the darkness, an observer on the beach might have considered the destiny of the Great King's armada. Perhaps the Persian fleet had looked more glorious at its inspection by Xerxes after crossing the Hellespont in June, when it was twice as large and half as tired, but never had it looked as brave as it did now, on its final journey to the fatal straits.

Aeschylus and Herodotus agree that the fleet was divided into three sections. Aeschylus portrays Xerxes' orders to his admirals:

Arrange the close array of ships in three columns,
And some, in a circle around the island of Ajax,
Guard the harbor entrances and the pathways of the roaring sea.

Aeschylus's words are vague enough to refer to an operation that closed off every port in Salamis; or one that closed off just those harbors on the eastern side, where the Greek fleet was moored; or one that closed off both the harbors where the Greeks were and also the western channel, near Megara, which was a possible escape route. It would be reasonable to describe a fleet that starts out from Phaleron Bay and wheels north and west into the Salamis straits as "circl[ing] around the island." Herodotus refers only to Persian operations in the Salamis straits, as does Plutarch. But a later historian says that the Egyptian contingent of two hundred ships rowed all the way around the island, to close off the escape route via the western channel between Salamis and Megara. Herodotus says nothing about the position of the Egyptians in the battle, but he specifies only the positions of the Phoenicians, the Ionians, and the Carians, the three most important contingents in the Persian fleet.

This later account is probably wrong. The Egyptians would have had to row all night to go around Salamis. The Greek fleet might have already fled by the time they arrived. When the Egyptians reached their destination, the western channel, they would have found a narrow strait only about 1,300 feet wide. If the Egyptians attempted to fight the Greeks there, they would have been at a substantial disadvantage against the heavier Athenian triremes, and they might also have been outnumbered. No ancient source mentions any fighting in this western channel, yet Aeschylus specifies that Egyptians were killed in the battle of Salamis. Finally, the later source has a nasty habit of improving earlier accounts, that is, inventing details. With all this in mind, we should imagine the Egyptians with the rest of the Persian fleet, heading northwestward from Phaleron into the Salamis straits. Indeed, it is plausible that the Egyptians formed the squadron that had been sent on ahead to secure Psyttaleia.

Herodotus's account, fortunately, is much more specific than Aeschylus's. According to Herodotus, after it left Phaleron Bay, the western wing of the Persian fleet—plausibly, the Phoenicans—wheeled toward Salamis. Indeed, this wing needed to do so: a look at the map shows that if it had continued in a straight line, the western wing would have missed Salamis and rowed toward Aegina. The rest of the Persian fleet, starting out from the eastern and perhaps central beaches of Phaleron Bay, was able to row almost in a straight line toward the Salamis channel.

The ability of one part of the Persian fleet to wheel around in the darkness while maintaining good order bespeaks enormous skill. This is another reason to suspect that the crack Phoenician squadrons were involved. It is also a reminder of how difficult it would be for the entire Persian fleet to enter the straits and to form a continuous, orderly line, without gaps, against the Greeks. If the Greeks were indeed in disarray and in flight, the Persians could afford a few mistakes. If, however, the Greeks formed up in battle order, the Persians would have to be perfect.

Meanwhile, the central-eastern part of the Persian fleet, says Herodotus, "was posted between Ceos and Cynosura." The Cynosura peninsula on Salamis is clear, but we do not know where Ceos was. In any case, we do know that the Persian fleet "held the entire passage with its ships all the way to Munychia." In other words, the Persian fleet stretched all the way from the western border of Phaleron Bay, past Piraeus, to the Attic coast opposite Psyttaleia, the islet where an advance squadron was unloading Persian soldiers.

To the extent that the Persian ships were visible in the dark, they would have made an extraordinary sight. The fleet would have looked like a bridge of boats between the mainland and the islet of Psyttaleia, a distance of about one and one-fourth miles. The bridge surely did not continue all the way to Salamis, because the Persians had to steer clear of the island in order to remain undetected.

Indeed, it would be a mistake to think of the Persian fleet as literally blocking the Salamis straits. Herodotus never mentions a blockade; instead, he speaks of the Persians "encircling" the Greeks or "surrounding" them or "guarding" the waterways. Triremes were not built to stand still, as in a blockade; they were built to move fast and agilely, whether attacking or fleeing.

The massing of the Persian fleet was something, marvels Herodotus, which the oracle-mongers had predicted. Well, almost predicted: these verses from the *Oracle of Bacis*, which predate the battle and which Herodotus cites, seem to envision a wider bridge than actually would have been found:

> *But when they bridge with boats the hallowed shore*
> *Of Artemis of the golden sword and seagirt Cynosura,*
> *Driven by manic hopes after they sack fertile Athens,*
> *Then shall awful Justice quench great Excess, the son of Pride,*
> *Raging terribly, planning to attack everywhere.*
> *Bronze will mix with bronze, and Ares will dye the sea*
> *With crimson blood.* Then shall the far-seeing son of Cronos*
> *And Lady Victory bring the day of freedom for Greece.*

The oracle is vague enough to be flexible: there were temples of Artemis on Salamis and on the hill of Munychia Hill and elsewhere in Attica; there were Cynosura peninsulas on Salamis and also at Marathon, site of past glory (near which there were also two Artemis temples). But the oracle clearly predicts a victory at sea over a big fleet after the sack of Athens. It is hard not to wonder whether it might not be a piece of propaganda, delivered before the Persian invasion, in favor of Themistocles' strategy of abandoning Attica and pinning all Greece's hopes in the fleet. It may even refer to Salamis.

In any case, the bridge of boats moved quickly. The leading column of the Persians entered the Salamis straits. But just how many ships followed them is a crucial question and, unfortunately, unclear. Before turning to it, consider the manner in which the Persians rowed up the straits.

Sailors always look to the sky. In September, the stars of the Bear, or, as the Egyptians preferred, the Thigh of the Bull, were low and bright in the early evening sky; we call these stars Ursa Major or the Big Dipper. But the main feature of the night sky was in the south, which in that season became what the ancients called the Water or the Sea Sky. The southern sky was filled with such constellations as the Goat-Fish, the Dolphin, the Southern Fish, the Water Bearer, the Sea Monster, and the Fish. So the Phoenicians and Greeks would have known them; today they are Capricorn, Delphinus, Piscis Austrinus,

---

* A pun in Greek, where the word for "crimson" is *phoinikeos,* just one letter away from the word for "Phoenician," *phoinikos.*

Aquarius, Cetus, and Pisces. But in the darkness of the early hours of September 25, the men of the Persian fleet are unlikely to have seen many stars. It is likely that they had chosen a cloudy night to enter the straits.

The Persian fleet entered the straits as silently as possible. "They did everything in an undertone," says Herodotus, "in order to keep the enemy from hearing them." It was impossible to move seven hundred ships in complete silence, but it was possible to drop the decibels to a minimum. Indeed, rowing undetected in the dark would become, if it was not already, a standard trireme maneuver. Salamis was not the only occasion on which the commander of a trireme fleet successfully moved his ships down one side of a narrow strait at night in order to avoid detection by an enemy whose ships were moored on the other side: the Athenian navy did just that when it rowed past the Spartans in the Hellespont in the narrows near Abydos in 411 B.C.

At Salamis in 480 B.C. the Persians no doubt kept their ships as far away from the island as possible and as close as they could to the Attic shore, that is, to Persian-controlled territory. In addition, they might have instructed rowing masters and pipers not to call out or pipe each stroke but, rather, to keep time by striking stones together—as a Spartan fleet did when successfully surprising the Athenians in the Saronic Gulf at night in 388 B.C.— or perhaps by leading the crew in humming or whispering a rhythmic song. They might have muffled the oars by keeping the stroke rate low and catching the water with soft and easy motions. Meanwhile, the roar of the Persian army marching westward along the coast of Attica would have drowned out much of the sound made by the fleet.

Besides sight and sound, the Persians might have given some thought to smell. The dried sweat of tens of thousands of rowers was a dead giveaway of the approach of a trireme fleet. The odor could be detected perhaps a mile or more away if the wind was blowing. The Persians could have reduced the odor by washing out their boats while at Phaleron. Otherwise, they had to hope that the wind wasn't against them.

Perhaps the Persians also reaped the benefit of Greek overconfidence. It does not seem to have occurred to the Greeks that the Persians were about to infiltrate the straits, and certainly not at night.

That very evening they had seen the enemy mass his fleet outside the straits. There seemed little danger that he would come back that same night to take the chance of entering unfavorable waters. But that is just what the Persians did.

Just before dawn, on a likely reconstruction, the leading ships of the Persian fleet had rowed into the straits and continued along the Attic coast for about two miles northwestward. They probably sat at the foot of Mount Aegaleos, opposite the islet of St. George, that is, the northernmost mooring point of the Greek fleet. These Persian ships now guarded the Greek escape route northward toward Eleusis, Megara, and the western channel separating Salamis from the mainland. The rest of the fleet extended along the coast of Attica for about four miles.

Although most of the Persian fleet had entered the straits, a large part had not. They were formed up farther to the southeast, east of Psyttaleia in the waters toward Piraeus, that is, outside of the straits altogether. Since the Persians expected the Greeks to be fleeing, they would have reserved a considerable contingent of ships to guard the southern exit from the Salamis straits, just as the Phoenicians now guarded the northern exit.

Within the straits, the Phoenicians and Ionians—along with, we may imagine, the other Greeks—anchored the opposite ends of the Persian line. Herodotus states that "the Phoenicians . . . held the western wing, that is, toward Eleusis" and "the Ionians . . . held the wing toward the east and Piraeus." The Ionians took up their stations about two miles to the southeast of the Phoenicians at the foot of Mount Aegaleos; plausibly, the Ionians were arranged opposite Ambelaki Bay and the southern end of the Greek mooring stations.

What Herodotus does not indicate is where the rest of the Persian ships were: that is, the Carians, Cypriots, Cilicians, Pamphylians, and Lycians; the Egyptians possibly were on Psyttaleia. He does mention two Carian ships in the thick of the fight, while Diodorus claims that the Cypriots, Cilicans, Pamphylians, and Lycians were arranged in that order from the Phoenicians to the Ionians; Diodorus has the Egyptians off at the western channel. But Diodorus's account of Salamis inspires little confidence, and the Carians might have joined the battle late.

HERODOTUS. Roman portrait bust, second century A.D. (Metropolitan Museum of Art, New York, Gift of George F. Baker, 91.8)

THEMISTOCLES. Roman portrait bust, possibly a copy of a Greek original. (Ostia Museum)

CYNOSURA PENINSULA. A view from the Salamis straits, looking southwest. Another part of the island of Salamis is in the background. (Barry Strauss)

ATHENIAN TRIREME. *Olympias* under oar at sea, a modern reconstruction of an Athenian trireme of the fourth century B.C. Note the ram. (Mary Pridgen by courtesy of the Trireme Trust)

XERXES. Relief sculpture of Crown Prince Xerxes standing behind King Darius on his throne, ca. 500 B.C. From the Treasury at Persepolis, Iran. (Oriental Institute of the University of Chicago)

CLASH OF CIVILIZATIONS. Greek infantryman attacking a Persian soldier. Attic red-figure amphora, 480–470 B.C. (Metropolitan Museum of Art, New York, Rogers Fund, 06.1021.117)

PERSIAN ATTENDANT. Relief sculpture of a beardless attendant with a cosmetic bottle and towel, possibly a royal eunuch. From the Palace of Darius at Persepolis, Iran. (Oriental Institute of the University of Chicago)

SPARTAN WARRIOR. Note the helmet and its transverse crest, the braided long hair, and the thin cloak draped tightly around the body. Greek bronze, 510–500 B.C. (Wadsworth Atheneum, Hartford, Connecticut. Gift of A. Pierpont Morgan)

CARIAN TREASURE. The skull and gold jewelry found in the tomb of an aristocratic lady of Halicarnassus of the fourth century B.C., the so-called Carian princess, indicating the kind of ornaments that Artemisia might have worn. (Don Frey)

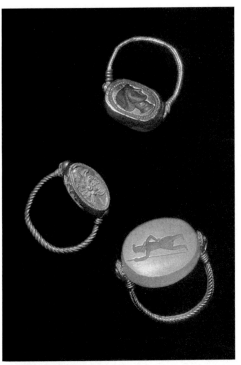

CARIAN RINGS. Three gold rings from the Halicarnassian tomb of the fourth century B.C. Note in particular the chalcedony signet ring of a Persian soldier (bottom), suggesting the loyalty that Artemisia had to Xerxes. (Don Frey)

PHALERON BAY. A view of the harbor where the Persian fleet moored, looking southeast toward Mount Hymettus. (Barry Strauss)

SALAMIS STRAITS. A view from the island looking toward the mainland and the hills from which Xerxes watched the battle. These are the waters in which the battle was fought. (Barry Strauss)

AMBELAKI BAY. The ancient harbor of Salamis Town, where part of the Greek fleet was moored before the battle of Salamis. The mainland of Greece is on the right (east) in the background, and the hills of Salamis are on the left (west). (Barry Strauss)

Some or all of the ships from Caria, Cilicia, Cyprus, Egypt, Lycia, and Pamphylia took up a position outside the straits.

Nor can we assume that those ships within the straits were lined up and ready in battle order when dawn broke. The length and difficulty of their journey in the dark, the need to maintain near silence, the great number of ships involved, the twists and curves of the straits, the expectation of an enemy in panic, the inevitable mistakes and confusion in any nighttime operation, all add to our understanding of why the Persians had to scramble when the Greeks came out to fight.

In any case, whether a Persian ship was inside the straits or outside, its crew was not at rest. A trireme fleet lined up in formation cannot maintain its order simply by dropping anchor. It is necessary for the rowers in each ship, or for a portion of them in turn, to alternate strokes in a continuous movement of rowing and backing, rowing and backing.

On every ship, calloused hands ignored the friction of the oar; muscles that had not rested from the afternoon's exertion pulled yet again. On and on they worked. "They didn't get even a little sleep," says Herodotus. Aeschylus writes:

> *The lords of the ships kept the entire rowing crew*
> *At their oars all the livelong night.*

Little by little, the hours of effort must have taken their toll. A commander who understood triremes would have thought twice before asking his men to go into battle so tired. The king of seafaring Sidon surely saw the danger, but Tetramnestus did not have the final say. Xerxes did, and Xerxes had never touched an oar.

Herodotus reports an anecdote about a Phoenician trireme on which Xerxes is supposed to have traveled after Salamis. A storm blew up, and at the pilot's advice, Xerxes ordered some men to jump overboard in order to lighten the boat's load. Xerxes had to choose between the Persian noblemen on deck and the Phoenician rowers below. Herodotus has no doubt about it: Xerxes would have sent the rowers overboard.

Herodotus rejects the story as just a tall tale, but even so, perhaps it reveals the Great King's sense of priorities. For Xerxes, the rowers were expendable; only the Persians on deck counted. He seems to have thought of oarsmen as human beasts of burden. But as a horseman, Xerxes should have known that even beasts break down, and every animal is limited by its body.

Had he ever scrutinized the men who rowed his ships, the Great King would not have delivered them to the enemy at dawn after a night spent pulling an oar.

CHAPTER EIGHT

~~

SALAMIS

The poet is going to war. Although he is forty-five years old, on September 25 he is ready to wear once more the same old breast-plate that he had worn ten years earlier at Marathon. This time he will surely want to fight on deck, as a marine, or to go below deck and pull an oar. Doesn't Athens need every man? Yet he will not complain if, in the end, the commanders decide that there are enough younger men to serve at sea and that he, instead, should line the beach at Salamis, waiting to drive his pike into any Persian survivor who is fool enough to stagger ashore. He is a patriot of the old school. He is also one of the most famous men in the city, having won first prize at the Festival of Dionysos only four years earlier, in 484 B.C. He is a local boy; from Salamis you can practically see his birthplace across the water at Eleusis, the birthplace as well of his brother Cynegirus, may the gods rest his soul, heroically departed a decade ago on the battlefield of Marathon. The son of Euphronius, he is the tragedian Aeschylus.

Eight years later, in 472 B.C., Aeschylus would again win first prize at the festival, this time for a tragic trilogy that included *The Persians*, his play about Salamis. He wrote from experience, because he had served at Salamis himself. So says Ion of Chios (ca. 480s—before 421 B.C.), a poet who came to Athens, knew Aeschylus personally, and published memoirs with a well-deserved reputation for accuracy. But after Aeschylus died in 456 B.C., his gravestone mentioned only Marathon

141

and not Salamis. Perhaps the poet had ordered that, in order not to look as if he was trying to outdo his brother Cynegirus.

But what might really have moved Aeschylus was snobbery. The better people in Greece, as the upper classes called themselves, loved Marathon but turned up their noses at Salamis. Marathon was won by good, solid, middle-class farmer-soldiers, but Salamis was a people's battle, fought by poor men who sat on the rower's bench. And Aeschylus, who grew ever more conservative with age, might have had ever less use for those people. So, the poet might well have preferred to forget Salamis.

But in 472 B.C. Aeschylus could still see the white horses of the sun rising over the earth that morning and the red stain widening in a Persian grandee's beard. He remembered things that he described in clichés, but they were earned clichés, as he might have thought; anyone who was there that day had the right to stumble in his words.

He remembered the power in the ship, when everyone was rowing, when you could hear the oars groan from rubbing against the leather

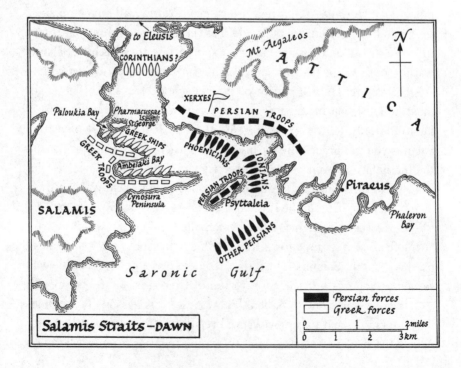

oar port sleeves, when you could hear the rushing sound of many oars rowing as one, striking the deep salt sea. He remembered the fishermen, who were everywhere on Salamis, grumbling about the moorings that they had lost to the fleet, then trading theories about strategy in the taverns. Only the fishermen really know the water and the winds and the wrinkles on the surface of the sea at sunrise. They could have spread their nets and picked up dead Persians that day, thick as tuna in the water, split open and boned like mackerel.

But if Aeschylus remembered the look on the Greek sailors' faces that night, when it was not yet morning, and the captains called them to their stations, and they knew that this was it, the day of death had finally come, and the Athenians among them had to worry about their wives and children here on Salamis—if Aeschylus remembered that, he did not tell. And yet, to anyone who was there, that was the story to remember. The looks of grit or discomfort or relief or fear or ferociousness: no one has recorded those.

It might have been hard for the Greeks on Salamis to sleep the night before the battle, on shore beside the ships, between the sound of Xerxes' army on the march, echoing across the straits, and the knowledge that the Greek generals were battling with words in Salamis Town. The generals from the Peloponnese were all for rowing westward and fighting for their homes, while they still had them. As for the Athenians, Megarians, and Aeginetans, they might have been ready to fight the other Greeks rather than give up the chance to stay at Salamis and drive the Persians back. The crewmen did not know if the fleet would hang together or split apart. They did not know where they would fight, but they knew it would be soon, that is, unless some renegade turned traitor to the enemy, but maybe that thought was too much to bear.

To relieve the tension, some men might have told jokes. They might have laughed at Themistocles' itchy fingers, for example, or at the spectacle of the gentry, pale and overweight, trying to pull an oar. They might have traded gripes about rowing masters. They might have argued over who had fought better at Artemisium. They might have wondered when the statues of Aeacus and his sons would ever get to Salamis.

And then it came: first the news that the enemy had snuck past the Greeks and surrounded them in the straits. Then the transcendent call rang forth. The Greeks would fight. It was a call of fear and a call of freedom. It was a battle cry to remind the men of why they had not surrendered to the Persians as most Greeks had: because, as Aeschylus puts it, they "are not called slaves nor subjects of any man."

And so the Greeks would fight at Salamis. At that hour, suddenly, there were no more Athenians, no more Spartans, no more Corinthians. There were only Greeks. For a brief moment, just before dawn on September 25, 480 B.C., the Greeks achieved a unity that had always eluded them. It was an imperfect unity, because a roughly equal number of Greeks were lined up across the straits, on Persia's ships, as fought on the Greek side. Yet the men at Salamis represented not just the flower of the city-states but a cross section of their male population. They ranged from the richest to the poorest, from cavalier to knave, from Panhellenic champions to losers at the childhood game of knucklebones, from representatives of families so old that they seemed to have sprung from the soil itself to immigrants from obscure villages somewhere in Thrace or Sicily. As a group they comprised citizens, resident aliens, and slaves. They spanned the ranks of the Greek military, from horsemen to hoplites (infantrymen), from marines to rowers, from archers to scouts. They were going to their ships to fight at last.

It should not have taken them long to get ready. All the Greeks had sharpened their weapons for battle; the debate concerned only where they would fight. The rowers needed just to grab their gear, including a little food and water to bring aboard. But first, they would eat. Since the Athenians had probably brought livestock with them to Salamis, the Greeks might have been able to add cheese to their pre-battle meal. It would all have been washed down with wine, diluted, in the ordinary Greek way, with water. This was the standard way of sending off a warrior with a shot of courage.

But seventy thousand men, the number of men gathered on the eastern shore of Salamis, ready to board their ships, cannot move at once. Thousands more men, Athenian hoplites, many of them presumably teenagers or quinquagenarians, stood ready to line the shore as soon as the ships pulled out. Nor can we be sure that there weren't other, even older men on the hills and in the town behind them, and women and children, too, peering down into the camp and onto the beaches, trying to grab a glimpse of their men, calling out advice and encouragement, and perhaps even clapping their hands and singing. It was a morning like no other.

From Paloukia Bay southward along the island's winding coastal curves to Ambelaki Bay, 368 Greek ships stood ready, moored at Salamis's shoreline, stern first. With the addition of the trireme from Tenos, they represented twenty-three city-states, from Athens, which had 180 triremes at Salamis, to Seriphos, which provided a penteconter. The civilization that we call Greece was made up of a variety of ethnic groups. They all spoke the same language and worshipped the same gods, but they had a variety of laws and customs. The sailors at Salamis represented a virtual cross section of Greek ethnic groups: they included Ionians and Dorians, which were the two main groups, as well as Achaeans, Dryopes, and Macedonians.

The Spartans provided the commanding general, so they were assigned the traditional position of honor at the extreme right of the line, at the southern end of Ambelaki Bay. The Greeks considered the extreme right to be the position of honor, because in an infantry battle, each hoplite held his shield in his left hand, which left his right flank exposed. Every man was able to protect his right by taking advantage of the overlapping shield of the man in line to his right, except for the man on the extreme right. He stood in the most dangerous and therefore the most honorable place.

Tradition also assigned a spot to the city that claimed the next position in importance: the left wing. At Salamis, that honor went to Athens, whose ships were presumably moored in Paloukia Bay. Aegina held the spot to Athens's right, to judge from the close communication between an Athenian and an Aeginetan commander during the battle.

According to this arrangement, the Spartans stood opposite the Ionians and perhaps other Greeks, while the Athenians and perhaps the Aeginetans faced the Phoenicians. In other words, the best Greek triremes were matched against the best Persian triremes. (It is not known where the other Greek contingents stood in the battle line.)

With full complements, 368 ships would have been filled with about sixty-two thousand rowers. As they took their seats, the rowers turned to one another and shook hands. These men were the backbone of the battle, and yet we do not know the name of a single one. Only a few captains and commanders are known by name. In fact, the ancient literary sources—histories, dramas, lyric poetry, philosophy—never mention a single rower by name, except for mythical heroes like the Argonauts. Their silence reflects both an age-old tendency in naval warfare to focus on boats instead of individuals and the upper-class bias of ancient literature. But in spite of the literary writers, the names of several hundred rowers in the Athenian fleet around 400 B.C. do survive, preserved in a public document, that is, in a lengthy inscription on stone. There we learn, for instance, of one Demochares of the deme of Thoricus, an Athenian citizen; of Telesippus of Piraeus, a resident alien; of Assyrios the property of Alexippos, a slave; and of Simos, a mercenary from the island of Thasos. These names, of course, mean almost nothing today, but perhaps that is the point. At Salamis, the freedom of Greece depended on ordinary men with undistinguished names. It was indeed democracy's battle.

On the Athenian triremes if not others, the all-important pilot or helmsman was also a product of democracy. Standing in the stern with a rudder handle in each hand (the trireme had a double rudder), the pilot steered the ship. He made decisions, sometimes split-second decisions, which might provide the margin of victory. Not only did a pilot have to be steady, knowledgeable, and dogged, he also had to be quick, intelligent, and independent. And these were precisely the qualities that Athenian democracy promoted. The society that produced Themistocles would prove to be a fertile recruiting ground for pilots.

Ace pilots might play a critical role at Salamis. The narrowness of the straits would leave little leeway for steering error. Furthermore, the large number of Persian marines and archers would render the Greeks vulnerable to a mauling if their ships were rammed and boarded. It was up to the pilots to avoid Persian rams while landing Greek rams in the enemy.

As they funneled into their ships, some sailors may have faced the possibility of death, while others shunned the thought that they would never step on the earth again. They probably knew that, should they die, even if they won the battle, they might never be buried, and the Greeks had a particular horror of leaving a corpse unburied. They even considered it miserable to have to settle for burial by strangers rather than by one's loved ones.

When someone dies in the water, his corpse floats for several hours, then loses the air in its lungs and sinks. Unless wind and waves deposit it on the shore sooner, a corpse will not resurface for several days, when bacteria in the abdomen generally emit enough gases to bring it floating up. But a puncture wound in the lung, such as from an arrow, a javelin, or a sword, allows gases to escape and delays the corpse's ascent. If not found within four days, a corpse's face will no longer be identifiable. On one occasion Spartan hoplites seem to have brought written identification with them into battle, but we know nothing otherwise of the primitive dog tags that ancient Greek combatants might have carried.

A sailor's body, therefore, might never be brought home. In later years, when Athens held an annual public funeral for its war dead, there was an empty coffin to symbolize the missing.

No doubt the cause and the camaraderie gave comfort to the men who came on board. But they might also have rallied and found faith in their ships. For the Greeks, triremes were not merely machines, nor even merely "wooden walls": they were alive and sacred, just as mountains and groves and springs were sacred.

Every warship had a name. Although we do not know the name of a single trireme that fought at Salamis, we do know hundreds of such names surviving from fifth- and fourth-century Athens. Ships were considered female. They were named for goddesses, like Artemis and Aphrodite; for demigods, like Thetis and Amphitrite; for ideals, like Democracy, Freedom, and Equality; for animals, like Lioness, Gazelle, and Sea Horse; for nautical locations, like Cape Sunium and Salamis; for weapons, like Javelin; for soldiers, like Hoplite or Ephebe (young recruit); and even for piratical notions like Rape and Pillage. Outside of Athens (and in some cases, outside Greece), we know of ships named, for example, after a sphinx, a snake, an eagle, a flower, a horse and rider, and for the heroes Castor and Pollux.

Every ship had its name depicted on a painted plaque attached to the prow. The name was possibly written out as well, but the painted image served several important purposes. It was relatively easy to identify in battle, it provided a symbol around which the crew could rally, and, not least, it was comprehensible. The majority of rowers in ancient fleets were almost certainly illiterate or only partially literate. Some of them would have had trouble making out writing, but the picture gave them something to remember.

Each trireme carried other decorations as well. Every stern pole was ornamented with a sculpted object. These represented a region rather than individual ships, and plausibly all the triremes in a given fleet carried the same stern ornament. It appears that Greek ships were all decorated with swan heads. Persian ships seem to have carried a human head in Persian clothing; perhaps this represented a heroic warrior or even the Great King. Stern ornaments were detachable, and were carried off as a victory trophy when a ship was sunk. Phoenician triremes also carried a bow ornament, possibly of a guardian god.

Finally, every trireme, indeed every ship, both in Greece and elsewhere in the ancient Mediterranean, had polished, painted-marble plaques on either side of the prow, each depicting an eye. Aeschylus calls triremes "the dark-eyed ships." The custom of depicting eyes went back to early Egypt. The eyes symbolized the ship's protective deity. Just as a human lookout sat in the prow and sent messages back to the pilot, so the eyes allowed the ship's deity to scan the horizon. Aeschylus refers to a ship's "prow that looks at the way ahead with its eyes obeying . . . the guiding rudder."

The eyes also marked the prow as sacred space. It was not by accident, for example, that when the Persians captured the trireme from Troezen off the island of Sciathos in August and sacrificed a Troezenian marine named Leon, they chose the ship's prow as the place to cut his throat.

The prow eyes, the ship's name (especially if it honored a divinity or hero), and the stern ornament all symbolized the faith and trust of the common sailor in the protection of the gods. Athena might have let her temples on the Athenian Acropolis be destroyed, but she would not let them go unavenged.

Men heading into battle are likely to pray, and the sailors on Salamis would have been no exception. The Greeks always sacrificed an animal before battle. We do not know if, at Salamis, they made one sacrifice on behalf of everyone or if the individual city-states each sacrificed separately. The Spartans always sacrificed a goat to Artemis, so if Eurybiades carried out the rite on behalf of the entire fleet, he certainly would have chosen a goat. The Athenians might well have done like-wise. They sometimes selected a different animal to kill before battle, but at Marathon in 490 B.C. they had vowed to sacrifice as many goats to Artemis after the battle as enemies killed. Since they slaughtered six thousand Persians at Marathon, that proved impractical, so instead they sacrificed five hundred goats a year on the sixth day of the month of Boedromion (roughly September). We might imagine, then, that at Salamis they would have been glad to stick to success and sacrifice a goat to Artemis.

In addition, the Greeks would have prayed to the gods for a safe trip. Just before the moment of departure, when every ship was fully loaded with its crew and the ladders had been pulled up, each com-mander would have carried out the ceremony. He would have recited prayers, followed by the singing of a hymn by his crew, and concluding with the pouring of a cup of wine from each ship's stern.

It was standard procedure to offer the gods animal sacrifice before battle and a libation of wine before departure. But myths clung to the ceremonies marking so momentous an enterprise as the launching of the Greek fleet at Salamis. It might have been on this occasion, for example, that, at a predawn moment when Themistocles was speaking from the deck of his ship, an owl was supposedly seen to fly through the fleet from the right and land on the halyards of his mast. Everyone who saw it took this as a favorable omen, since the owl was Athena's bird and had come from the right, that is, the auspicious side.

More lurid is the story of Themistocles' sacrifice. According to the philosopher Phanias of Lesbos, who was a student of Aristotle, Themis-tocles sacrificed three human victims beside his trireme. Decked out in gold jewelry, they were high-ranking Persians indeed, no less than the sons of Xerxes' sister Sandauce and her husband Artaüctus. Apparently an animal sacrifice was in progress when they were brought to Themis-tocles. At that point, a seer named Euphrantides claimed to witness a conspicuous flame shoot up from the altar and to hear a sneeze from the right. Thrilled, he clasped Themistocles by the hand and told him to sacrifice the three young men to Dionysus Carnivorous if he wanted a victory. Themistocles refused, but the crowd dragged the Persians to the altar and slit their throats. Plutarch, who repeats the story from Phanias, thinks it has merit, but he also tells what seems to be another version, in which Aristides captures the prisoners later, during the battle, before Themistocles allegedly has them sacrificed.

At daybreak, around 6:15 A.M., the outline of the Persian ships across the straits was visible. The Greek generals held an assembly. It was not unusual to launch a fleet before sunrise, but it would have been impractical to hold an assembly of more than three thousand men in the dark. In addition, the Greek commanders had other reasons to delay the launching of the fleet, as will become clear presently.

The assembly consisted of only the marines. It may seem strange that the rowers were not invited, but this was standard procedure in the pre-battle assemblies of ancient Greek navies. An assembly of the marines of over three hundred ships amounted to more than three thousand men; to include the rowers would have meant an assembly of more than sixty thousand men, and there wasn't a hillside in Greece big enough to accommodate such a crowd. Besides, it would have delayed the fleet's embarkation dangerously to wait until after the assembly to fill so many ships with so many men. Far better to have the rowers file onto their benches aboard ship first, while the assembly was in session, and then to have the marines clamber onto the deck.

The purpose of the assembly was to inspire the men. Greek generals usually addressed their troops before sending them into battle. The rowers certainly needed to be inspired as well, but perhaps the marines seemed to be in greater danger, considering that they sat on deck and might well have to engage in hand-to-hand fighting.

But there was a final reason to address the marines and not the rowers, and that was the prestige of the armed man. Marines carried sword and spear but rowers did not. In 480 B.C., the marines were probably drawn from the social class that supplied Greece's infantrymen: the men of middling wealth, most of them farmers. These men came from families that, for generations, had supplied the backbone of the Greek armies. The rowers, meanwhile, certainly included men of modest wealth: the rowing benches could not be filled without them. But many of the rowers were poor men, sometimes dirt-poor, and Greek manpower needs dictated that they would even include slaves. Poor men in Greek land armies served only in a supporting role, as light-armed troops, and sometimes served not at all. By addressing the marines, therefore, the commanders paid homage to the martial tradition of the Greek people. They also reminded the marines, at least symbolically, that they were elite troops.

So the marines gathered round. Each is likely to have worn a short-sleeved, belted tunic and perhaps also a cloak against the morning chill on the water. He would be carrying a shield, a spear, and a sword. Many would be wearing a breastplate.

Various commanders spoke, but Themistocles seemed to say things best. What the others said is not recorded, and only the gist of his remarks survives. Herodotus reports:

> *All his words contrasted the better with the worse in human nature and the human condition. He told the men to choose the better, he finished his speech resoundingly, and he gave orders to board their ships.*

At first sight, Themistocles' words are disappointing. Then, on a second look, they reveal the eloquence of simplicity. There may have been no better way to tell the men how much depended on their behavior during the next day.

Or maybe, for once, Themistocles knew when to hold his tongue. Nothing that he said could have affected the men as powerfully as the sacrifices or the prayers or the omens. Indeed, at the very last minute, when Themistocles had finished and the marines were boarding their ships, another augury of success appeared. The trireme from Aegina, sent to fetch the statues of the sons of Aeacus, arrived. If seventy thousand voices had cried out in unison "The gods and heroes are with us!," the effect could not have been greater.

If Themistocles noted the arrival from Aegina with approval, he no doubt focused on the fleets. His men, fresh from a night on shore and fired to avenge their gods and defend their homes, faced an enemy whose ships were still finding their places in line and whose captains had perhaps begun to fret. The Persians had expected to find a broken fleet on the verge of flight; instead, they faced a battle-ready foe, while they themselves had tired crews and boats positioned for the wrong assignment. Within the space of a day, the Greeks had gone from despair to the real possibility of victory. The gods had given the Greeks an opportunity that most of them had never imagined.

The gods, that is, through their faithful servant, Themistocles. The

Athenian was irreverent to men but he was a lifelong devotee of Artemis. He owed the goddess more than a goat for the advantage bestowed upon the Greeks by his ruse with Sicinnus. And yet, it may be that Themistocles had still more tricks to play before the battle began. The ancient sources are so difficult on this subject that we can do no more than judge these tricks as plausible: we do not know if they actually happened or if they only grew in legend later. But when dealing with Themistocles, it would be unwise to ignore any possible ploy.

The first trick has to do with the role of Corinth in the battle. Years later, around 430 B.C., when Corinth and Athens had become the bitterest enemies, the Athenians insisted that, at the outset of the battle of Salamis, the Corinthians hoisted their sails and fled instead of fighting. In other words, they behaved just as the Samians had at Lade in 494 B.C. Yet all the other Greeks denied this. Furthermore, before 430 B.C. the Athenians had allowed the Corinthians to set up victory monuments on Salamis. Herodotus, who reports the facts, is neutral.

The story about Corinth might amount to nothing more than slander, but then again, it might contain a grain of truth. Suppose the Corinthians indeed had raised their sails and fled, but only to deceive the Persians. In that case, the Persians would believe with certainty in the Greek collapse. Softened up by deception, they would have been shocked by the fury of the Greek charge. In the meantime, the Corinthians could have quickly furled their sails and entered the battle.

The second trick, involving winds and waves, is even more complex. It is said that only the fishermen really know the winds. To earn their livelihood, fishermen must know when it is safe to go out to sea and when they must stick to shore; they need to know if they can sleep until dawn or if they must be up earlier, in order to find a smooth sea on which to toss their nets. A good fisherman can make a fair guess, the night before, about the winds that the next morning will bring.

A smart naval commander knows, therefore, that fishermen are valuable resources. We may imagine that Themistocles took the trouble to get to know the fishermen on Salamis personally. In his usual politician's manner, he might have learned their names, kissed their babies, and asked about the winds.

It seems a good guess that as soon as he finished addressing his marines that morning, Themistocles had his finger up to the wind, because the fishermen had already given him information. They had told him that within two hours of dawn, the *aura* would begin to blow.

The *aura* is a sea breeze. In the region of Attica, it blows in from the south, off the Saronic Gulf. The *aura* is a gentle breeze, rarely blowing as much as four or five nautical miles per hour. In the Attica region, the *aura* usually begins to blow between 8:00 and 10:00 A.M. Another common phenomenon is for the *aura* to be proceeded by a north wind, blowing off the land.

If Themistocles expected an *aura* on the morning of September 25, the information might have been of great interest to him. He knew that the *aura* was intensified by the narrow Salamis straits, by what meteorologists today call the channeling effect. No doubt he had seen the results himself. He did not expect a hurricane, but he knew that the *aura* would make boats bounce and waver on the water. And that might make a difference in the battle.

Here the historian enters intriguing if dangerous ground. Herodotus says nothing about the winds at Salamis. Then again, he says nothing about the winds in any naval battle. Our information comes from Plutarch. Although he wrote six centuries after Salamis, Plutarch had access to several fifth century B.C. accounts besides Herodotus, accounts that no longer survive today. Plutarch was, in general, a careful scholar, with a habit of labeling tall tales clearly. He was a Greek to boot, so he knew the weather.

Plutarch reports that Themistocles waited for the *aura* before he gave the order for the Greek triremes to charge. He waited for "a brisk breeze . . . from the sea and a swell to roll down the straits." He expected that these conditions might give the Persians trouble because he knew that their triremes "rose high in their sterns, and had bulwarks and would come down heavily." In other words, the waves would upset the Persian ships because of their height. Themistocles worried little about the effect of the swell on the Greek ships, because "they had light drafts and lay low in the water." Indeed, Themistocles may have been right, because other evidence confirms that Phoenician triremes contained bulwarks. This feature, aimed at protecting the large number of men on deck, rendered the ships vulnerable to wind.

We might also add that the Greeks had the advantage of knowing what awaited them. The Persians, by contrast, were sailing blind: they had no locals to ask about the wind, since Attica had been evacuated. They had to rely on the exiled family of the ex-tyrant of Athens, most of whom hadn't seen Athens in thirty years, and none of whom was likely ever to have spent much time with the fishermen there.

If Plutarch is right, then Themistocles had yet another card to play against the Persian fleet. But only a very few men of the tens of thousands in the Greek fleet can have shared his knowledge of the strategic overview. Most of them made out only the threatening mass of the enemy triremes and the back of the oarsman astern of them or the early light reflected on a forest of spear points or the blood dripping from the sacrificial goat's throat.

Somewhere in the crowd, either on a trireme or in the ranks along the shore, a poet, we may imagine, intermingled obligation with iambic meter not yet sung. Phrases like "lord of the oar," "rich in hands and rich in rowers," "to join in battle with their triremes' rams," and "to shut out the invincible wave with sturdy walls" rushed through his mind in turn. Yet however many lines he may have spun, Aeschylus kept returning to one verse in particular: *theoi polin soizousi Pallados theas.* "The city of Athena will be rescued by the gods."

As for Themistocles, he had achieved all that he had sought. In spite of every effort by his allies to avoid it, in spite of every effort by his enemies to wage it on better terms, one cunning Athenian had created a clash of a thousand warships precisely where he wanted it, and precisely when. Themistocles had arranged the perfect battle. All that remained was to fight it.

THE BATTLE

CHAPTER NINE

≈

SALAMIS STRAITS: MORNING

The admiral Ariabignes, commander of the Ionian and Carian squadrons in the Persian fleet, son of Darius and half brother of His Majesty the Great King Xerxes, sits in the stern of his flagship. The ship, which is unusually large, has a towering stern and high bulwarks. We may imagine Ariabignes in the stern, shortly after dawn on September 25, pondering his uncertainty. Perhaps he absentmindedly fingers the twists of the gold torque that hangs heavily around his neck. The noble blood of Gobryas, a Persian of great courage, runs in Ariabignes' veins, and it is too rich for seawater. But battle is battle, wherever it takes place, and the admiral is a seasoned warrior. He knows that confusion gets in the way of victory, and he has reason to be confused.

He had expected to catch the cowardly Greeks in the act of sneaking out of their harbors on Salamis during the night, which is why the entire Persian fleet has been deployed in darkness in the straits. Yet not a Greek ship has budged all night except for a trireme that rowed *into* rather than out of the straits; unbeknown to Ariabignes, it was Aristides' ship. If indeed the forty Corinthian ships had hoisted sail at dawn and fled, then Ariabignes might have been reassured: how like the Greeks to be so paralyzed by talk that they could not even turn tail in a

timely manner. But still, he might wonder why the other Greek triremes had not followed the first to flee.

It is unlikely that Ariabignes suspects that the Persian fleet has blundered into a trap. Royal admirals do not like to admit mistakes, especially not mistakes that might discredit their brother on the throne. Xerxes himself had ordered the navy into the straits, and Xerxes himself was there at Salamis. Aeschylus writes of the king:

> *He had a seat in full view of the army,*
> *A high hill beside the broad sea.*

Xerxes observed the battle from the slopes of Mount Aegaleos on the mainland. The Great King sat on a golden throne, looking down like a god from Olympus on the men who were about to die for the sake of his ambition.

Ariabignes might have comforted himself with the thought that his men would fight well regardless of what awaited them. If the sight of Xerxes on high were not enough to ensure their loyalty, then the presence of Iranian and Sacae marines on every ship should have made up for it. Since the Great King's ships had crossed the Hellespont in May, only six triremes, all Greek, had defected from the Persian navy to the enemy side. So Ariabignes might have reasoned, but it is doubtful that he had an inkling of what lay ahead.

Meanwhile, about a mile away on the other side of the straits, the Greeks made full use of the advantage they had over the Persians: the knowledge of the truth. They prepared to shock the enemy with an attack.

Surprise is a weapon. Often underestimated, it is one of the most effective and cheapest of all force multipliers as well as one of the most versatile. It is possible to surprise an enemy not only in the time or place of battle but in the manner of fighting. Ariabignes and his other commanders knew that the entire Greek navy faced them. What they did not know, and what they could perhaps hardly fathom, was that the Greeks were ready to do battle. And yet, that morning at around seven o'clock if not earlier, events would force Ariabignes into admitting the truth. The Persians had been swindled.

Themistocles knew, as a modern military maxim puts it, that it is devastating to "come down on the enemy with thunder before he sees the lightning." The ancients put it more simply: panic, they believed, is divine. And so, the Greeks on Salamis unleashed the storm of war on an enemy that had expected a drizzle.

Shortly before 7:00 A.M., as soon as Themistocles and the other Greek generals had finished their send-offs and the marines had boarded their triremes, an order was passed from ship to ship. Up the row of triremes moored in the harbors and opposite the beaches of Ambelaki and Paloukia bays, the command went out, perhaps by sounding the trumpet, perhaps by raising a purple flag, perhaps by holding aloft a gold or silver shield—or perhaps by doing all three: the Greeks would launch their ships.

On the far side of the straits, the first sign of trouble for the Persians was an unexpected sound from the Greek harbors. "A song-like shout sounded triumphantly from the Greeks," reports Aeschylus, "and

at the same time, the island's rocks returned the high-pitched echo."
This was the paean.

It was a peculiarly Greek custom, Dorian in origin but eventually
adopted by the other Greeks. Aeschylus describes the paean as a "holy
cry uttered in a loud voice, . . . a shout offered in sacrifice, emboldening
to friends, and dissolving fear of the foe." When an army marched into
battle or a navy left the harbor to wage war at sea, the men sang the
paean. It was a combination of prayer, cheer, and rebel yell.

The Persians had heard the paean before, most recently at Artemisium and Thermopylae. But in the last weeks, as they beat down nearly
defenseless foes in Euboea, Phocis, and Attica, they had become used to
its absence. It was the last thing they had expected this morning.
Aeschylus is blunt about its alleged effect on the Persian audience
aboard ship:

> *All the barbarians felt fear because they had been deprived of*
> *What they expected. The Greeks were singing the stately paean at that time*
> *Not for flight but because they were hastening*
> *Into battle and were stout of heart.*

Next the alarmed Persians heard the blaring of the Greek trumpets, an unambiguous call to arms. The ancient trumpet, or *salpinx*, was
a long, straight, narrow tube flaring into a small bell. The *salpinx*
ranged from two and a half to about five feet long: the *salpinx* was
hardly handy, but it was certainly loud. Homer compares the sound of
the *salpinx* to the terrible cry of Achilles. An ancient music critic, Aristides Quintilianus, calls the *salpinx* "a warlike and terrifying instrument," "masculine" and "vehement."

Next came the sound of enemy oars being rowed on command,
crisply and in unison, in what Aeschylus calls "the regular stroke of the
rushing oars together." Ominously, the Greek word for stroke, *embolē*, is
the same word used for "charge" or "ramming." There was no mistak-
ing the meaning of that sound.

By now, the Greeks had left the shadow of the shore and were
clearly visible to the Persians. Only a few minutes had passed between
the sound of the paean and the sight of the enemy. Unlike the Greeks,

who had put together a battle plan on shore and had enjoyed at least a little time to think things through, the Persians had to scramble.

From his flagship, Tetramnestus, king of Sidon, no doubt assessed the situation. Two other Phoenician monarchs were also present nearby: Matten, king of Tyre, and Merbalus, king of Aradus. Since the three of them represented the greatest naval tradition in the world, they are likely to have responded calmly. But a surge of emotions, from the lowest seaman to the loftiest courtier, stood in the way of an unperturbed reaction to the Greek challenge. Besides, the Persian commanders Megabazus and Prexaspes had the final say, and they probably did not enjoy the same ease at sea as the Phoenicians.

We can only imagine the range of feelings on the Persian ships. For the captains, it may have been fear; for the rowers, fury; for the pilots, frustration; for the squadron commanders, finger-wagging; for the skeptics, self-satisfaction; for the admirals, fantasies of revenge. The Phoenicians blamed the Ionians; the Ionians blamed the Egyptians; the Egyptians blamed the Cypriots; and everyone blamed the Persians. And it's likely that the Persians nervously fingered their necks, thinking of Xerxes' anger at those who failed him.

Whatever their feelings, the Persians were professional enough to hustle into order. To their credit, they rowed out from the coast of Attica toward the far side of the straits in order to meet the Greek fleet. "When they [the Greeks] launched their ships," writes Herodotus, "the barbarians were upon them without delay."

Meanwhile on Salamis the Greek fleet got under way. As was customary, the right wing, here headed by the Spartans under Eurybiades, led the advance. Aeschylus writes:

> First the right wing in a good arrangement
> Leads in order, and second the whole fleet
> Advances.

But where did they advance to? Herodotus offers clues, and the rest may be surmised from the ancient way of war. Triremes were, as the poet says, "bronze-rammed floating chariots." The key to trireme battle was maximizing the chance to ram the enemy while minimizing his opportunity to ram back. Under perfect conditions, an attacker would approach a victim from the victim's stern, to protect himself from the ram at his victim's bow. Bow-to-bow ramming became feasible only after first strengthening the bow timbers of one's ship, a tactic invented by Corinthians in 413 B.C. Since an enemy would not voluntarily present the sides of his triremes, ramming usually meant having to maneuver around or through an enemy fleet. The attacker would then ram his victim in the victim's quarter, that is, the stern portion of the ship. In that position, the attacker's own oars would be clear of the rammed ship, and he could back away quickly and easily. Furthermore, by attacking at a narrow angle, the attacker minimized the danger of wrenching his own ram off sideways.

But conditions are rarely perfect, and the attacker sometimes had to ram the enemy amidships. And sometimes he might risk coming at the enemy's bow and then quickly turning to ram. In that case, the attacking pilot might try to use his ram to hit the oars of the other trireme and break them against the stem of his own ship, after having his own crew pull in their oars. This was a difficult maneuver but probably deadly to the enemy rowers, whom it knocked about.

The basic tactic at the start of battle was to arrange one's ships in line abreast while, at the same time, keeping gaps from opening between ships and also protecting one's flanks. The smaller and slower a fleet, the more important it was to cover the flanks, and the Greeks were outnumbered by an enemy with lighter, faster, and more agile ships.

When they came out of their narrow-mouthed harbors, the Greeks rowed first in single file and then deployed in line abreast. Leading the ships out from Ambelaki Bay, the Spartans anchored the right end of the Greek line near the tip of the Cynosura peninsula. The Athenians, who were probably in Paloukia Bay, anchored the left end of the Greek line either at Cape Trophy (the modern name), which is the tip of the Kamateró peninsula, or at the southeastern end of the islet of St. George. In either case, the Greek line enjoyed the advantages of land bastions at both ends and a friendly shore at its rear.

The channel to the north and east of St. George was all but closed off. Today, a reef sits to the east of St. George, between that islet and the mainland of Attica. But in antiquity the sea level in the straits was at least five feet lower than it is today. The reef, therefore, was itself an islet in 480 B.C. The islet-reef and St. George are probably the little archipelago that the ancients called the Pharmacussae Islands. The distance between the two was perhaps as little as six hundred yards, too narrow for either fleet to risk entrapment.

Extending between Cynosura and either Cape Trophy or St. George, the Greek line was between two and two and a half miles long. It was too short for the Greeks to deploy all their triremes in a single line, but it was perfect for two lines, the formation that the Greeks might also have used on the last day at Artemisium. The triremes in the rear line could stand ready to counterattack any Persian ships that tried to pass through the front line and ram Greek triremes there.

The Athenians held the left end of the Greek line; the Spartans held the right. The Aeginetans probably stood next to the Athenians. The other Greeks were deployed in between, although we do not know where. If the Corinthians had indeed sailed northward to incite false confidence among the Persians, they surely quickly returned to the Greek line, in a position near the left end.

The Persians deployed their ships in battle order in line abreast along the Attic coast, where their infantrymen held the shore. Since the Greeks' flanks were protected by the terrain, the Persians could not outflank them. So they probably arranged their ships opposite the Greeks in two or three lines, depending on how much of the Persian fleet had entered the straits by dawn. The Phoenicians held the right end of the Persian line, opposite the Athenians and Aeginetans. The Ionians (and perhaps other Greeks) held the left end. We do not know where the other contingents in the Persian fleet were stationed, nor is it clear which contingents were stationed outside the straits.

The Greeks had launched their ships and the Persians had rowed out to meet them. The fleets came close enough to each other for them each to hear the trill of the other's pipers, keeping time for the oarsmen. The *aulos*, or Greek pipe (sometimes mistakenly called a flute), was a cylinder with finger holes, sounded with a reed. Normally pipes were played in pairs, one pipe fingered by each hand. A cloth band around the player's head and face was used to support the cheeks. The sound of the pipe was so stirring that Greek conservatives thundered against it because it might lead youths astray. For the same reason, the pipe proved invaluable in focusing the minds of the oarsmen on the trireme.

It served as both a metronome and distraction from the awfulness of what lay ahead.

Perhaps it was now that the Persians heard what Aeschylus calls "a mighty battle cry" from the Greek ships:

O sons of the Greeks, advance:
Liberate the fatherland, liberate
Your children, your women, and the abodes
Of your ancestral gods and the graves
Of your ancestors. Now is the battle for them all!

And the Persians answered in turn with what—to the Greeks— sounded like "the noise of the Persian tongue."

It was a historic moment. For centuries, Phoenicia had been the eastern Mediterranean's greatest sea power. Now, a Greek upstart, a city with a newfangled system of government—democracy—and a brand-new fleet, challenged that supremacy.

The two fleets confronted each other, yet the battle did not begin at once. The Greeks flinched first. Or so it seems: at any rate, their ships begin to back water, that is, they continued to face the enemy but rowed backward, stern first, toward the shore of Salamis. If this was panic, it was not panic on the part of the rowers. Below deck, most of the rowers could see nothing. The decision to back water came from the generals and was transmitted to captains and helmsmen by a pre-arranged signal.

Seen from above, which was Xerxes' perspective, the opening stage of the battle might have looked like a standoff between two schools of fish. The swordfishlike Phoenician triremes, with their long narrow rams, pursued the hammerhead-shark-like Greek vessels, with their short and stubby rams. The sharks seemed to have lost their nerve.

But the Greeks probably knew just what they were doing. We may imagine that gaps had opened up in the long Greek line; by backing water, the ships were able to close ranks. They also drew the Persians close enough to Salamis to put them in range of Athenian archers on shore: protected by their shields from Persian archers, the Athenians could attack the enemy on deck or wait for Persian survivors of wrecked ships to take to the water. Still another reason for the Greek decision to back water might have been the desire to wait as long as possible for the *aura* to blow.

But the plan did not work out that way. As often in the history of battle, the first blood was shed not on a general's order but at the initiative of a subordinate who had grown tired of waiting.

On the western end of the Greek line, an Athenian captain, one Aminias of the deme of Pallene, put his ship out to sea again and rammed a Phoenician trireme. He may have seen that some Greek ships had backed too far, since they actually ran aground. He might have taken this as a sign of the jitters and might have worried that the Persians would seize the moment. And so Aminias took matters into his own hands.

Who was this man who lit the spark of battle? Assuming that Aminias fit the usual Athenian mold of a captain, he was a man of substance but not of advanced age. He owned land and a house in Attica, had legitimate children, and was less than fifty years old. Since Athenian men tended to marry around the age of thirty, Aminias was likely in his thirties or forties. He was also wealthy, since captains had to pay their own crews. Since Pallene, his home, was a farming district in central Attica, Aminias probably owed his wealth to olives, grapes, figs, and grain. We may imagine him as fit and tough, as farmers often are, and we know that he had guts. A captain as courageous as Aminias surely had men loyal enough to follow him anywhere. But it no doubt helped that most of his rowers probably came from Pallene and many would have known each other their entire lives. Trust came easily to such a crew.

It had to, because ramming was a group effort. When Aminias decided to break out of the line and ram an enemy ship, he had to pass the order on to his helmsman, and he in turn to the rowing master, who then had to inform the crew. The marines and archers on deck had to brace themselves for impact by sitting firmly, but it was on the oarsmen's shoulders that the main burden fell. They would have to power up the boat rapidly from a standing start—or even worse, from backing water—to ramming speed.

It would not take long from the moment that Aminias gave the order to the point of impact. Athens's heavy ships could not achieve the speed of a fast trireme, which, tests suggest, could accelerate from a standing start to nine or ten knots within about sixty seconds. But

Aminias's trireme did not have to go nearly that fast. The Phoenician ships were either standing still or moving toward the Athenian ships, so the Athenian attacker did not have to outrun the enemy. Aminias merely had to go fast enough to penetrate the planks of a Phoenician ship. Depending on whether Aminias's trireme struck its victim amidships or in the quarter, a speed of two to four knots would have been sufficient.

Once the captain ordered the attack and the pilot passed the word on, the rowing master would rapidly move the crew up to a high stroke rate, perhaps approaching fifty strokes per minute. At that pace, every rower had to devote all his attention to the task at hand. For no more than a minute it might seem to him as if nothing existed except a narrow, stinking tunnel of 170 men bent over in unison, as if rowing a single oar. Still, the mind might wander to home and happy times, to games and feasts, to anything except the split-second shock of collision. Muscles strained and lungs sucked in air; it seemed as if the agony would never end. And then suddenly, just before the moment of impact, the rowing master, primed by the pilot, ordered the men to switch to backing water, in order to keep the ram from penetrating the enemy ship too far. Then the crash came, and if all went well, the vulnerable attacker would already have begun backing off. Although working at extreme intensity, the men would have to work harder still, rowing the ship in the opposite direction from before.

Aminias's crew had slammed into a Phoenician trireme and given their captain the first kill of the day. It was a great prize but came at a price: the ram had penetrated too far into the Phoenician ship, and the men could not extract it. The attacker's goal was always to withdraw as quickly as possible after ramming. Otherwise, if his ram remained stuck in the enemy's hull, he ran the risk of counterattack by the enemy's marines and archers, either from their own deck or after boarding his; and the Persian deck troops outnumbered the Greeks.

Aminias's men knew all this. Below deck, they no doubt backed furiously but still could not move their ship. Above, they could hear the footsteps of their marines and archers as they took their positions to protect the trireme. They could also hear the shouts of the Persian marines eager to board Aminias's boat. It was at this dangerous moment that other Greek ships came to Aminias's defense. Up and down the line, the battle had begun.

Meanwhile, the Phoenicians coped with the paradoxes of ramming. The trireme's ram was as lethal as it was dramatic, but at first it proved deadlier to the victim's hull than to its men. The opening made by a ram was perhaps only about one foot square in size. Water would pour into the rammed ship through the hole and would swamp the ship but not make it sink; there was time for the crew to get out. At the point of a ram's impact a few men might die or be injured. Elsewhere on the vessel, other men might be injured by the force of the impact. But most men would probably make it through the ramming unharmed. Danger, however, lay ahead.

Imagine a shower of arrows and javelins between the ships, parried when possible by shields but sometimes finding their mark. Imagine men collapsing on deck or being speared and then thrown into the water. Others would jump into the water voluntarily to escape a foundering ship, first removing helmets and armor to keep from sinking. Meanwhile, aboard the ships, some of the marines may have made it onto the enemy deck and settled matters in hand-to-hand combat. Sword clashed with dagger and with battle-ax, spear collided with spear.

Hand-to-hand combat; close-quarter fighting; coming to grips; coming to blows: the Greeks delicately called all this the "law of hands." Greek crewmen, as Herodotus notes, had a good chance of surviving the battle if they made it through the law of hands, since they could swim to safety. Not so the Persian and Mede marines: few of them knew how to swim, and so, many of them drowned.

In the end, the Greeks managed to overpower the enemy and free Aminias, his crew, and their vessel. The triumphant victors carried off the stern ornament of the Phoenician ship, probably a figurehead in the shape of a human head. They might have lost a man or two in the fight, but there would be no time to mourn them, let alone to wash the blood off the deck.

And so the battle of Salamis began—at least that is what the Athenians said. The Aeginetans told a different story. They claimed that the first Greek ship to start the attack was not the Athenian vessel of Aminias but the Aeginetan trireme bringing the statues of the sons of Aeacus. And they attributed the initiative to a miracle. The Aeginetans said that while the Greeks were backing water, there appeared an apparition of a woman. She exhorted the Greeks into battle in a voice loud enough for the entire Greek camp to hear. First, however, she gave them a piece of her mind. "Gentlemen, just how long are you going to keep on backing water?" she asked.

Herodotus, who reports both stories, does not choose between them. Aeschylus says merely that a "Greek ship" began the ramming. He was perhaps not being politic so much as realistic. Not only was it difficult to reconstruct a battle years after the fact, it would have been difficult the next day. The Greeks had no official historians to record the details, and no timepieces aside from sundials and water clocks to mark the hours. Besides, Greek city-states were nothing if not competitive; Athens and Aegina, old enemies, were both naval powers; it would have been considered bad form for them to do anything less than argue over bragging rights to having drawn the first enemy blood. But the most important thing of all to remember is the confusion that reigned on the ancient naval battlefield.

The vast majority of the men were below deck, where most could see nothing of what happened outside. Those on deck were generally too busy with matters nearby to take in the overall scene—a common problem in ancient warfare, as Thucydides remarks. The interplay of sun and clouds—and both were present at Salamis—could play tricks on one's eyes, and so could fear and excitement.

And then there was the noise. In a world without machines, the din of battle was perhaps the loudest sound imaginable. And no battle was noisier than one at sea. The clamors, shouting, and cheers of a naval engagement were commonplaces of classical literature. After the trumpets, the hymns, the battle cries, the rushing oars, and the piping, there came the cacophony of bronze-sheathed wooden rams crashing into wooden oars and ships. There was the twang of bowstrings and the whiz of arrows, the whirring of javelins and sometimes the metallic clang of swords. Afterward there came the screams of the dying. Meanwhile, the shores on both sides of the straits were lined with armed men, and it would not have been surprising if some women and children were present as well. The spectators emitted "wails, cries—winning, losing—and all the other various things that a great force in great danger would have to utter," as Thucydides writes of a later naval battle. At Salamis, all of this was magnified by the echoes of a narrow space ringed by hills.

Through it all the rowing masters constantly cried out to their men. They called out not merely orders but appeals—pleas for harder effort, invocations of patriotism or of the greatness of empire, promises of rewards or threats of Xerxes' wrath, references to national tradition and the need to live up to it. Well-trained crews knew the importance of keeping silent, both to preserve energy and to be able to hear the rowing masters.

So—to return to Herodotus's reluctance to choose whether Aegina or Athens drew first blood—the historian tacitly concedes the difficulty of fishing out the truth from the roiled and noisy waters of the straits. And yet another problem faced the historian: religion. Like the Aeginetans, many of the men who fought at Salamis came away convinced that only the gods could have won the battle for Greece. The numbers of the Persian fleet were so large, the preceding disasters at Thermopylae and on the Athenian Acropolis so awful, the situation of the refugees on Salamis so precarious, the defensive position at the Isthmus so shaky, that it seemed hard to believe that unaided human action had reversed the expected outcome. The Lady of Salamis is not the last divine intervention to be reported of the battle.

Afterward, some claimed to have seen a great light shine out from the direction of Eleusis on the mainland, a few miles north of the straits. They also said that they heard the sound of voices filling the Thriasian plain beyond Eleusis, from the mountains to the sea, as if a crowd of men was participating in a religious procession—as in the Eleusinian Mysteries, which were held annually around the very day of the battle. Then out of the shouting crowd a cloud began to rise up little by little from the earth and land on the triremes.

Others said that they could see the shades of the sons of Aeacus with their hands stretched out to protect the Greek triremes. Others insisted that the hero Cychreus (in Greek mythology, the first king of Salamis) appeared to Athenian crews in the form of snake. And it appears that some Aeginetans may have seen something in the sky above the straits—clouds? the morning star? electrical discharges?—that symbolized the god Apollo and the Dioscuri (the sons of Zeus, the heroes Castor and Pollux).

So the high-pitched religious emotions, the noise and confusion of naval battle, and the Greek habit of competitive bragging all made it difficult to say afterward exactly how the battle had begun. In fact, it was hard to reconstruct the battle altogether. Herodotus, for one, admits that he "can say little precisely about how each of the barbarians or Greeks fought." Yet he provides invaluable clues, as does that other fifth-century source, Aeschylus, to say nothing of other ancient writers. Nor does Herodotus have the least doubt about why Salamis turned out as it did. More on that presently: first, let us return to the beginning of the battle.

After the Athenian or Aeginetan trireme rammed the Phoenician trireme, the next ship to join the battle came from the Aegean island of Naxos, captained by one Democritus. Then, all along the straits from St. George to the Cynosura peninsula, ship after ship began to aim at each other.

But the crucial confrontation of the morning involved the Phoenicians and the Greeks opposite them. To understand how events unfolded, let us return to Aminias. When other Athenian ships came to the aid of Aminias's vessel, they might have turned and so created an opportunity for Phoenician ramming. But the Phoenicians are unlikely to have picked off more than one or two Athenian ships, because the Athenian line did not break. What happened next may well have come about as follows:

The Phoenicians tried to row their agile ships around or through the Athenian line, but either flank was protected by a protruding headland. The Athenian triremes held firmly together in mid-line (protected by a second line in the rear to counter any Phoenician breakthrough). The fast-sailing Phoenician ships feinted and darted, but the Athenians would not give them an opening. The Phoenicians charged and retreated, charged and retreated. These superb seamen would do everything that could be done under the circumstances, but they fought under a handicap. The fresh and confident Greeks could afford to make a mistake or two, but the tired and shocked Phoenicians could not.

In this opening stage of the battle, "at first the flood of the Persian host held firm," according to Aeschylus. But the Persians were not able to maintain their formation. "The barbarians," says Herodotus, "did not remain drawn up in order of battle." The Greeks kept in line.

Several things went wrong for the Phoenicians. The confined space of the straits made it impossible for them to carry out their signature maneuvers. As an Athenian admiral put it later, a fast and nimble fleet needs space to get the enemy in its sights from some way off, and it needs room to make sharp turns. In the narrows off Salamis, the Phoenicians' speed offered them no help.

They were crowded, so if the Phoenicians tried to maneuver in spite of the obstacles, they might run afoul of their own ships, which were closely packed together. In the straits, having more ships turned into a disadvantage. Something similar would happen to the Athenian fleet sixty-seven years later in 413 B.C. during another trireme battle. By then, three generations after Salamis, the Athenian fleet no longer consisted of heavy ships; it had become as light and agile as the Phoenicians were in 480. In 413, Athens ran into trouble in the harbor of the Sicilian Greek city of Syracuse. There, Athens was the invader and Syracuse defended its homeland, just as Athens had done in 480. The Syracusan fleet managed to push the Athenians backward and into confusion in the narrow space of the harbor. To be sure, the Syracusans had a force multiplier, because they had strengthened the bows of their ships enough to allow bow-on ramming.

The Athenians at Salamis had not strengthened their bows, but they, too, had a force multiplier nonetheless; indeed, they had several. The Persian enemy was exhausted from all-night rowing. He suffered from the aftereffects of shock at the Greek attack. When the morning sea breeze, the *aura*, began blowing between eight and ten o'clock, his boats might have been pushed to their sides.

The breeze and the wave "struck the barbarians' ships and made them totter and delivered them sideways to the Greeks, who set on them sharply," says Plutarch. In his reconstruction of the battle, the poet Timotheus refers to the "the boat-wrecking breezes (*aurai*)," which may point to something similar. Since their ships had bulwarks and also a higher center of gravity than the Greeks' ships, the Persians were especially vulnerable to the breeze.

For any or all of these reasons, the Phoenicians fell out of order and exposed their sterns to the enemy. The Greeks simply took advantage of it. They charged and charged and did all the damage that could be inflicted by the greatest force multiplier of them all: the heavy weight of their triremes directed against lighter ships.

Timotheus paints a picture of the shock of impact—perhaps from ramming, perhaps from having the oars sheared off, or perhaps from both. If a smashing blow, he writes, "was inflicted on one side, all the sailors fell backwards together in that direction, but if a [. . .] on the opposite side shattered the many-banked sea-going pines, they were carried back again."

Not at first but eventually, within a matter of hours, the Phoenician line fell apart completely. Many of their ships had been rammed. The rest decided that it was better to live and fight again another day than to suffer certain defeat. Some of the survivors, including high-ranking Phoenicians, made it to safety on the nearby Attic shore. They either found refuge on a neighboring ship or they swam.

The rest of the surviving Phoenician triremes turned and fled to the southeast. If they hugged the Attic shore, they would have seen the struggle on the Persian left continue in the center of the channel. The battle on the Persian left was not decided as quickly as the battle on the Persian right. Herodotus insists that the Ionians and other Greeks on the Persian left did better than the Phoenicians; the Carians were probably on the Persian left as well. Very few Ionians took up Themistocles' challenge to fight badly in order to help the Greek cause. On the contrary, the Ionians made a stronger showing in the service of Persia than they had at Artemisium, precisely because of Xerxes' watchful presence at Salamis. Furthermore, we may imagine that some of the Persian ships outside the straits were able to row the short distance to come to the Ionians' assistance. On top of that, the Persian left did not have to deal with the crack Athenian or Aeginetan squadrons. As a result, the ships on the Greek right could do no better than to hold their own until the Greek left had finished off the Phoenicians and was able to come to their aid.

From his throne at the foot of Mount Aegaleos, Xerxes had a front-row seat at the humiliation of the Phoenician fleet. Greek poets portray him bewailing his fate, but the lord of Persepolis was not a man to let down the facade in public. More confidence is inspired by Herodotus's description of Xerxes during the battle: asking for ship identifications from a military aide and then turning every so often to a scribe to have him record the name of a rare captain who had done well—and the name of his father and his country.

It was not the scene on the water that got Xerxes' dander up so much as the Phoenician survivors who approached the royal presence on land. The Phoenicians blamed everything on the Ionians. The Ionians had destroyed Phoenician triremes, they claimed, because the Ionians were traitors.

But the accusers suffered from bad timing. Just as the Phoenicians made their denunciation, a clash of ships unfolded in the straits below. First, a trireme from the Greek island of Samothrace, fighting for Persia, rammed an Athenian trireme. Then an Aeginetan trireme rammed the Samothracian in turn. But the Aeginetan ram must have become stuck in the Samothracian ship, because the Samothracian marines were able to storm onto the Aeginetan ship, javelins in hand, and overpower it.

The indomitable Samothracians were not Ionians, but they were Greeks, and that was good enough for Xerxes. He turned to the Phoenicians, angry beyond measure, and had them hauled away to have their heads cut off. He did not want to let bad men slander their betters, he said, in a lame attempt to justify his rage.

We do not know about the fate of Tetramnestus, king of Sidon. He probably survived the battle, because he is not named in Herodotus's or Aeschylus's lists of prominent casualties. Nor is Xerxes likely to have had a king executed, since monarchs do not like to remind their subjects that royal blood can be spilled. But one thing is certain: Tetramnestus never again enjoyed the status in Xerxes' eyes that he had on the day before Salamis. There may even be some truth in a later story of Phoenician triremes fleeing all the way back to their home ports in the eastern Mediterranean rather than face the Great King's wrath.

Ariabignes would have been lucky to fare similarly. He fought in the thick of battle on what was no doubt a splendid flagship, and every Greek within eyesight must have aimed for it. Ariabignes represented a trophy and a strategic prize.

Because their generals joined the fray, ancient armies were vulnerable to decapitation. Persian armies were organized in obedience to the Great King and his family and tended to collapse if the commander was killed. The Persian military was hierarchical and not given to individual initiative, while the Greeks excelled at improvisation. The Spartans at Thermopylae, for example, kept fighting after the death of Leonidas. When, 150 years later, King Darius III fled from Alexander the Great at the battle of Issus in Syria in 333 B.C., the Persian line collapsed.

Knowing the importance of the Great King in battle, a clever enemy general would make him a target. At the battle of Cunaxa in Mesopotamia in 401 B.C., for example, the rebel prince Cyrus the Younger aimed to kill King Artaxerxes but succeeded only in losing his own life; interestingly, Cyrus's army, made up of Greek mercenaries, continued fighting to victory.

At Salamis, Xerxes was not available to strike at, but his stand-ins were his half brother Ariabignes and his full brother Achaemenes, admiral of the Egyptian fleet. Ariabignes did in fact die in the battle, as Herodotus confirms, which makes Ariabignes by far the most famous casualty of Salamis.

Herodotus does not record how or when Ariabignes died. But there are stories in other ancient writers about an unnamed Persian "admiral" or Xerxes' brother "Ariamenes" (apparently a conflation of *Aria*bignes and Achae*menes*) killed early in the battle, after which the Persian fleet fell into disorder. The details in these two accounts do not command trust, but they serve as a reminder that, whenever and however he was killed, Ariabignes' death probably contributed mightily to the plight of the Persian fleet.

And there is poetic truth in Plutarch's assertion that the drifting body of "Ariamenes" was recognized by Artemisia, who then brought it to Xerxes. Rarely have the mighty fallen further.

CHAPTER TEN

≈

SALAMIS STRAITS: AFTERNOON

By midday on September 25, Aminias of Pallene wears his vanity like a victory wreath. Seated on the deck of his trireme, he spits out orders to the pilot, thinking now and then of the choice beasts that he will later sacrifice in gratitude to the gods. Or so we might imagine, because if Athena Nike, the Lady of Victory herself, had stretched out her hand to him that day, he could not have found a better guide to glory. Now he can hold his head above other Greeks; now he is no longer a man without a city, no longer a refugee from spear-won land: he is a man who defends what is sacred and holy and who returns the violet-crowned land of the goddess to the children of Athena, a city made great and strong again.

His trireme stalks the Salamis straits in search of Persian ships in flight. They are not few in number, since All-Powerful Zeus has instilled fear in the enemy's hearts. And like Diomedes cutting down Trojans on the windy plain of Troy, Aminias brings black death to the men of western Asia. The difference between the two, of course, is that Aminias cannot in fact wage a private war. Unlike the hero Diomedes, he depends on the cooperation of 199 other men, the crew of his ship. Many of them are Aminias's demesmen of Pallene, and they share his self-satisfaction; they are all the hardened members of a very small club. At Artemisium and now at Salamis they know the rule: strike or be struck down.

Aminias represents the many Athenian and Aeginetan captains who turned and attacked the Ionian and Carian squadrons after having routed the Phoenicians. He scored more kills than his comrades, but otherwise his experience was not unusual. The terrible thrusts of the Greek rams—"the utterly ruinous rams," as Aeschylus calls them—cut apart the Persian fleet. The Sacae archers tried to defend their ships by firing at the enemy as he approached, but shields usually protected the Greek marines, and decks sheltered the rowers. Furthermore, if the *aura* did indeed upset the Phoenician ships, it might have made it difficult for the archers to take a steady aim. "The arrow," reports Aeschylus,

> *Offered no help, and the whole force was undone,*
> *Conquered by the shock of the ships' rams.*

Salamis Straits—AFTERNOON

The mighty Iranian arrow, long the favored weapon of shock of Persia's mounted aristocrats, had been vanquished by the humble instrument of fishermen and ferrymen: "by the single sweep of the oar." It was a world turned upside down, and the men of Aminias's ship were in the vanguard of the revolution.

The defeat of the Ionians and Carians can be told through the experience of captains like Aminias. Trireme battle began with lines of ships in order, but it quickly devolved into a series of single combats. And these combats depended less on any rulebook than on the character of the captain. The ideal captain was cunning, quick, flexible, and ruthless. His success depended less on his knowledge than on his innate ability to size up a situation and to anticipate the enemy's next move. Today's experts call this ability situational awareness. The captain must be able to improvise. To quote a modern military maxim, "Nothing is true in tactics." At Salamis, Aminias lived by that absence of rules—and he lived to be embarrassed by it before the day was done.

By midday, Aminias's crew would have been as exhausted as it was exhilarated. In late September, the air temperature in the Salamis straits might have been about 70 degrees Fahrenheit around noon. At this season, the Greek sun is warm and bright without being overwhelming, as it is in summer. But it is nonetheless uncomfortable to sit in, hour after hour, especially with its effects increased by reflection off the water. The marines and archers on deck must have dripped with sweat. Only the captain was protected by a canvas canopy. The men below deck sat in a cramped and poorly ventilated space. Even the *thranitai*, the top level of rowers, were denied the fresh air that usually blew through the open-sided outrigger. In battle, side covers, made either of canvas or animal hide, were hung over the outrigger to protect the men from arrows.

As long as a trireme was moving under oar, the men on deck had to remain seated, just like the rowers below. The marines were compelled to learn how to throw a javelin from a seated position in order to be able to attack the enemy's marines on a ship approaching to ram. Difficult to master, the seated javelin throw also puts strain on the back and arm muscles, which have to do all the work that would normally be shared with the leg muscles. And rarely if at all would a marine have the opportunity to stand up and stretch his legs, let alone take a stroll.

The rowers would have their own aches and pains to complain of. Modern rowers are able to take full advantage of the strength of their leg muscles via the use of a sliding seat. The ancient oarsman sat on a sheepskin cushion atop a fixed seat. Since his feet were fixed to the floor, a rower would slide slightly back and forth willy-nilly on each stroke. Therefore, he could make some use of the leg muscles, but more of his work was done by the back and arms than is ideal. Confined to a narrow space, ancient oarsmen had not the least bit of privacy. Continually thirsty, they had to make do with a limited supply of water and a few snacks during a hard day's work. Urination was rarely a problem for rowers, since the body tended to sweat off its waste products; a man who had to urinate during battle would have to do so where he sat. (The one woman, Artemisia, no doubt had her own chamber pot.) The thalamians in the hold suffered from the sweat of two upper levels of rowers dripping down on them.

There would be no chance for chitchat with the man on his side, since an oarsman had to stay silent in order to hear the piper and the rowing master. But the silence might be broken from time to time by the cry of someone who needed the help of the ship's carpenter. During lulls in the battle, he would be a busy man indeed.

And in a battle as long as Salamis, which lasted from sunup to sundown, there would be many lulls. Crews would rest; ships would regroup; lines would re-form. After successfully ramming an enemy vessel, for example, a ship's crew would need time to recover. Since the shoreline was so close, it was possible to ferry the wounded and the dead back to base, possibly on small boats dispatched for that purpose. And once the Greeks had the Persian fleet on the run, there might have been time for triremes to return to shore to make repairs or pick up food or to exchange rowers if any fresh men were available.

One other ingredient in the men's psyches should be kept in mind: as the day wore on, almost everyone saw friendly forces die. This was especially true of the Persians, but it also applied to the Greeks, who, for all their success, did incur losses. Pious Greeks believed that the Fates stalked the battlefield, eager to drink human blood. The Fates could not have been disappointed at Salamis. On both sides, ships were rammed, men were slashed by sword, speared by javelin, pierced by arrow, and occasionally smashed by battle-ax or other exotic weapon.

The marines were most at risk, because even a ship that escaped the enemy's ram might lose a man or two on deck to a hostile arrow striking an unshielded body part.

Some men would survive their wounds, while others would linger for days until infection killed them. But some would die immediately in the straits, especially if they were hit in the abdomen. The death was sometimes painful, desperate, accompanied by gushing blood and by the victim's screams. Some saw friends or allies die and came away more determined than ever to fight. Others felt fear at what they saw. Still others stopped noticing the slaughter after a while.

The men were exhausted and inflamed in turn, cowering or callous, scrappy or scared stiff. And no doubt some just kept on sitting on deck or rowing below, telling themselves that as long as they kept a grip on the wooden handle, they would hold on to their soundness of mind. Others might lose themselves in the group, buoyed up by the close contact of so many men in so small a space.

After the Athenians broke through the Phoenician line in the narrows, the combat zone at Salamis began to resemble nothing so much as the battlefield of the Heroic Age. By the afternoon, the battle was a melee in which heavy Greek triremes hunted lighter Persian triremes fleeing from the straits, and a clot of fresh Persian triremes unknowingly blocked the exit.

The battle devolved into a series of individual duels between Persian ships seeking safety and Greek ships seeking blood. The straits had become, as Herodotus says, a *thorubos*—using once again the Greek word for chaos, the same word he used to describe the panic of the Greek commanders on Salamis just two days earlier, when they learned that the Persians had taken the Athenian Acropolis.

It was a terrible moment for the grand Persian fleet, the hour of its suffering. More Persians died in the confusion of ships coming and going than at any other time of the battle. Aeschylus writes:

> *They all hastened in disorderly flight,*
> *Every ship in the barbarian force.*
> *And then they struck them with broken oars*
> *And the fragments of shipwrecks and*
> *They boned them like tuna or some catch of fish.*

Some of the Persians might have made it back to the mainland, but some swam to the Salamis shore, only to be killed by angry Greek soldiers. Many Persians died in the water. The Persians did not die alone, but they were lonely, "sojourners in a harsh land," as Aeschylus puts it. They were "wretched with their struggling hands" before they drowned. And the last sight that some of them saw might have been the bronze of an enemy ram about to run them through on its way toward the side of another ship.

Aminias's path of glory had begun around seven o'clock that morning, when he ordered his crew to slam into a Phoenician trireme, which gave their captain the first kill of the day (or possibly the second, as the Aeginetans insisted). When Aminias and his crew next appeared in the battle record, the Persian fleet had collapsed. In that moment of confusion, Aminias homed in on his most extraordinary opponent yet: Artemisia, queen of Halicarnassus.

By noon in the straits, Artemisia was able to watch the disintegration of Xerxes' fleet. Her Carian squadron was posted on the left wing of the Persian line, or rather, of what had been the Persian line. It was a critical moment and suddenly Artemisia saw Aminias's trireme bear down on her ship. We might imagine the Athenian's ram plowing through the scum of broken oars, shattered planks, and floating corpses, a froth of blood churned up by its passing.

To understand what happened next, we have to appreciate the role of the forgotten man of ancient sea battle, the pilot. He stood on the quarterdeck and operated a pair of side rudders. These were actually oversize oars, each hung at a slant to the hull and each operated by a tiller. The ends of the two tillers were close enough together for the pilot, standing between them, to operate one with each hand. The Greeks called the rudder's blade the "wing," its loom the "neck," and its tiller bar the "pole" or "shaft," as in a vine prop or a spear. The size of a trireme or merchantman made the tiller bar look downright petite, which set philosophers thinking.

"How is it," asks an unknown writer whose works have come down with Aristotle's, "that the rudder, although small and at the extreme end of the ship, has so much power that the great bulk of ships can be moved by a little tiller and one man?" The Roman-era Greek writer Lucian says of a huge grain ship named *Isis* that, despite its bulk, it was steered by "some little old man" employing "a delicate pole and turning the big rudders."

Using only his naked eye and the tillers, the pilot maneuvered his trireme out of harm's way or toward the prey. Side rudders proved highly efficient: they could turn a ship quickly, tightly, and with a relatively small loss of speed. And yet, paradoxically, the pilot had to use the rudder as little as possible, since the more often the rudder was clear of the water, the less drag on the ship. During the run up to ramming, in particular, the rudder was best left disengaged. Knowing how to use the rudder effectively and minimally was in itself an art.

Since he set the ship's course, the pilot had to keep his ears cocked to the orders of the captain, who sat directly behind him in the stern. He had to be calm, quick, and uncomplaining. It is no exaggeration to say that the lives of everyone aboard depended on the keen sense and the cool hand of the pilot.

When Aminias called out "Ram!," his pilot would have turned the rudder as needed and then cleared it from the water. With every rapid beat of the trireme's 170 oars, Artemisia's doom came closer.

But she had her own pilot to call on and her outstanding ingenuity. Artemisia ordered her pilot to take evasive action but of a kind that might have put Penelope to shame. That heroine of Greek epic said she would marry as soon as she finished weaving a shroud for an old man. But she undid her weaving every night in order to keep the suitors at bay and retain her loyalty to her missing husband, Odysseus. Artemisia undid her own work even more dramatically. She commanded her pilot to turn and ram one of her fellow Carian ships.

She did not have the luxury of choice. Artemisia could not escape the straits, because the way was blocked by the pile-up of friendly ships, some in flight themselves, others still trying to make their way to the front in order to prove themselves beneath the Great King's eyes. Nor could Artemisia go further into the straits, because the enemy ruled those waters, and she was in the thick of Greek ships. So she turned on her own men.

The victim was the trireme of a local potentate, Damasithymus, king of Calynda, a Carian city southeast of Halicarnassus. As near neighbors, Queen Artemisia and King Damasithymus might well have been rivals. The two of them had quarreled at the Hellespont in May or

June, and Herodotus speculates that Artemisia may still have carried a grudge in September. It occurs to him that since Artemisia had foreseen the Persian catastrophe at Salamis, she might even have planned the attack in advance. Then again, Damasithymus might merely have been the victim of bad luck, a man whose ship happened to be in Artemisia's way. In any case, she gave the order, and Artemisia's men rammed their ally's ship and sank it.

Damasithymus and his crew must have been shocked. Maybe their marines fought back by shooting arrows or hurling their javelins at Artemisia's ship. Perhaps they merely went down cursing the traitor's name.

What followed was a double boon for the wily queen. Aminias saw Artemisia's ship ram Damasithymus's. So Aminias probably concluded that Artemisia's ship was a friend after all, probably a Persian ship that had defected to the Greek side; otherwise, it would not have rammed a Persian trireme. He may have considered the possibility that his lookout had made a complete misidentification and that Artemisia's was in fact a Greek ship. This mistake would have been understandable. After all, Halicarnassian marines wore Greek armor, and although there were Iranian and Sacae marines on Artemisia's ship as well, in the confusion of battle, the Greek armor might have caught the lookout's eye. In any case, Aminias decided to leave Artemisia alone. Aminias now ordered his pilot to change course and attack another ship instead.

But Aminias had been tricked. He had not seen Artemisia herself, since she sat beneath an awning. Had he in fact recognized the queen, he would have risked everything in order to get her. Aminias would not have rested until either he captured her or he was captured himself. Like every Athenian captain, Aminias knew about the thousand-drachma reward for taking Artemisia alive, to say nothing of the honor of avenging Athenian manhood. So Aminias continued attacking enemy ships at Salamis that afternoon, but he had just missed the greatest prize of all.

Artemisia escaped the wrath of Aminias, yet she still had Xerxes to contend with. And that was the second part of the wages of her treachery. Far from being angry with Artemisia for ramming one of his ships, Xerxes thought more highly of her. It seems that he was tricked as well as the Athenians. From his throne on the hills above the straits, or so the story goes, Xerxes had been told that Artemisia's trireme had rammed another ship. His courtiers identified Artemisia but mistook Damasithymus for an enemy. "Master," they asked the Great King, "do you see how well Artemisia is fighting?" No doubt they were excited to have any good news to report.

It had been a long morning for the King of Kings. We can imagine the usual hum of activity around the royal personage. Eunuchs would carry parasols to shade him from the sun, slaves would serve refreshments in gold tableware (tasted first, of course, by the royal taster), advisers like Ariaramnes and the ever-present Mardonius would comment on the battle below, runners would dash down to the shore to bring his commands to officers who might ferry them out to the fleet, and secretaries would record his every word. At first, everyone would no doubt praise the resilience of the Persian navy and its ability to turn the tables on the perfidious Greeks and their so-called ambush, itself a puerile attempt at the strategy that only a man of Persian sophistication could execute. But as the sun rose high above the straits, it became ever more difficult to hide the truth.

And the truth was one thing that nobody wanted to tell the Great King. An incident from the days just before the battle illustrates the wariness of his courtiers. As the story goes, two Greek exiles at the Persian court, Demaratus of Sparta and Dicaeus of Athens, were in western Attica, among Persian troops who were devastating the countryside. No doubt they were guiding the looters when they saw a striking omen. A huge cloud of dust rose from the vicinity of Eleusis, accompanied by a loud noise. To Dicaeus, it sounded like the annual procession of the Eleusinian Mysteries, held at this season. He told his companion that the sign represented an omen of defeat for Xerxes. If the cloud drifted toward the Isthmus, his army would lose a battle; if it headed for Salamis, his navy would lose.

"Shut up! Don't tell this story to anyone," replied Demaratus. "If these words reach the King, it's you who will lose something—your head. Neither I nor any other person will be able to help you. Keep quiet and let the gods take care of the army." As Demaratus spoke, the cloud drifted toward Salamis and the two men knew what disaster lay in store. But they said nothing until afterward, when Dicaeus and his descendants repeated the tale.

Although Dicaeus's story may be too good to be true, it relies on what was common knowledge: the fear of Xerxes among his own men. So as they watched disaster unfold beneath them at Salamis, the Great King's men would have denied what their master's eyes saw. They might have told Xerxes that his ships were merely regrouping for a devastating offensive. They might have pointed out the power of the squadrons that were ready to enter the straits and hurl themselves against an exhausted enemy. They might have speculated aloud about how they could send a messenger to Themistocles with an offer of a fat bribe—perhaps even now he was merely holding out for some such prize. If all else failed, they might have comforted Xerxes with the thought that men had died crying out the glory of his royal name.

And they surely grasped at whatever straws were available. For one thing, they could have noted that one of Xerxes' plans had worked out brilliantly, precisely as he had intended. Just as the king had said, his presence made the men fight better at Salamis than they had at Artemisium. Never mind that they were moved less by inspiration than by fear; they were moved nonetheless. And they were also moved by rivalry.

The Phoenicians and Ionians were both subjects of Persia, but they had no love for each other. They were both naval powers; the Phoenicians were Xerxes' favorite fleet, but the Ionians dearly wanted that status for themselves. Two things were necessary to get it: first-rate performance at sea and friends in high places. Nothing got done in Persia without a patron at court to grease the wheels. By the same token, the top courtiers all looked for clients to champion. Nothing gave a man prestige like having an eager foreigner pay him court. So each of Persia's peoples had its patron at the palace and every Persian council meeting had its share of faction.

Ariaramnes, the leader of the pro-Ionian group at the Persian court, no doubt pointed out to the Great King just how well the cities of that rich region were battling on behalf of their monarch. Very few of them paid attention to the propaganda of Themistocles to fight badly on purpose. On the contrary, the Ionians excelled at Salamis in the number of kills to their credit. "I have a list of many names of captains who captured Greek ships," says Herodotus, although he refers to only two.

They both came from the island of Samos, just off the coast of Anatolia. One was Theomestor son of Androdamas and the other was

Phylakes son of Histiaeus. If the question of disloyalty to Greece troubled either man, he could have turned to his island's history for comfort. Whatever virtues Samian moralists might have preached, fidelity was not one of them. In a world of opportunists, Samos stood out.

For two generations, Samos had seesawed. In 525 B.C. the Samian tyrant Polycrates threatened to help Egypt against Persia. Then, around 517, Persia conquered Samos, evicted Polycrates, and replaced him with his brother Solyson, a loyal Persian client. Next, in 499 when the Ionians revolted against Persia, Samos joined the rebels. That is, they joined them at first: it was the Samian contingent on the Greek right wing at the naval battle of Lade in 494 B.C., sixty ships strong, that turned tail before the fight, thereby saving themselves but dooming the rebel cause.

Theomestor could have justified what some saw as treason to Greece by calling it service to a higher cause: the greatness of empire. Or he might have contented himself with a lower cause: the rewards that a grateful Xerxes was likely to give him.

As it turned out, Xerxes was short of heroes to bestow honors on after Salamis, and so the Samians had a claim on a grand prize. Theomestor was named tyrant of Samos. Phylakes was given a large estate and was named one of the Great King's benefactors, or *orosaggai*, an elite corps.

And then there was Artemisia. When his courtiers pointed out her great feat of ramming an enemy ship, Xerxes displayed a wise skepticism. "Is it really Artemisia?" he asked. Xerxes' question shows that it was difficult to make out the details from where he sat. No wonder a Roman-era writer told a fabulous story about a serpent, with eyesight good enough to see for two miles, who sat with Xerxes under a golden plane tree and reported on Artemisia's exploits below. The real Xerxes no doubt had sharp-eyed scouts in his service, and they insisted that they could clearly see the "distinguishing mark" on Artemisia's ship.

Conceivably, what they made out was the painted plaque on the prow with the ship's name. Another possibility is that Artemisia's ship was marked by something large and visible, like the ram in the shape of a boar's snout used in Samian penteconters or the figureheads that might have decorated the prow of a Phoenician trireme. But in that case, Aminias should have recognized her ship as well.

There is also a story that Artemisia had planned ahead and carried a set of Greek signal flags on board. When she decided to ram Damasithymus, she had her ship's Persian flags replaced with Greek flags. But then both Aminias and Xerxes' courtiers would have thought Artemisia's ship was Greek, so this is no doubt a tall tale.

Is it possible that Xerxes' men knew perfectly well that Artemisia had rammed a Persian ship but they lied in order to give the Great King something to think about other than executing everyone around him? Ariaramnes, enemy of the Phoenicians, might have eagerly twisted the truth in order to have more evidence of Phoenician incompetence. We might even consider the chance of a prearranged conspiracy between him and Artemisia. But all of these possibilities are only speculation.

However it was achieved, recognition by Xerxes was good news for the queen. Yet it would backfire if survivors from Damasithymus's ship denounced her. Luckily for her, there were no survivors. This was a godsend for Artemisia, since rarely were all hands lost after a ship was rammed. The men usually had time to abandon ship. Except for the Persians and Medes, most of Damasithymus's crew knew how to swim because they were islanders.

Or was it luck? The 230 sailors on Damasithymus's ship could not have died to the last man unless someone made an effort to kill them. That person might have been Artemisia. She had more than one motive for a massacre. Not only did she fear survivors telling tales and not only did she dislike Damasithymus: she needed to convince her Athenian pursuer that she was on his side. The best way to do so was to follow standard procedure, and that meant ordering her archers to shoot the Calyndian survivors. She might even have sent her marines onto Damasithymus's deck as a boarding party.

Artemisia surely had the nerve to order a bloodbath of her allies, but would her men have obeyed? They were probably so devoted to the queen that they would have stormed Xerxes' throne if she had issued the command. Long before Salamis, Artemisia would have chosen the crew of her flagship with care and would have treated them with attention. Her Carian rowers and marines would have received high wages and an easygoing rowing master. The commander of her Iranian and Sacae marines would have been accorded a full measure of flattery from the queen.

She would have taken to addressing each of them personally and telling them how she had known their fathers and would pray for the health of their sons. She would have accorded the best of them the honor of guarding her tent. She would have doled out dicta to her commanders with a Delphic inscrutability. She would have done nothing to discourage her men from picking fights with other crews for insulting them as followers of a female.

By the time she was done, Artemisia would have molded most of her men into her willing instruments—and the rest would have been too frightened to put up resistance. And if Damasithymus had insulted their queen, then, by the gods, he deserved to have his ship sunk in order to defend the honor of the men who served her. And if Artemisia had wanted her marines to dirty their own hands, they would have drunk Calyndian blood if that is what it took to please her.

Yet, for all that, it might have been simply the proximity of the Greeks that doomed Damasithymus. After all, why ask her men to do something that they might later regret, Artemisia might have reasoned, when the Greeks themselves would take care of silencing Damasithymus's crew for her? Her own men, she might have concluded, had been compromised enough—by having rammed an ally's ship—to ensure that they keep their mouths closed later.

With so many Greek vessels around, there were plenty of ways for Calyndians to die. Swimming in the blue Aegean was one thing; swimming through the corpses and debris of a great naval battle was another. Some men might just never make it. Even good swimmers might have been brained by a passing trireme's oars or have been pulled under a ship and drowned. Others might have been speared by enemy javelins. But the greatest threat was the archers, for whom men in the water made easy targets.

The Greek sources, understandably, say nothing about Greek brutality to enemy swimmers at Salamis, but there might have been plenty of it. Savagery at sea was a by-product of grudge fights and do-or-die struggles. A trireme battle in 433 B.C., for example, pitted a furious Corinth against what it considered the ingratitude of its former colony, Corcyra. Corinth won the battle, and normally its captains would have then sailed among the wrecks and salvaged disabled enemy hulls for their own use. Instead, the Corinthian captains looked for Corcyrean survivors and butchered them in the water. In 413 B.C., Syracuse was fighting for its life against an Athenian invasion. While triremes battled in their harbor, the Syracusans added small boats to the struggle, some staffed by teenagers who used pitchforks to kill Athenians who had jumped from their wrecked ships.

Stones, too, made good weapons to throw at men in the water, and we know that Athenians used stones against Persian land troops during the battle of Salamis. Small boats were present in the Greek fleet at Salamis, and the Athenians for one were angry enough to use them on a mission of vengeance, just as Athenian captains were ready to slaughter the men who had desecrated their temples.

Timotheus makes the intriguing suggestion that Greeks fired flaming arrows at the Persian ships. He refers to "covers burning with fire on ox-[. . .] splints of wood; and their thronging life was slaughtered beneath the long-winged bronze-headed string-[. . . arrows]." He also says that "the strong and smoky fire will burn them [Persian young men] with its savage body." The Persians had used these weapons in their attack on the Acropolis and may have used them again at Salamis; Timotheus's account of the Greek view of the battle has not survived.

Whether they used flaming arrows, spears, pitchforks, stones, or their own hands, the Greeks dealt brutally with the Persians in the water at Salamis. We can be sure of that, because in their invasion of the Greeks' homeland, the Persians had abused a royal corpse, looted private property, burned temples, and raped, enslaved, and killed civilians. The Greeks would have had to have been angels not to have taken whatever revenge they could. And so between Artemisia's men and the crews of the nearby Greek ships, Damasithymus and his men did not have a chance.

But Xerxes, if Herodotus's informant was right, did not know that Damasithymus's crew was the victim of the cunning queen. He thought that Artemisia had rammed a *Greek* ship, which would have been a great deed on such a black day for his cause. But it was a bitter deed, too, as Xerxes is supposed to have noted by speaking a line that sums up Persia's discontent: "My men have become women," the Great King cried, "and my women have become men."

Aminias no doubt felt comfortable in his manhood, even if a mysterious vessel had beaten him to a fresh kill. There were plenty of other victims available for his fury. We are not certain how many enemy ships he rammed that day at Salamis, but we know that Aminias won a prize for valor after the battle. And his name lived on. Herodotus and Plutarch wrote about him. For a century and more, every schoolchild in Pallene is likely to have heard of Aminias as the deme's favorite son— an honor for which the sleepy town in the Attic countryside provided no other candidates. When they visited the local temple of Athena Pallenis, the youth of Pallene might well have been able to see war booty deposited there by Aminias in the customary gesture of thanks to his hometown goddess. So a century after Salamis, when the Athenian navy commissioned a ship named *Pallenis* after the deme of Pallene, all thoughts might have turned to the glory days of Aminias in the fatal straits.

CHAPTER ELEVEN

~~

SALAMIS STRAITS: EVENING

Polycritus son of Crius, heir to a family that is second to none in Aegina either in lineage or wealth, sits in the stern and waits. His squadron prowls the passage at the exit of the straits. There, whenever a Persian ship comes hurrying by in flight toward Phaleron, a bronze-beaked Aeginetan killer stalks his prey. And every time a ram smashes into the side of a Persian ship, great-hearted Polycritus imagines hearing the music of a bard, singing of the glory of the greatest man in the greatest navy in all Greece. Never mind the numbers of Athenian ships: only the democratic rabble could confuse mass with excellence. The thirty triremes of the Aeginetan company are as superior to Athens's rowboats as a nobleman is superior to a mob. Or so we might imagine Polycritus thinking.

Enervated and dehydrated, calloused and cramped, bleeding from scrapes and superficial arrow wounds, panting and perspiring, famished but furious, the oarsmen of Aegina row on, hour after hour, kill after kill. Deaf to the screams of the dying and the shouts of the spectators, stubborn in stifling the roar they want to bellow, they hear nothing but the orders of the rowing master and the sharp sound of the pipe. Below them was a scene of "the emerald-haired sea . . . reddened in its troughs by the drops from the ships, and there were battle cries mingled with screams." Meanwhile, on deck, the Aeginetan marines rallied and filled any gaps in their ranks caused by Persian arrows.

Shipwrecked men suffered from "spray [that] foamed and took over their esophagi"; they gasped and belched back sea brine; they gnashed their teeth and shouted insults; they shivered and raged at the approaching darkness. Phoenician rowers who had made it to the Attic shore sat "naked and frozen on the shore of the sea." And still the triremes of Aegina rowed on, hunting new victims.

The Persians did not give up their resistance until evening. This innocent-sounding fact underlines the remarkable nature of Persia's rout. Once the Greeks had broken the Persian line and turned the Phoenicians and Ionians to flight, the battle should have effectively been over, except for the Greek pursuit. And yet the struggle went on for hours afterward. Geography and politics were to blame. The narrowness of the straits

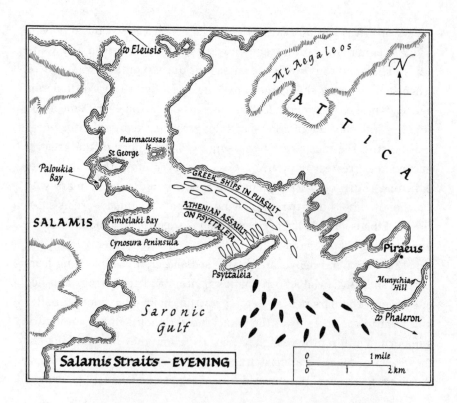

made it impossible for Persia's front lines to flee toward Phaleron without crashing into the ships that were still coming forward.

Aeschylus describes the collision that resulted:

At first the flood of the Persian host
Held firm. But when the mass of ships
Crowded into the straits, there was no help for one ship from another,
In fact they were struck by their own bronze-mouthed rams,
And the whole oared armada began to shatter.
The Greek ships very intelligently started to strike around
In a circle, and the hulls of ships lay upside down,
And the sea could no longer be seen because it was
Full of shipwrecks and of the slaughter of men.

The Greek poet Timotheus writes in a similar vein: "The barbarian Persian army went backwards in flight, rushing along; and one line of ships, sailing the long neck [of the sea], shattered another. . . ."

But why did Persian triremes continue to come forward after their best squadrons had been thrashed? Surely, somehow the message of defeat was spread from ship to ship. The problem was not communications; on the contrary, the more news of defeat, the greater the ambition of the rear ranks to get to the fore. Persian captains jockeyed for a place in the front lines in order to ram an enemy ship while Xerxes was watching and thus to be recorded in his list of men to reward afterward. While the Greek contingents at Salamis managed to put aside their rivalries and each fight for the common good, the Persian contingents each thought about its separate relationship with the Great King.

By the same token, the Persian ships had little interest in continuing a struggle past the point where they might collect their reward. Compare the Spartan willingness to fight to the last man at Thermopylae with the Phoenicians' decision to turn and leave the line at Salamis after they realized that they could not defeat the Athenians. The Spartan king Leonidas served a transcendent cause, while the Phoenician king Tetramnestus merely calculated the odds. Freedom was worth dying for, but there was no percentage in giving one's life in exchange for power from the Great King that one would never enjoy.

By the evening of September 25, the Greeks had pushed the chaotic mass of Persians back. The action in the battle of Salamis had returned to where the Persians had begun the night before, at the eastern end of the straits. While the Aeginetans lurked at the exit of the channel, the Athenians inside the straits drove Persian ships into their hands. Meanwhile, an Athenian commando unit had landed on the islet of Psyttaleia, which lay just to the south of the Aeginetan squadron. There, another proud man brought back bloody spoils and glorified his name. He was the Athenian Aristides son of Lysimachus. Rivals though their cities were, Aristides and Polycritus had one thing in common: hatred of Themistocles. And the ships of other Greek cities, too, recorded impressive kills; we may mention only Croton, Naxos, and Corinth.

For Aegina's ambush to succeed, we may imagine that it was crucial first to remove the Persians from the islet of Psyttaleia. Had they remained there, they could have signaled to their ships about the ambush, which would have allowed some of the Persian triremes to escape by speeding up, by hugging the coast, or perhaps by steering a zigzag course. On top of that, if the Aeginetans had tried to hide their vessels in the shadow of Psyttaleia, the Persians might have threatened the men with arrows. And so the Persians had to be removed. Besides which, the Athenians were in a mood to sweep the foreigner from any inch of their soil, however small, that they could.

The mission was entrusted to a corps of Athenian infantryman under Aristides' command. This "brave man," the "best of the Athenians," does not seem to have had command of a ship during Athens's greatest naval battle. That is not surprising, considering that he was a returned political exile. Instead, he had his great moment when the Greeks broke the Persian line and chaos reigned among the Great King's triremes. At this point it was safe to thin the ranks of the Athenian infantrymen lining the Salamis shore. Aristides gathered a large number of them—we do not know how many—and put them on small boats. They landed on Psyttaleia and slaughtered the Persians there down to the last man. A Roman-era source claims that there were four hundred Persians on Psyttaleia. Here is clear evidence of the spirit of revenge and bloodthirstiness that motivated the Greeks at Salamis.

Aeschylus describes the incident with these dramatic words in the speech of a Persian messenger:

When God had given the glory of the naval battle to the Greeks,
That same day, after they had fenced their skin with well-bronzed armor,
They leapt out of their boats and circled around the whole island,
And we [Persians] were trapped without a thing to do. Many fell to the
* ground,*
Killed by stones from the Greeks' hands or by the bowstring's arrows.
In the end they rushed upon us as one, striking us, hacking like meat
Our unhappy limbs until the lives of all were utterly destroyed.

Slaughtering the trapped Persians was a neat feat but not a difficult one.

Both the carnage on Psyttaleia and the Aeginetan ambush represented mopping-up operations. The Persian navy had been defeated. Now was the time to kill as much of it as possible. As long as they retained their land army in Attica, the Persians could hold Phaleron as a secure base for the fleet. The Greeks, therefore, could not prevent all of Persia's ships from escaping, but they would try to ram as many as they could.

At Salamis, the Aeginetan navy fulfilled the promise of its magnificent tradition. Like the cities of Phoenicia, Aegina was a land of seafarers. Its merchant traders piled up wealth: the Aeginetan Sostratus son of Laodamas, for example, was the richest businessman in sixth century B.C. Greece. Thanks to its commerce, Aegina supported a population of about forty thousand, even though the small island had only enough farmland to feed about four thousand.

The Aeginetan navy ruled the Saronic Gulf for decades. Even its gods were respected as mighty protectors in war at sea, as witnessed by the request of the Greeks at Salamis for the statues of the sons of Aeacus the day before the battle. Aegina's navy had once been so dominant that before building its new fleet in 483 B.C., Athens was reduced to renting extra warships from Corinth in order to fight with Aegina, and the rentals secured only a temporary victory for Athens. On a memorable occasion long before, perhaps in the seventh century B.C., the Aeginetans had beat an Athenian invasion force so badly that only one man lived to tell the tale—and as soon as he straggled home, he was promptly murdered by a mob of angry Athenian widows. They stabbed him to death with the pins they used to fasten their dresses.

At Salamis, the sailors of Aegina wanted not only to beat the Persians, they wanted to prove that they, and not the Athenian upstarts, deserved to rule the waves. On top of that, Athens's democratic government sent shivers down the spines of Aegina's upper classes. Barely ten years earlier, they had been forced to put down a democratic revolution on their island; they were incensed enough to hack off the hands of a revolutionary seeking sanctuary in a temple. Athens had been behind that revolution, so at Salamis, Aegina's marines and commanders, who were prosperous to a man, were fired up to demonstrate the superiority of their oligarchic society to Athenian democracy, which they thought of as mob rule. Whether it was true that an Aeginetan and not an Athenian trireme had been the first to ram a Persian ship at Salamis, the Aeginetans no doubt felt that they deserved the honor.

Aeginetan mistrust of Athens may help explain why Aegina had not sent all its triremes to Salamis. The Aeginetans kept other ships at home while their best triremes participated in the battle. Perhaps they feared that Athens might make a deal with the Persians, and so they wanted to maintain a reserve to defend their island. Another concern was defense against Persian raiders.

Polycritus son of Crius was a man whose pride in his pedigree would have shown up a Persian grandee. Every ancient Greek name had a literal meaning, and Polycritus was a man to set store in the significance of his appellation, the same name borne by his father's father. Polycritus was "Excellent Beyond Measure," son of the "Ram." Ten years before Salamis, the Athenians had dishonored the Ram. In 490 B.C., while the Persians prepared to invade Athens at Marathon, Aegina gave earth and water to Persia as signs of submission. No doubt the islanders were glad to join so powerful an ally against their hated foe.

But the Athenians struck back by enlisting the help of Sparta, a strongly anti-Persian state even then. The Spartan king Cleomenes sailed to Aegina in order to arrest the men he regarded as traitors to Greece. But he was stopped by a strong-willed Aeginetan, none other than Polycritus's father, Crius. Crius was not intimidated by the Spartan, whom he accused of having taken bribes.

Livid but stymied, Cleomenes promised to return with reinforcements. With a dry but menacing Laconian wit, he said to the man whose name means "ram,"

Better plate your horns with bronze, ram, because you are bringing down a heap of trouble on yourself.

Cleomenes soon returned and arrested Crius, along with nine other prominent Aeginetans, and he sent them all as hostages to their bitterest enemies, the Athenians. Afterward, neither diplomacy nor force could get them back to Aegina. We do not know whether they ever returned home or died in Athens.

For the sake of a common front against the barbarian in 480 B.C., Polycritus could forgive the Athenians all their crimes except one: he could not forgive the ruin of his father, caused by Athens's alliance with Cleomenes. Polycritus was ready to shove his father's name down every Athenian throat that he could. At the exit to the straits, he went far towards doing just that. While the Athenians drove Persian ships out of the channel, the Aeginetans closed the net. Herodotus writes:

When the barbarians were put to flight and were sailing out toward Phaleron, the Aeginetans lay in ambush in the passage.

"The passage" in Herodotus refers to the area just outside the Salamis straits, where the sea widens. We might guess that the Aeginetans hid their ships behind the Cynosura peninsula or behind the island of Psyttaleia, after Aristides had led the operation to drive the Persian soldiers from it.

"Quiet, boys," the rowing master would have told the men as Polycritus's ship kept out of sight. We can imagine them sitting in silence until the next Persian ship flew by, hell-bent for Phaleron. Polycritus would have chosen carefully before ordering the attack, pausing just long enough to establish a good, long run-up for ramming without letting the Persian vessel get far enough ahead so that it could escape.

Cooperation with Athens gave Aegina the opportunity to upstage its old enemy. It happened just after Polycritus's trireme had rammed a fleeing ship from Sidon. Whether he knew it or not, this was a special prize, because the ship had been rated by the Persians as one of the ten fastest ships in their entire fleet. Polycritus then caught sight of Themistocles' flagship, which happened to come near him while chasing an enemy vessel in flight. At this point in the fading day, Athenian triremes were fighting two different battles, one against enemy ships that made a stand and resisted and another against those that had given up and were in flight. But the resistance must have reached its finale for a commander of Themistocles' importance to be willing to leave the straits.

Apparently what happened next is that Polycritus ordered his pilot to bring his trireme between Themistocles and an enemy ship, presumably the one that Themistocles was chasing. The Aeginetan vessel came close enough for Polycritus to be able to shout to Themistocles. He mocked him for criticizing the Aeginetans for Medizing, that is, for being pro-Persian. It seems that this was a common theme of Themistocles, maybe something that he had a habit of throwing in Aegina's face at councils of war. Now, Polycritus said words to this effect: "Medizers, are we, Themistocles? I'll show you who's a Medizer!" And with that, Polycritus rammed an enemy ship. Themistocles' response, if any, is not recorded.

While he savored that settling of scores, Polycritus could also marvel at the discovery just made when his marines boarded the Sidonian ship they had rammed. They found one of their countrymen, Pytheas son of Ischenöos.

In August, Pytheas had been serving as a marine on an Aeginetan trireme captained by one Asonides when it was captured by the enemy near the northern Greek island of Skiathos. The Persians also captured two other Greek triremes, one from Troezen and one from Athens. The Athenians beached their ship and the men fled; the Troezenian crew was taken and one of its marines had his throat slit as a human sacrifice. Most of the marines on the Aeginetan trireme were captured quickly, but Pytheas resisted. He threw the attackers into disorder.

This was before the battles at Artemisium and marked the first encounter between Greek and Persian vessels. Although the Persians outnumbered the Greeks, ten ships to three, the Greeks might have put up a stiffer fight. Pytheas was the only one to exemplify the spirit of resistance. "He proved to be the bravest man that day," Herodotus comments. Pytheas kept on fighting until his entire body bore vicious wounds.

When he finally fell he was still breathing. A high percentage of the marines on the enemy ships were Persians, and the Persians greatly admired bravery. So they made an effort to save Pytheas. They dressed his wounds with myrrh, an aromatic resin gathered from desert shrubs on the shore of the Red Sea and used in ancient times for healing because of its anti-bacterial effects; myrrh was also used for burning as incense. The Persians bandaged Pytheas with long strips of fine linen cloth, the same kind used in ancient Egypt to wrap mummies. Then they brought him back to their camp in Therma in northern Greece and exhibited him admiringly to the whole army. The other Aeginetan captives were treated as slaves.

Pytheas should have been dead, but at Salamis, he was held aboard the same Sidonian vessel that had captured him. The Greek cause had come full circle. The first man to resist the Persians at sea was released by his own countryman on the day of Greece's greatest naval victory.

Pytheas's is but one of the remarkable stories at the battle of Salamis. Another is that of Phayllos, a trireme captain at Salamis who came from the Greek colony of Croton in southern Italy. Phayllos was already famous in Greece for his three victories in the Pythian Games at Delphi: one in the footrace and two in the pentathlon, a grueling program of discus, javelin, jump, footrace, and wrestling. The Pythian Games were Panhellenic games, like the games at Isthmia and at Nemea (both near Corinth) and the most famous games of all—the Olympic Games. His athlete days were behind him in 480 B.C., when Phayllos was in his fifties, but his name lived on. The graying champion came out of his comfortable retirement to help the Greek cause at Salamis. Phayllos was an aristocrat and very wealthy: he paid for the crew of his own trireme, which was filled with Crotoniates who lived in Greece. This was the only ship from Greek Italy or Sicily to serve at Salamis, and it fought with distinction. Phayllos's men captured more than one Persian ship in the battle (we do not know the precise number). After the war, Phayllos advertised the victory by putting up a statue of himself on the Athenian Acropolis.

But the most successful Persian-hunter at Salamis was probably the Greek captain Democritus of Naxos, the third man to begin the battle, right after Aminias of Pallene and the Aeginetan ship carrying the statues of the sons of Aeacus. Naxos had sent four triremes to Salamis, but to fight for Persia, not Greece. A large island in the Aegean, Naxos had been sacked by Persia in 490 B.C. and its government had no stomach for revolt. But Democritus did. He was merely a ship's captain but was one of the best-known men on the island, and he talked the other Naxians into joining the Greeks at Salamis rather than the Persians at Phaleron. (The island of Paros, Naxos's neighbor—and rival—also stayed away from Phaleron, but Paros did not help the Greeks at Salamis. The Parians liked Athens as little as they did Persia, since Athens had tried to conquer Paros in 489 B.C. So they stayed aloof, waiting to see who won the battle.)

Democritus had a great day at Salamis. The contemporary poet Simonides celebrated him with these words:

> *Democritus was the third to begin the battle, when at Salamis*
> *The Greeks met with the Medes to fight at sea.*
> *He took five ships which he cleaved asunder and he captured a sixth,*
> *A Dorian vessel that had been dragged off by the barbarian's hand.*

In other words, Democritus took five Persian ships in all, and he recaptured a Greek ship from the Persians. We may imagine that each of these ships had been rammed but not beyond salvaging by the victor.

For a single captain to take no fewer than six ships is a stunning battle record. There are not likely to have been many men like Democritus in either fleet, and yet, afterward, he did not win the prize for prowess. That went to Polycritus of Aegina, followed by two Athenians, Aminias of Pallene and one Eumenes of the deme of Anagyrus, a captain of whom we know nothing. We also hear of another Athenian captain or perhaps cocaptain (the captain's position was sometimes shared) named Sosicles of the deme of Paeania. We do not know whether these men disabled more Persian triremes than Democritus or whether they owed their fame and honor to the influence of their cities. Regardless, Democritus's performance at Salamis symbolizes the Greek achievement in that battle.

Corinth had its share of the glory. A Corinthian captain named Diodorus captured an enemy vessel, and there were other successful Corinthian captains whose names are unknown. Corinthian seamen risked their lives at Salamis with their fellow Greeks, and some Corinthians died and were buried in a place of honor outside Salamis Town.

The Corinthian contingent might have begun the battle of Salamis at dawn, by sailing northward, as a decoy to lull the Persians into thinking that the Greeks were in flight and perhaps also as a way of drawing off some Persian ships. To continue this possible reconstruction, as soon as the battle began, a Greek dispatch boat rowed after the Corinthians to call them back. They furled their sails, rowed quickly back, and joined the fray near the Athenians and Aeginetans and contributed to the destruction of the Phoenician fleet.

Or so we might reconstruct the Corinthian battle experience. By the time Herodotus approached the subject in the mid-fifth century B.C., Corinth and Athens had become bitter enemies. Athenians now claimed that Corinth had disgraced itself in battle, while Corinth and the rest of Greece said just the opposite. The other Greeks insisted that Corinth had fought in the first ranks of the battle. In fact, war memorials at Delphi and Olympia had Corinth's name engraved in third place, after Athens and Sparta. On top of that, no fewer than four epigrams praising Corinth's role at Salamis survived into the Roman era, which means either that the Athenians slandered a rival or that Corinth worked hard to cover up its failure. That Athens, which controlled Salamis, allowed Corinth to set up one of those epigrams on the island, outside Salamis Town, on the tombstone above the grave of its men who died there, suggests slander.

The Corinthian admiral Adimantus, or so the Athenian story goes, fled in terror at the moment when the two fleets first came to blows. He spread his sails and headed north, followed by his whole squadron of forty ships. But a speedy dispatch boat, "sent by divine intervention," caught the Corinthians off the coast of Salamis. A messenger denounced Adimantus as a traitor and told him that the Greeks were winning. Adimantus and his men returned, but in time only for the end of the battle.

Since the battle lasted for about twelve hours and Salamis is a small island, it can hardly be true that Corinth missed most of the battle. The epigrams tell a tale of Corinth's valor. The gravestone epigram on Salamis reads:

> *Stranger, once we lived in the well-watered town of Corinth*
> *But now Salamis, the island of Ajax, holds us*
> *Here we took Phoenician ships and Persians*
> *And Medes: And so we protected sacred Greece.*

A Corinthian commemorative plaque was set up in Corinthian territory at the Isthmus, in the sanctuary of Poseidon, where the biennial Isthmian Games were held. The epigram is eloquent:

> *When all Greece was balanced on the razor's edge*
> *We protected her with our souls and here we lie.*

This cenotaph (a memorial over an empty tomb) stood in the general area to which the Corinthian admiral Adimantus had wanted to move the Greek fleet from Salamis. He did not get his wish, but at least he got it memorialized. We may imagine that the cenotaph stood nearby the Persian ship captured at Salamis that, according to Herodotus, was still preserved at the Isthmus in his day, around 430 B.C.

The Corinthian Adimantus had a proud epitaph at Corinth that read:

> *This grave is Adimantus', through whom*
> *All Greece put on a victory wreath of freedom.*

Perhaps also as part of Adimantus's publicity campaign, he named his daughters "Victory with Ships" (Nausinice), "Pick of the Booty" (Acrothinium), and "Defense Against Force" (Alexibia); his son was named "The Bravest" (Aristeus).

There is also a dedication, in a temple of the goddess Leto, by the Corinthian captain Diodorus, which states:

> *The rowers of Diodorus took these weapons from the hostile Medes*
> *And dedicated them to Leto as a memorial of the naval battle.*

Traditionally, warriors dedicated an enemy's shields, but perhaps Diodorus's ship left stern ornaments.

Finally, there is a story that the women of Corinth prayed to Aphrodite that their men "throw themselves heart and soul into the fight against the barbarians." This was an inspired prayer, because the Greek word for "throw themselves into" also means "to ram." (Ancient comics made hay out of the sexual double meaning of "to ram.") On top of that, Aphrodite was worshipped at Corinth by sacred prostitutes, and some ancient writers say that it wasn't all the women of Corinth but just the prostitutes who made this prayer. Eventually, bronze statues of women were set up in the temple of Aphrodite on the Acropolis of Corinth with this inscription:

> These statues of women have been set up because they prayed to the Cypriot
> Goddess on behalf of the Greeks and their citizens who fight fairly and openly.
> Bright Aphrodite had no intention of surrendering
> Her Acropolis to the arrow-bearing Medes.

This remarkable inscription manages to celebrate Corinth while taking a swipe at Athens and Athenian manhood. The reference to Aphrodite's Acropolis might remind a visitor of Athena's Acropolis and its capture by the Persians. The reference to fighting "fairly and openly" might contrast favorably with Themistocles' cunning that bordered on treachery. Finally, the Greek word for "fight fairly and openly" can also mean "fight with an erection"—an appropriate prayer to Aphrodite, after all. The Greeks were not prudes, and what they said was, in effect, that the Corinthians were big men in every sense, and so they stuck it to the Persians.

At midday during the battle of Salamis, a Persian sentry atop Munychia in Piraeus would have looked out over a sea whose colors ranged from turquoise to blue to silver to gray. Looking southeast, he would have seen Phaleron Bay, where the Persian fleet had left its harbor the night before. Beyond, the hills rolled clear toward the southern horizon, all the way to Cape Sunium.

Turning behind, looking northeast, the Persian would have had a clear view of the ruins of the Athenian Acropolis. Mount Hymettus, famed for its honey, rose like a curtain wall behind it to the south. Mount Pentele, rich in marble, loomed to the northeast, while the pine-forested Mount Parnes closed the Attic plain to the north. Turning now to the southwest, the Persian would have faced the low, rugged hills of the island of Salamis in the distant haze, with the conical peak of Mount Oros on the island of Aegina behind it. Looking back to the east, following the turn of the Attic coast, he would have seen the entrance to the bay of Salamis.

As he surveyed the scene, the Persian lookout would have seen victory behind him and uncertainty ahead. As the day wore on, if he kept looking, he would have watched as Persia's ships fled back to Phaleron, chased by their victorious enemies. It was a spectacle of horror on an early autumn afternoon when the sea was all silvery blue in the shimmering light. Everything was blue and gray and silver—and blood red.

There was no place of honor for the Persian dead, and they vastly outnumbered the Corinthians; indeed they outnumbered all the Greeks. We do not know how many Persian crewmen died at Salamis. Herodotus does not try to give numbers. He simply says that many well-known Persians, Medes, and their allies died besides Ariabignes. Greek losses were few. Unless they died in "the law of hands," the Greeks tended to swim to safety, unlike the enemy, at least the Iranian and Sacae marines and officers. The Ionians and other Greeks in the Persian fleet, as well as maritime peoples such as the Phoenicians and Carians, would surely have mastered the skill of swimming.

Aeschylus, too, speaks of some Persians dying in hand-to-hand combat and others surviving that struggle, only to drown. He names nineteen Persian "chiefs" who died at Salamis; most of them are mere names, perhaps chosen by the poet for their colorful sound, but one is the king or syennesis (a formal title) of Cilicia. He was an important man from a wealthy region in southern Anatolia. Herodotus does not mention his death, but if Aeschylus is right, it was a significant blow for Xerxes. And likewise the range of countries from which Aeschylus's casualties come, if it is credible: besides Persia, there is Bactria, Cilicia, Egypt, Lydia, Mysia, and Phoenicia.

An author of the Roman era, perhaps citing a fourth century B.C. Greek source, writes that the Greeks lost more than forty triremes at Salamis, while the Persians lost over two hundred; that is, a ratio of 1:5. This suits the lopsided outcome of the battle. It also fits the fact that Xerxes continued to have a large number of triremes even after Salamis. So these figures may be roughly correct.

Using them only as a guideline, it appears that the Persians lost more than six thousand marines as well as a small number of elite officers. If, at a guess, an equal number of oarsmen in the Persian fleet were killed during the "law of hands," then the total number of Persian deaths at Salamis would be over twelve thousand. Remembering the fate of Damasithymus's men, all of whom were massacred, this figure should perhaps be considered a minimum. It would not be surprising if the Persians lost twenty thousand men or more.

Aeschylus's Persian messenger sums up the disaster of Salamis thus:

> *Be sure of this: never in a single day*
> *Has so great a number of people died.*

And even after every Persian ship was rammed or had escaped, there were still survivors, clinging onto debris, who could be picked up if they were Greek, or killed or left to die if they were Persian. Their wailing, says Aeschylus, could still be heard at sundown, which occurred in Athens at 7:18 P.M. on September 25.

By then, the wind and waves would probably have begun the ghoulish delivery of corpses onto the shore, a process that continued for several days. These corpses were mainly from Persian ships, since they formed the overwhelming majority of the casualties. Aeschylus states that

> *The shores of Salamis and every nearby place*
> *Are full of corpses, rotting ill-starredly.*

And:

> *The sea-dyed, much-driven bodies*
> *Are carried, after death . . .*
> *In wanderings in both directions.*

And:

> *Lost from a ship of Tyre near the headlands*
> *Of Salamis, they lie on the rugged headlands.*

"And the starry sea swarmed with their [Persian] bodies," says Timotheus, "and the shores were laden." While some corpses ended up on

Salamis, most of them seem to have been blown toward Attica. At the end of the day, a zephyr, a west wind, blew up, and eventually it drove wrecks, oars, and corpses onto the Attic shore around Cape Colias, not far south of Phaleron.

After the battle, Mardonius, Xerxes' chief adviser, threw the accusation of cowardice in the face of the Phoenicians, the Egyptians, the Cypriots, and the Cilicians. He may have been right if by cowardice he meant that after a certain point they chose to flee rather than fight. By no means did these squadrons go without casualties, but each probably preferred to cut its losses.

The Persian navy was ill-suited to battle an opponent who could neither be intimidated nor bought off—an opponent like the Greeks. The Persian fleet was less a naval than a political organization. It was not a single structure but, rather, a group of chieftains each vying for the favor of the overlord. It was less a navy than a floating royal court.

And so, by turns too confident and too cowardly, the Persian fleet at Salamis fought well but never wisely. Had it been willing to fight on, the Persians could have inflicted more losses on the Greeks, thereby increasing the odds of ultimate victory should Xerxes be willing to continue the fight at sea another day. On the other hand, had they retreated without each unit trying its luck, the Persians would have saved their strength for later. In the end, they did neither.

The most important question left by the clash at Salamis is this: Why did the Greeks win the battle and the Persians lose? Herodotus, who understood Salamis as well as any ancient writer, gives his answer succinctly: good order versus disorder. The Persians fell apart; the Greeks did not. Herodotus writes:

> *Since the Greeks fought [with each ship] in order and [with every ship] in the order of battle, while the barbarians neither remained drawn up in order of battle nor did they do anything wisely, it was only to be expected that things turned out for them as they did.*

But the student of history wants to go a step further and ask why the Persians fell apart. For this, there are three answers: shock, command, and geography.

At dawn on September 25, the Persians were shocked to discover that the Greeks were ready to fight. The Persians were not prepared for this mentally or physically. They had expected an easy pursuit of a broken enemy, not a tough fight. Even at first light, the Greeks possibly kept the enemy off guard by sending the Corinthians northward on a phony flight. At Salamis the Greeks were in top form psychologically and had spent the night sleeping on dry land rather than in wakeful and exhausting rowing. Shock made it easier for the Greeks to break up the good order of the Persian fleet.

Many Persian commanders were killed in battle, including the highest-ranking admiral, Xerxes' half brother Ariabignes. Persian navies (and armies) were more vulnerable to decapitation than Greeks because Persia was more centralized. Nor did Persia encourage individual initiative the way the Greeks did, especially a democracy like Athens. Unlike the Greeks, Persian commanders had little loyalty to a cause; instead, they fought mainly to impress Xerxes. They had no incentive to fight to the death. The Persian way of command contributed to a breakdown of good order at Salamis.

Finally, the Greeks took every advantage of the unusual geography of the Salamis straits. The narrow space made it impossible for the Persians to use their superiority in speed. By the same token, the channel turned the heaviness of the Greeks' triremes from a liability into an advantage. And it turned the superiority of the Persians in numbers into a disadvantage, because their boats collided with each other. If, on a likely reconstruction, the regular morning sea breeze began to blow, the result would have unsteadied the Persian ships more than it did the Greeks'. So the straits' geography contributed to the disorder of the Persian fleet.

Shock, command, and geography: three simple building blocks, deployed in a deadly way, turned the battle of Salamis from a hammer blow by Persia into a trap laid by Greeks. Persia hoped to crush the Greeks with its superiority in numbers but blundered into an ambush in which its very mass worked against it. Rarely have so many been hurt so much by so few.

Between the two of them, Athens and Aegina accounted for most of the Persian warships that were disabled during the battle. Both achievements were extraordinary, but Aegina's was outsize, since its 30 triremes represented only one-sixth as many ships as Athens's 180. No doubt Aegina disabled other enemy vessels in the morning besides the one rammed by the ship bearing the statues of the sons of Aeacus, but what really distinguished Aegina at Salamis was the ambush it carried out in the afternoon. The Aeginetans "exhibited achievements worthy of mention," says Herodotus: high praise indeed, considering his promise in the opening sentence that his book would be "an exhibition of . . . great and astonishing achievements" so that they not be forgotten.

THE RETREAT

CHAPTER TWELVE

≈

PHALERON

As the west wind picks up in the evening of September 25, it bends the crowd of warships like a field of grain in the afternoon breeze. The Persian navy is in flight, its men all but dead in their seats. On one of the triremes, the lookout gives the word that the enemy has stopped his pursuit, but the petrified rowers keep pulling. As they pass Piraeus on the port side and the pilot starts adjusting the rudder for the turn into Phaleron Bay, the captain shifts her thoughts to the shore. The queen of Halicarnassus is always thinking, and she knows that Xerxes will call a war council. She has to ponder how best to make use of the credit she will have won from ramming what she hopes the high command will have thought was an enemy ship. She understands not to overplay her hand, now that her forecast of naval disaster has come true. Meanwhile, as Artemisia knows, she must keep her men content and quiet about what they really did at Salamis: or so we might imagine.

As the surviving ships pulled back up to the beach at Phaleron on the end of the worst day in the history of the Persian fleet, the men are likely to have scrambled ashore and rushed to their camp. The soldiers stationed there will have run down to the ships to help them, sending whatever slaves were available to carry off the wounded and the dead. The corpses would be cremated, the wounded brought to doctors.

And there were many corpses. In the days after the battle of Salamis,

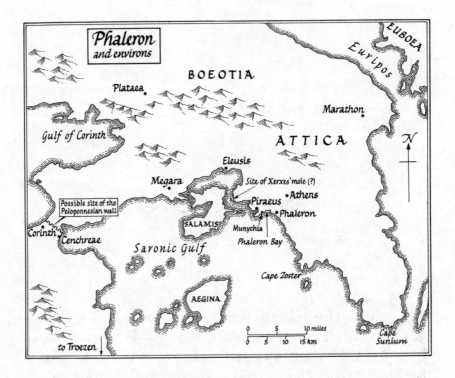

Phaleron and environs

the shores of Attica became the most ethnically diverse graveyard in human history to that date. It was a testimony to the diversity of the Persian Empire and to the folly of its leaders.

As for the men injured in battle, those with flesh wounds to their limbs, simple fractures, or sprains had a fair chance of surviving. Wounds would be swabbed with myrrh, fig juice, or wine to reduce infection and stop the bleeding, and then they would be bandaged with linen or cotton. A fractured limb would be extended and adjusted; rubbed with an ointment containing a mixture of fat, resin, and herbs; and then carefully bandaged to effect a light compression. After a few days, the bandages would have to be checked and changed. Sprains and dislocations could be adjusted and the pain managed with herbs and massage, but not always with success. Xerxes' father, Darius, for example, once suffered so much from a dislocated anklebone that not even his Egyptian doctors—then considered the world's best—could heal him; only Democedes of the Italian-Greek city of Croton, who happened to be in the Persian Empire, was able to do the trick.

The odds of survival were poor for anyone needing surgery. Ancient doctors carried bronze medicine chests, about five inches long by about three inches wide, whose tools included scalpels, hooks, forceps, and drills. Ancient surgeons were well aware of the importance of cleanliness. Greek and Near Eastern physicians had some success in extracting arrow- and spearheads from wounds. They had some ability to reinflate collapsed lungs, and they experimented with bores and augers to treat skull wounds. Yet the survival rates for most of these procedures were poor.

"A healer is worth many men in his ability to cut out arrows and smear soothing medicaments on wounds," says Homer. But it is doubtful that there were enough doctors available at Phaleron Bay for all the wounded after Salamis. So, as ineffective as most ancient doctors were by our standards, some men had to settle for even worse: fumbling medical help from their comrades or attempts at magic from the camp followers, who offered nostrums, spells, prayers, and amulets. The numbers of dead surely mounted in the hours and days after the battle.

Meanwhile, the living could at least be fed and given water and wine to drink. After nearly twenty-four hours on the sea, they must have been as hungry and thirsty as they were tired. Still, the talk is likely to have turned to pulling out of Phaleron immediately that night, before the Greeks could attack them. As darkness fell, torches would have lit the dispirited camp. Moans of pain and crying for the dead would have mingled with rumor, blame, and scheming.

Whether or not Xerxes visited the fleet that night, he was not idle. He felt danger hanging over him. Xerxes knew that when Darius invaded Scythia (today's Ukraine) in 513 B.C., the Persian army had nearly been trapped when its bridge over the Danube had almost been cut. Now Xerxes feared for his bridges over the Hellespont. He intended that the remnant of the Persian fleet race back across the Aegean in order to protect the expedition's lifeline.

And yet he wanted to hide his plans. So immediately after the defeat at Salamis, apparently the very next day, Xerxes ordered his engineers to begin constructing a causeway between the mainland and Salamis. They tied together Phoenician merchantmen, presumably ships that had brought supplies to Greece for Phoenician warships. The

Persians planned to use these ships to serve both as a pontoon bridge and as a wall behind which they could build the causeway. In other words, since they had failed to reach Salamis by sea, they planned to attack it by land. They probably rowed the merchantmen into the straits along the Attic shore, guarding them with some of their remaining warships. With a large enough naval escort, the Persians might create the impression that they were planning another naval battle, which was just the disinformation that they wanted to feed the Greeks.

On September 26, the day after the battle, Xerxes called a war council. Unlike the last time, Xerxes did not meet with all the kings and squadron commanders in his service. This time, he consulted only Persians, with the exception of Artemisia. The queen of Halicarnassus had emerged from the wreckage of the straits like Aphrodite arisen from the sea. She was now not merely the most powerful woman in Xerxes' entourage, she was the most influential of all the king's non-Persian allies.

In council, Mardonius advised Xerxes to make little of Salamis. "Our struggle is not to be decided by pieces of wood but by men and horses." And he added:

> *The Persians have nothing to do with what has happened, nor can you say that somehow we have been cowardly men. If the Phoenicians and Egyptians and Cypriots and Cilicians have been cowards, this disaster has nothing to do with the Persians.*

It was a sentiment to strike a chord in the Persian elite. When the bad news from Salamis reached Susa, the Persians

> *all tore their tunics and cried and made boundless lamentations and blamed Mardonius. The Persians did this not so much because they grieved about the ships as because they feared for Xerxes himself.*

In strategic terms, the ships were at least as important as the king, but the Persians thought just the opposite.

After hearing from Mardonius and his other Persian advisers, Xerxes did an extraordinary thing. He dismissed them and his bodyguards as well. For once, the royal tent was empty except for the Great King and the counselor who most inspired confidence. If he had listened to Artemisia's advice before Salamis, he might now be the master of Greece. At least he had finally learned whom to trust.

Artemisia might be forgiven if she had stopped to savor the moment. After all, she was the half-Cretan widow of the petty ruler of a small Anatolian city nearly two thousand miles away from the imperial capital. She had barely escaped with her life from a naval disaster, and she had done so only by treacherously turning on her ally in full view of witnesses. She was a woman in a society whose ruling elite considered it the most terrible insult to call a man "worse than a woman." And yet she had climbed the peak of power.

If he had not done so already, Xerxes was soon to honor her with the prize for bravery in battle. The story is told that Artemisia received a full suit of Greek armor as a sign of her achievement. At the same time, Xerxes gave a spindle and distaff to "the admiral of the fleet." A distaff is a rod on which wool is wound before being spun into thread. In Greece, it was a symbol of womanhood. So to give a distaff to a naval commander was surely an insult.

We do not know which commander is meant by the phrase "admiral of the fleet": the chief candidate is probably Megabazus son of Megabates, one of the two Persian commanders of the Phoenician squadrons (along with Prexaspes son of Aspathines). Megabazus may have held a hereditary position as "the admiral," to judge from official documents at Persepolis. In the Roman era Megabazus was called the admiral in chief of 480 B.C., which may be an echo of such a status. But Megabazus's fortune may have sunk after Salamis, since neither he nor the other two surviving Persian admirals, Achaemenes and Prexaspes, was reassigned to a naval command the following year.

If the spindle and distaff were an insult, the full suit of Greek armor was meant as a compliment. In both Greece and Persia, prowess in battle, especially land battle, was considered the height of manliness. And surely Xerxes' gift represented nothing but the best in materials and craftsmanship: certainly something with the finest horsehair for the plume and with a design incised on helmet, breastplate, and greaves, and with a stunning blazon on the shield, perhaps one of the lions or winged bulls favored in Persian art.

If it is really true that Xerxes gave Artemisia a *Greek* suit of armor, as opposed to Persian armor, that might reflect the standards of Caria, where Greek influence was very strong and soldiers were armed in the Greek fashion. In Athens, a suit of armor and a wreath were the standard prize for valor. The Persian monarchs were nothing if not sensitive to the customs of their subjects.

But no one at the time would have considered Xerxes overly generous in his gift to Artemisia. After all, Theomestor was rewarded with the tyranny of Samos, and Phylakes was given an estate and enrolled among the King's Benefactors. Two generations later, the rather poor country of Acarnania rewarded an Athenian general with not one but three hundred suits of armor. But that general had *won* his battle; Artemisia merely salvaged some specious honor during a disaster.

The conference met in Xerxes' tent on September 26: it was the hour of Xerxes' anxiety, and Artemisia was there to reassure him. Leave aside her charm and coquetry: Artemisia was the best naval strategist in Xerxes' service. His half brother, the Carians' and Ionians' commander, the admiral Ariabignes, was dead; his brother Achaemenes, commander of the undistinguished Egyptian fleet, was disgraced, as were the three Phoenician kings and the two Persian admirals, who outranked the kings. Samian and Samothracian captains had scored kills in the battle, and so had others. But Artemisia alone had predicted the disaster that would lie ahead if the Persians fought at Salamis. On top of that, she had fought brilliantly, or so it appeared to Xerxes and his courtiers.

We hear nothing of an interpreter at Artemisia's private session with Xerxes. Unless one is to be supposed, we must conclude that the supple queen had learned to speak good Persian, since the King of Kings would hardly have stooped to speak in a language other than that of the ruling people.

Mardonius had suggested that Xerxes choose between two courses of action. Either the king should order the full Persian army into action against the Greeks at the Isthmus or he should have the entire navy and a portion of the army withdraw from Greece entirely, and Xerxes with them. In that case, Mardonius would stay and command the rest of the army; and he promised to subject all Greece to the Great King's authority. Mardonius preferred the second course of action, says Herodotus, because it might allow him to reestablish his reputation after the failure of the expedition for which he had beaten the drum so loudly.

Xerxes asked Artemisia which course of action she recommended. She replied that Mardonius should be left in Greece with a portion of the army. In that case, the risks would all be his, while Xerxes could take the credit if Mardonius managed to succeed. Nor need the king concern himself about any Greek threat. "If you and your house survive," Artemisia said, "the Greeks will have to run many races for their lives and possessions—and they will have to do so often." Besides, she added, he had in fact burned Athens.

Artemisia had told Xerxes what he wanted to hear. Even if every man and woman in his entourage had told him to stay, Herodotus adds cattily, Xerxes was too frightened to have remained in Greece. Yet even Herodotus concedes that Xerxes made a considered and timely decision. Xerxes had lost a battle, but he did not give up the war. The only question was the strategy with which to fight. The king was quick to grasp the full extent of the naval disaster. With equal speed, he understood that the results of Salamis raised a more important issue than Greece: Ionia.

At Salamis, the Greeks had won control of the sea. Unchecked, they could in time use it to wrest back the empire's hard-won gains of the last generation: northern Greece, the Aegean islands, and, the greatest prize of all, Ionia. The question was how to keep the Greeks in check.

In just a few days, in fact, in as little as twenty-four hours, Xerxes came up with an answer, a new strategy that he immediately began to put into practice. Conquering Greece was no longer his priority. Because it could no longer turn the enemy's flank by sea, his army would not attack the Greeks at the Isthmus. Instead, his policy would be to withdraw all the Persian navy and part of the Persian army. Xerxes left just enough military force on the Greek mainland to keep the Greeks off balance and disunited. In the meantime, he would personally relocate to the part of the empire that most needed his attention: Ionia. Within two months of Salamis, Xerxes had moved to Sardis, the provincial capital. He would stay there for the next year, until the autumn of 479 B.C.

It turned out very badly. Within a year of deciding to withdraw from Athens, Xerxes had lost not only the Peloponnese, but nearly all his possessions on the Greek mainland as well as the main Greek islands of the eastern Aegean, with the city-states of Ionia and Caria on the way out. The other islands would follow a year later. Twenty years after the outbreak of the Ionian Revolt, in 499 B.C., a Greek alliance on the mainland was driving the Great King out of the Aegean and back from the Aegean coast of Anatolia.

What went wrong? Xerxes made three mistakes, but calling off the Isthmus attack and withdrawing to Sardis was not one of them. In fact, it made perfect sense to pull back from Greece. Conquering the Peloponnese—the only part of Greece still free of the Persians—would have brought Xerxes glory and a source of mercenaries but little else. The Persian Empire was vast and rich, but Greece was small and poor. In spite of the elegant meters of Aeschylus's choruses and the 200,000 words of Herodotus's *Histories*, in spite of the stockpiles of booty taken from the Persians and the marble monuments that would commemorate Greek victory, in spite of the skill of its spearmen and the force of its fleets—in spite of all that, Greece had little to offer. The Persian kings already had more wealth in the city of Persepolis than there was in the entire Greek peninsula.

The main advantage of conquering Greece, besides glory, was defensive. Left unchecked, the Greeks might expand. The Aegean islands, Ionia, and Egypt were all waiting to be shaken loose from Persia. And leaving Greece unconquered set a bad example for the other restive peoples of the empire. In short, Greece represented less a resource than a threat.

On top of that, time and treasure added to the war in Greece had to be subtracted from the resources available to police the rest of the empire. On first glance, it might appear that by choosing to withdraw from Athens, Xerxes demonstrated his cowardice. In truth, the Great King showed his maturity. His presence represented a limited resource. Wherever the Great King went, his servants performed better. It would have been irresponsible to stay in Greece when he was needed in so many other parts of his realm.

Already at Phaleron after the battle of Salamis, Xerxes was thinking about his other border trouble spots. Or so we may conclude from a telltale detail: the Egyptian ships in his fleet, once two hundred strong, returned home. But their marines stayed behind, to form part of the Persian land army under Mardonius. It was an interesting choice.

On the one hand, the Egyptians had won the prize for bravery at

Artemisium, where they captured five Greek ships, crews and all. With their boarding spears, large battle-axes, long knives, and large daggers, they made picturesque soldiers and perhaps potent ones. There were no Egyptian foot soldiers in the Persian land army, a gap that these marines could fill. On the other hand, the Egyptian squadron had found a place on Mardonius's list of cowards at Salamis. Perhaps he blamed the captains and not the marines for their spinelessness. Or perhaps the decision to retain the Egyptians was more political than military. The admiral of the Egyptian fleet was Achaemenes, Xerxes' brother, and governor of Egypt. Perhaps Mardonius chose to flatter Achaemenes in order to improve his standing with Xerxes' family.

And then there was a negative reason to keep the Egyptians in Greece: they would not be in Egypt. The province on the Nile had revolted from Persian rule only half a dozen years earlier. If Egypt's ships had survived storms and battles relatively unscathed—as their prowess at Artemisium and absence at Salamis might suggest—then the marines would have numbered two thousand or more. When two thousand armed men had seen the Great King's failure firsthand, why send them home to a disloyal land? Within a generation, Egypt would rebel again; in 480 B.C., the Persians might have seen it coming.

Of course, Ionian marines also represented potential rebels, but unlike the Egyptians, the Ionians had proven themselves loyal and effective sailors at Salamis. Better to save their marines for another naval battle than to waste them opposite a Spartan hoplite's spear.

The Egyptian ships are not heard of again in 480 or 479 B.C. Apparently, Xerxes felt he could dispense with them, as well as with those of the Cilicians, Cypriots, Lycians, and Pamphylians. All that remained was the Carians, Ionians, and Phoenicians, the traditional core of the Persian fleet. And that fleet would now be based in the East.

This was part of Xerxes' new strategy. By pulling his fleet back from Greece, Xerxes changed the power equation. Without that fleet, Persia would find it hard to stop the Greek fleet and maintain control of the Aegean. But it was not impossible. Paradoxical as it seems, the Persian army could defeat the Greek navy. It could do so by conquering Greece and cutting the Greek navy off from its base. But how could the Persian army conquer Greece without a Persian navy to give it the mobility to leapfrog Greek defenses?

Xerxes' answer, after the disaster at Salamis, was for Persia to return to the old way of dealing with the Greeks: bribery. "Ares," the god of war, says Timotheus in his poem about Salamis, "is king: Greece does not fear [Persian] gold." It was a nice boast, but it was not true. The Great King's riches could still buy Greek traitors. The pro-Persian leaders of Thebes thought so. They told their masters how to conquer all Greece without a battle:

Send money to the men who have the most power in the cities and you will divide Greece. Then, with their help, you will easily defeat those who are not on your side.

This was good advice. The Spartans were seriously worried that Athens would cut a deal with the Persians, and it might have happened. If the Persians had pursued a major charm offensive after Salamis, if they had made a grand gesture offering Athens a substantial concession in recognition of its victory at sea, then the Persians might have been able to make a deal. But the Persians made only a stingy offer, and they followed it with a painful but nonlethal attack.

Athens, the Persians reasoned, could be bought cheaply. Athenians had returned to what was left of their homes a few weeks after Salamis, when the Persian army withdrew northward. In the spring of 479 B.C. the Persians sent the king of Macedon, both a Persian vassal and an old friend of Athens, on an embassy. He reported that Xerxes now offered the Athenians an amnesty for their past crimes against him; he offered them autonomy, the expansion of their territory, and a promise to rebuild their temples at his expense. In return, Xerxes expected to add Athens's naval power to his side.

When the Athenians turned down the proposition, Mardonius invaded Attica a second time, in June 479 B.C. Once again, the Athenians evacuated their territory for Salamis. Once again, Mardonius sent an ambassador to them, now on Salamis, to repeat Xerxes' offer. When a member of the Athenian council named Lycides proposed hearing the ambassador out, he was stoned to death by his angry countrymen. Not to be outdone, a crowd of Athenian women made their way to Lycides' house and stoned to death his wife and children.

To Mardonius, the Athenians were obstinate. An unbiased observer

might have said "determined." The second invasion of Attica only stiff-
ened Athenian resistance. It galvanized them to threaten Sparta that
unless it ventured out from Fortress Peloponnese and risked its crack
army in defense of Attica, the Athenians would, in fact, make a deal
with the Great King. The Spartans agreed: the Persians had provoked
the very thing they most wanted to avoid. In short, the Persians proved
no shrewder in negotiation than in naval warfare.

Diplomatic ineptitude was Xerxes' first mistake; his second was
trusting Mardonius to lead the remaining Persian forces in Greece.
Once negotiations had failed, a more cautious general would have
avoided a set battle with Greece's heavily armed infantrymen. And if
battle proved inevitable, he would have insisted on choosing terrain
where he could make the most of Persia's superiority in cavalry. But the
bigheaded Mardonius plunged his men into a confrontation on ground
where he could not deploy his horsemen. Left to face the iron advance
of the Greek phalanx at the battle of Plataea in August 479 B.C., Mardonius lost both his army and his life.

Xerxes' third mistake was failing to rebuild his fleet in the East. It
turned out that Greece's victory at Salamis was not merely naval but
psychological, because it shook the enemy's confidence in his sea forces.
"They had been struck a great blow," says Herodotus of the Persians:
"On sea, they were broken in spirit."

Whether by accident or design, the Greeks had hit the keystone of
Persia's naval policy at Salamis by devastating the Phoenician fleet.
Never a sea power itself, Persia had put its confidence in the Phoenicians. For all the ships in his armada, even after the losses in storms and
at Artemisium, Xerxes had little trust in any of them except for the
Phoenicians. And it was precisely the Phoenicians who had most disappointed at Salamis.

After the Phoenicians, the two best squadrons in Xerxes' fleet were
the Carians and the Ionians (along with other Greeks). But the Carian
contingent was never large and the Ionians were rarely trustworthy.
Xerxes' very first thought after Salamis was that the Ionians would
betray the bridges at the Hellespont to the Greek fleet. Besides, precisely because the Ionians had stood so firm at Salamis, they, too, had
suffered losses in the straits. The best squadrons in the Persian fleet
were bleeding, and the unwounded units were dubious.

Persia had lost a naval battle, but rather than continue the war at sea, Persians found it all too easy to virtually write off their navy. Indeed, they seemed almost relieved to be forced back onto their natural element: the land. The war with the Greeks continued at high intensity for another year, but the Persian fleet hugged the coast of Anatolia. They did not expect the Greek fleet to venture across the Aegean to challenge them. When the Greeks did just that in August 479 B.C., the Persians were too afraid of the Greeks to fight them at sea. Instead, they beached their ships on the Anatolian coast at Mycale, opposite the island of Samos, only to lose the land battle that followed. The Greeks burned the Persian ships on the beach at Mycale.

Two other things are striking about the Persian fleet at Mycale. It amounted to only 300 triremes, a far cry from the around 700 triremes at Salamis, not to mention the 1,207 triremes after Persia crossed the Hellespont. Nor did it include the Phoenicians, whose units had been sent elsewhere before the battle. Whether the Persians wanted to use the Phoenician ships elsewhere, say, in Thrace, or whether the Persians wanted to ensure that at least one part of their fleet survived, is unclear. Either motive testifies to Persia's naval weakness.

But the Great King's treasury was not empty in 479 B.C., and he would have been wise to use it to build ships. To bribe Ionian admirals. To soothe the egos of unhappy Phoenicians. To buy his captains whatever equipment they said they needed. In the long run, the cheapest way to hold on to Persia's Aegean empire was to fight for it at sea.

Xerxes had developed a new strategy, after the defeat at Salamis. It was a good strategy, but he and his generals executed it poorly. And so, Persia failed.

On top of everything else, Xerxes underestimated democracy. He understood neither its ferocity nor its ability to learn from its mistakes. The day after Salamis, Xerxes' nightmare was pursuit to the Hellespont by a Greek fleet. A year later, he no longer considered that likely. Surely, he reasoned, if the Athenians had not sailed to Anatolia in their moment of triumph after Salamis, they would not do so in 479 B.C., after proving unable to defend Attica from a second invasion. The autocrat had no conception of the power of a people in arms who had been provoked.

But his captains did. Twenty-four hours after the end of the slaughter at Salamis, the remaining ships of Xerxes' fleet left Phaleron Bay for the last time. They had timed their departure for night, in order to keep it secret from the Greeks. They managed to move undetected but not unafraid.

Near Cape Zoster, not far from Phaleron, the lookouts mistook a series of promontories for enemy ships. In their eagerness to flee them, the Persians broke formation. Eventually, they realized their mistake and regrouped.

The Persian ships were impatient to reach the bridges, so they set the fastest course, cutting directly northeastward across the Aegean toward the Hellespont. But at least one squadron followed the longer route along the coast of the Greek mainland, which offered more shelter from the wind. Or so we might guess, judging from the fate of two Carian ships captured by ships from Peparethos (today, Skopelos), a Greek island in the northwestern Aegean, north of Euboea.

Peparethos was not a member of the Hellenic League against Persia. It was a fertile island with a good harbor, and it probably could have managed to build and man a few triremes. Or perhaps it was Peparethian pirates who attacked the Carians; the ships might have been stragglers and therefore easy to pick off. In any case, the people of Peparethos commemorated the feat at Delphi after the war. There, they commissioned a prominent Athenian sculptor to set up a statue to Apollo, the patron god of Delphi. The statue, which was bronze and stood almost twice life-size, is long gone, but the inscription still exists. It reads:

Diopeithes the Athenian made this.
Because the Peparethians captured two ships of the Carians at spearpoint
They gave a tenth of the booty to far-darting Apollo.

Artemisia was not among the victims. Xerxes had given her the honor of bringing his illegitimate children to Ephesus, a port city in Ionia. Hermotimus the eunuch was assigned to join her and serve as the children's guardian. We can imagine the two masters of cunning aboard the same ship, each trying to extract information from the other without giving up anything in return.

Xerxes had a less pleasant journey. He did not leave with the fleet.

Xerxes and the Persian army stayed in Athens for about a week after the battle of Salamis. They left probably on October 2. The Spartans at the Isthmus were, it seems, ready to harass the enemy in his retreat, but they changed their minds because of a bad omen: while King Cleombrotus was sacrificing, there was a partial eclipse.

The Persians marched to Thessaly, about two hundred miles north of Athens. There, Xerxes left Mardonius and his forces for the following year's campaign. The Great King and a portion of the Persian army continued about three hundred miles to the Hellespont. They kept up a rapid pace. All in all, it took forty-five days to travel the distance of about 550 miles from Athens to the bridges, about half the time of the Persians' three-month trip to Athens. Xerxes probably reached the Hellespont around December 15.

It was a tough trip. The Persians planned to "live off the land," to use the ancient euphemism for stealing and extorting food from the locals. But as a result of the Persians' trip south a few months before, the northern Greeks knew what they were in for, and presumably many of them headed for the hills with their food stores. The Persians were reduced in some places to eating grass, herbs, leaves, and bark. Dysentery struck, and some men were sick and had to be left behind, while others died.

When they reached the Greek city of Abdera in Thrace, Xerxes made a treaty of friendship with the men there. As signs of friendship, he gave them a golden dagger and a tiara with gold detail. Presumably they fed the Persians better than the Persians had been used to. At any rate, the Abderans claimed that Xerxes had been so worried on his trip that Abdera was the first place that he loosened his belt since leaving Athens—but Herodotus discounts this story.

When Xerxes' men finally made it to the Hellespont shortly afterward, they met up with the Persian fleet that had sailed north from Phaleron Bay at the end of September. The ships ferried the men across the Hellespont, because the bridges had been shaken loose by storms. In the city of Abydos on the Anatolian side of the strait, the men finally found plenty of food, but their troubles were not over. The hungry men gorged themselves, and that and the change in water led to many additional deaths. The rest of the army continued south to Sardis with Xerxes.

Herodotus, who has little regard for Xerxes as a warrior, says nothing about the Great King's activity in the following year other than the passion he developed for one Artaünte. She was the wife of his brother Masistes, and Xerxes happened to spend time with her in Sardis. He did not consummate the affair until later, when they were both back in Susa. The results were ultimately disastrous, including murder and a rebellion. The moral drawn from all this by Herodotus is that Xerxes was a slave to his lust—and to women.

But although Xerxes may have embarrassed himself in this affair, he is likely to have done serious political and military work in Sardis. In fact, we may imagine him lobbying and pleading and threatening the Ionians to maintain their loyalty to the Great King. And it would be surprising if during the nine months that he spent in Sardis, Xerxes did not consult the strategist who lived only about two hundred miles to the south, the queen of Halicarnassus, who made him think that she fought better than any man in his fleet.

CHAPTER THIRTEEN

≈

ANDROS

There is a strong smell of salt air on the island of Andros, even in the tent, and a man who steps outside will feel a breeze off the water. The sea is dark at night, but the sound of it lapping against the shore is a reminder of its presence. To Eurybiades son of Eurycleides the sea is an unstable thing and sailors are untrustworthy. Although he is commander in chief of the Greek navy, he has never gotten used to sea people and their habit of defying their betters. And being a Spartan, he considers himself to be better than any foreigner. For two months he has had to put up with the disrespect of Themistocles, and he is doing so again tonight in the Greeks' war council. Eurybiades might have wished that he had stayed in Sparta, where he could feel the earth below him and count on the lesser folk to know their place.

So we might imagine the frustrations of the Spartan as his allies continued to argue. It was probably the night of September 27, two days after the battle of Salamis. The Persian fleet had stolen out of Phaleron Bay on the night of September 26. When the Greeks learned that the enemy had given them the slip, they immediately decided to follow. With the Persian navy gone, it was safe to leave just a token force of Greek ships on Salamis.

The Persians had sailed to Athens that summer by following the coast of mainland Greece. That route made strategic sense when they hoped to crush the Greek navy at Artemisium, but it was the long way from Anatolia. Now that they were in a hurry to reach the Hellespont in the fall, the Persians would surely island-hop directly across the Aegean Sea. So the Greeks figured, and they headed straight from Salamis to the enemy's logical first stop: the island of Andros.

Andros is about eighty nautical miles from Salamis, and even oarsmen tired and short-handed after a battle could have made the trip in a day. But hurry as they did to reach Andros, the Greeks did not see any Persian ships there. If they wanted to catch up to the enemy, they would have to head farther away from home. The Athenians were game, but it was more than most of the Greeks had bargained for, so they held a council to decide on their next step. What to do was by no means obvious, because their fortunes had swung back and forth in the past days.

As the Greek triremes had pulled back to Salamis on the evening of September 25, the cheers and congratulations no doubt gave way to the same rush of postbattle activity as in the Persian camp. Surgeons, soldiers, and slaves hurried to help the living and attend to the dead. The

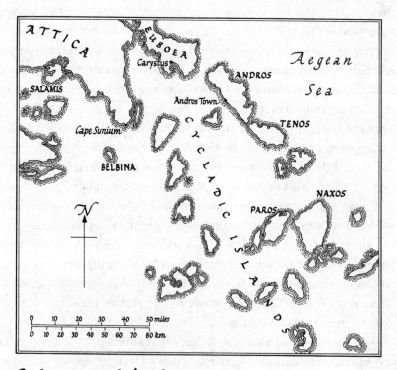

Salamis and Andros

difference, of course, is that at Salamis there would also have been prayers of thanksgiving and maybe even family reunions on the part of Athenian men and their refugee wives and children. And there would have been additional jobs to do.

The Greeks would have hauled onto Salamis whatever wrecks of either fleet were worth saving. After a naval battle, the victors always salvaged boats and towed them ashore. The buoyant wooden hulls of triremes often remained afloat, even after having been rammed. The shipwrights would immediately get busy with repairs to make them seaworthy again. Greek scavengers would scour the straits for hulls, as long as they avoided the Persian archers on the Attic coast, which Xerxes' men still held. It was a reminder that Greece's victory at sea was astonishing but not absolute.

In fact, the Greeks braced themselves after the battle for another attack. They knew that in spite of the damage they had inflicted on Persia's ships, the majority of the enemy's triremes had escaped. In the confusion of battle, the Greeks probably did not know how high a percentage of their kills consisted of the enemy's best ships. And the Greeks' victory was not bloodless: they, too, had suffered casualties and lost ships, if far fewer than the enemy had.

Herodotus calls the Athenian fleet "the salvation of Greece," but the Greeks did not know that yet on the day after the battle of Salamis. They had won a great victory over the Persian fleet but not so great as to destroy it. What they did not understand at first was how great a blow they had struck at Xerxes' will.

When they saw the Persians begin to build a causeway, the Greeks might have groaned at Xerxes' terrible exuberance. Suddenly they had to fear an attack by land as well as by sea. Then came the shock of discovering on the morning of September 27 that the Persian fleet had left Phaleron Bay. We do not know just how the Greeks learned this information, since the enemy vessels had departed at night. Perhaps when no ships approached Salamis that morning, the Greeks sent a small force of ships to investigate and so learned the truth.

The day before, the Greeks would have marveled at the spectacle of Persian corpses on Salamis. Some were men who had tried to struggle ashore, only to be killed by Greek soldiers. Others had washed ashore, but a strong west wind blew up after the battle and carried the dead away from Salamis and toward Attica. Besides, after sinking within a few hours of death, many of the bodies would have stayed at the sea bottom for days until the gases of decay caused them to rise. Eventually, the shores of Salamis and Attica would have stunk of the unmistakable odor of decomposing human flesh.

The dead rowers would have been near naked, but the Persian marines wore gold jewelry, and the grandees even more of it. Booty belonged to the state or, in this case, to the Greek alliance, to be distributed after it was all collected. Still, everyone was a potential freelancer, unable to resist helping himself to whatever piece of treasure he could get away with taking. Consider in this context a story told about Themistocles and a friend. They were walking along the shore after a naval battle, perhaps Salamis, and they saw corpses wash up with gold torques and bracelets. When his friend pointed them out, Themistocles replied, "Help yourself, for you are not Themistocles." A general could not afford to get caught with dirty hands.

We hear nothing about prisoners at Salamis, although there were usually prisoners in naval battles. Wealthy captives would be ransomed and the rest enslaved. It may be that at Salamis the Greeks were too angry to spare enemy lives and the Persians too hard-pressed to stop to take captives. The Persians did capture at least five hundred Athenian civilians in Attica, but they were probably marched back east rather than given valuable space aboard the ships.

The Persian fleet was in a hurry to pull out of Phaleron in any case. To catch them in flight, on September 27 the Greeks launched their "swift ships" of Salamis, as an Athenian victory monument later called them, until the avenging armada reached Andros.

Andros island is big and nearly vertical. Its steep hills, terraced for grain cultivation and for growing figs, olives, and grapes, rise precipitously from the sea like a tan-colored screen, streaked with green, set above an enamel-blue background. Andros is a stepping-stone to Euboea, from which it lies about seven miles away, and to Attica, whose southern tip at Cape Sunium is about forty-five miles away. Andros's location was both its fortune and its bad luck. Eyeing it as a useful stopping point for their ships, the Persians had conquered Andros in 490 B.C. and imposed a tribute, a tax. After Artemisium, they forced the Andrians to contribute ships to their fleet. With Salamis so near, the Andrians had no excuse to sit on the fence. We do not know how their ships fared in the battle, but now that an angry Greek fleet had descended on Andros, the islanders would have a great deal of explaining to do.

Andros Town, the classical city, commanded a wide bay. It sat on the west coast of Andros island, where its harbor was sheltered from the winds. The city was located about halfway down the coast of the long and narrow island, beneath the two peaks of Andros's highest mountain.

Because Andros was hostile to the Greek cause, the commanders probably held their war council outside the city, in one of the tents pitched on the shore beside the moored fleet. It was there that Eurybiades had to put up with Themistocles' challenge. Themistocles behaved with the ease of a man who was still in Salamis, staring across the straits at the familiar hills of Attica. He pressed his case against his commander in chief like a mathematician unveiling a new equation.

Themistocles argued that the road to the Peloponnese ran through the Hellespont. Let the Greeks sail beyond Andros, pursuing the Persian fleet through the islands all the way to the bridges connecting Europe and Asia. The Greeks could finish the job they had started at Salamis: they could defeat the Persians with their ships. Cut off and terrified, Xerxes and his men would practically swim home in their haste to escape.

Even if he was not to be moved by pity for the dispossessed, surely Eurybiades was ready to bow to Themistocles' strategic genius, now that it had proven itself in the bloodstained sea at Salamis. No, yielding was un-Spartan. Tyrtaeus, favorite poet in Sparta, summed up the national ethos in his ode to battle: "So let each stand his ground firmly with his feet well set apart and bite his lip."

But Eurybiades stood up to the Athenian and drew others to his banner. The commanders from Aegina and other islands might have agreed with Themistocles, but the mainlanders surely thought that victory had driven him mad. Even as the Greeks sat on Andros, Xerxes still occupied Athens, and the Persian army was marching toward the Isthmus. Raised in a world where battles were decided by men who fought on land, most Greeks would have thought it obvious that the road to the Peloponnese ran through the Isthmus of Corinth. What good would it do to break the bridges at the Hellespont when the Persian army was still at large and dangerous in the Greek homeland?

Eurybiades argued that far from trapping Xerxes in Greece, they should do everything to encourage him to go home. Leave the bridges alone; allow Xerxes to cross them. To isolate him in Greece would be like cornering a hungry lion. The barbarian would then spring back more ferociously than ever, threatening to conquer the cities of Greece one by one. In fact, it was likely that the Persians would now leave Greece, since they no longer had a navy and since they were short of food.

We might imagine that Eurybiades had another, perhaps unspoken, reason for opposing Themistocles' plan. To concede the supremacy of sea power would amount to announcing the supremacy of Athens.

Themistocles was only speaking for his countrymen, since most Athenians agreed with him. They were in no mood to sit in exile on Salamis and wait patiently while the Persians decided what to do. Victory in the straits had convinced them of what they might have suspected at Artemisium: they had built the most effective navy in the eastern Mediterranean. From the Adriatic to the Nile, no sea power could challenge the Athenian fleet. And having realized this, the Athenians wished to shout it from the rooftops.

But they were not prepared to do it over the opposition of the rest of the Greeks. Or rather, Themistocles was not ready to lead his countrymen down that road alone. When he realized that he could not win the debate in the war council, Themistocles decided to give in. He would accept the argument of the majority of the allies and turn the fleet back to the mainland. First, he had to convince the Athenians. The men of the Athenian fleet would not have hesitated to leave their allies at Andros and go after the Persians on their own.

Themistocles left the council and called a meeting of the Athenians. Sitting outside near their ships, they would have represented no small gathering of men. Athens had mustered 180 triremes at Salamis. Assuming that it had lost some ships in the battle, that others needed repairs, and that others had been left to guard the island, Athens might easily have sent a hundred ships to Andros. No doubt some of these boats had lost men in the battle, and no doubt some of the crews were slaves and so ineligible to attend assemblies, but it would not be surprising if about fifteen thousand Athenian citizens or more heard Themistocles on Andros.

Themistocles sounded three themes: strategy, religion, and Athenian self-interest. Now that he had established himself as a military genius among his own people, Themistocles spoke in the sharp, short sayings of a man polishing his reputation. "Forced to fight," he said, "defeated men battle back and repair their earlier cowardice." He agreed with Eurybiades that it would be dangerous to trap the Persians in Greece.

Turning to religion, Themistocles said that it was not the men of Greece who had pushed back "a great cloud of men," but rather it was "the gods and heroes who were jealous that one man—and an impious and wicked man—should rule both Asia and Europe." Then he recited a list of Xerxes' crimes against temples, statues of the gods, and even the sea, which he had whipped and fettered as punishment of the Hellespont for spoiling the Persians' first attempt to bridge it.

Tempted to pass over these nods to piety, the modern reader should remember how fine a line there was for the Greeks between the human and divine worlds. For example, when a Greek wanted to say that he understood the limits of naval technology, he might have said he was a god-fearing person who respected the power of the sea god, Poseidon. And when he wanted to say that the Greeks had cleverly made use of nature at Salamis, from the narrowness of the straits to the force of the wind, he might have cited the help of the gods and heroes.

Finally, Themistocles advised the Athenians to think about their families, to rebuild their homes and plant their crops. In the spring they would sail for the Hellespont and for Ionia. Since the Persians were still in Attica, he was promising something he could not deliver—like many a politician. No doubt it was unnecessary to explain to his listeners that the Persians could not stay in Attica much longer, since they lacked food. But it was bold to promise a naval offensive in the next year, and one that would not stop at the Hellespont but would include Ionia!

Themistocles won the day with these words. He had done some fast talking, but he then followed it with outright treason. Or so Herodotus says: he reports that Themistocles sent a small ship back to Athens, perhaps a ten-oared vessel with a sail. He had staffed it entirely with close associates, men whom he trusted to stay loyal even if tortured. His slave Sicinnus was among them. They made for Phaleron and the Persian camp. There, while everyone else stayed aboard ship, Sicinnus got off and delivered a message to Xerxes.

It is a sign of how terrified the men were that they stayed on board. A small boat could not have reached Attica quickly from Andros, and the crew would normally have been eager to get on dry land. But they were also eager to survive. The intrepid Sicinnus told the Great King that he had a message from Themistocles. The clever Athenian wanted to do the king a favor, so he reported to him that the Greeks were following his fleet and planned to break the bridges at the Hellespont. The coast was clear for Xerxes to depart overland in peace.

It may seem strange that, after Salamis, Xerxes was willing to hear out Sicinnus again instead of having him hauled off and beheaded. But the story may show just how slippery Sicinnus and his master were. They might have argued that Themistocles' message before Salamis was true as, after all, it largely was. If Panaetius the Tenian deserter had not warned the Greeks, they would have been surprised by the Persians and Xerxes would have won. And so, having delivered a second message, Sicinnus would have made everyone happy, even if the message was completely false. Xerxes and his army, who had to decamp for the winter, would leave Attica all the sooner; Themistocles had the satisfaction of having contributed to the liberation of his homeland while also keeping open his pipeline to the enemy; and Sicinnus and his crewmates escaped back to Andros.

But a question remains: was Eurybiades right in holding back the Greek fleet? In the short term, he probably was right, because autumn, with its risk of storms, was the wrong season for a naval offensive. But in the long term he was wrong. The Greeks would have been foolish not to attack the Persian fleet in the following year, before the Persians had a chance to repair their broken navy. If the Greeks could keep the enemy from projecting naval power across the Aegean Sea, they would make it very, very difficult for Persia to conquer Greece. As for Eurybiades' argument that holding Xerxes in Greece would only force him to attack, the big question was whether the Persians could beat the Spartan-led Greek army at the Isthmus before the Persians' food supply ran out. An answer would have tested Sparta forcefully: no wonder Eurybiades preferred not to seek the answer.

Deprived of his naval offensive, Themistocles next did a remarkable thing. He and his allies had stood up to Persia in the name of liberty. They preferred death to giving the Great King earth and water and submitting to his demand that they pay tribute. The islanders of the Aegean had been forced by the Persian navy to do just that. Most of them, like

Andros, had fought for Xerxes at Salamis, but it would have taken exceptional bravery to have done otherwise. Now that the Greeks had defeated the Persian fleet, they sailed to Andros and announced its freedom.

But Themistocles asked the Andrians to pay tribute to *his* fleet. In other words, he told them that they had, in effect, exchanged one master for another. The Andrians, who might have been dumbfounded by the demand, refused. Never at a loss for words, Themistocles said that Athens had two great goddesses who would demand the money: Persuasion and Necessity. Not to be outdone, the Andrians replied that they had two great goddesses of their own, Poverty and Hardship, and could not pay.

The wordplay was elegant but it gave way to force. The Greeks laid siege to Andros in order to get the money they had asked for. Andros Town sat on a steep hill that climbs spectacularly from the sea to the acropolis, which enjoys a height of about 1,250 feet, more than twice as high as the Acropolis of Athens. The city was protected by a well-built stone wall that connected harbor and acropolis. A sensible man would have shuddered at trying to take a fortress like this by siege. By even attempting to conquer the city, the Greeks might just have been trying to put the best face on the Andrians' refusal to meet their demand for tribute. In any case, the siege could not have lasted long, since the Greeks moved on next to Euboea and then Sparta. Then the sailing season was near its end. Andros remained unconquered.

Yet quietly and apparently without a moment of hesitation, the Greeks had started a paradoxical venture. If a philosopher had asked Themistocles how he could defend Athenian freedom in one breath and attack Andrian freedom in the next, he might have shrugged off the contradiction. People on a god-given mission to liberate their homeland tend not to let inconsistency stop them.

Besides, the Greeks made no bones about the victor's right to the spoils. After the battle of Marathon in 490 B.C., Athens's triumphant commander Miltiades led a naval expedition to the island of Paros. It was a Persian ally and a very wealthy island. Miltiades promised his fellow citizens gold on Paros. But their siege of Paros failed. Miltiades was wounded, and all he got for his pains when he returned home was a jury that imposed a big fine on him for incompetence; he would have had to pay it, but he died first of his wounds. No wonder Themistocles was relentless at Andros.

He certainly did not single out Andros in his desire for money. After Sicinnus and his crew returned from Phaleron, Themistocles sent them to the other nearby Greek islands that had supported Persia. Their message was the same as at Andros: pay up or suffer siege and destruction. Paros, which had held its triremes back from Xerxes until the outcome of Salamis was clear, yielded to the demand, as did Carystus, a city in southern Euboea. Other islands may have contributed as well; the evidence is unclear.

It would be easy to criticize Themistocles for extorting money, especially because he kept it secret from his fellow Greek commanders. But remember that all of the cities that Themistocles held up had supported the attack on Athens; that a navy was very expensive to maintain; and that Sparta and the other Peloponnesian states had been ready only a few days before to abandon every last inch of Athenian territory. And if Themistocles kept for himself some of the money that was collected, remember, too, that he was not paid a thing by Athens for his public service.

But Themistocles probably should be taken to task for the attack on Carystus. When the siege of Andros failed, the Greek fleet made a short journey northward to Euboea. Carystus was the main city of southern Euboea. Its steep acropolis lay several miles inland from the coast. A siege would have been no more successful than it had been at Andros, so the Greeks contented themselves with doing some damage to Carystus's countryside. This might have meant looting farmhouses, trampling on grapevines, and hacking at some olive trees while a terrified populace huddled within the walls of the town. If Eurybiades had known that the former Persian ally already was paying protection money to Athens, he might have spared it. Then again, it seems that Carystus had skimped, compared to Paros, which paid Themistocles enough to deter an attack, so the Euboean city bears some blame for its misery.

The Greek navy next returned to Salamis. By now, Xerxes and the Persian army had pulled back from Athens into northern Greece. That meant, first and foremost, that the Athenians could go back to their homes. From Troezen and Aegina, and above all from Salamis, there was a mass movement of return. We would expect that the Athenian navy helped people get home, just as it had taken part in the evacuation.

Attica itself was probably largely intact. The Persians had not been there long enough to inflict deep devastation on the land's infrastructure. But they had gone after prestige targets. Besides destroying temples and overturning statues, they had carried off works of art with them back to Anatolia. The most famous losses were a bronze statue of the goddess Artemis, taken from her rural shrine at Brauron, and a set of statues of the heroes Harmodius and Aristogeiton. The images of these two men, honored as tyrant slayers, were taken from the Athenian Acropolis to Xerxes' palace at Persepolis, in southwestern Iran. When Alexander the Great arrived there as a conqueror in 330 B.C., he arranged for the statues to be brought back to Greece. The originals have disappeared, but Roman-era copies of excellent quality still survive.

On Salamis, the commanders had the breathing space to take care of an important post-battle ritual: distributing booty. It was standard procedure for the victors to comb the field—or the ships and the shore—for anything worth taking. Afterward, it was up to the commanders to parcel out the loot. It was to be expected that each commander would keep something for himself. And valor on the battlefield would also be rewarded.

After the battle, all the talk was of the bravery of Aegina, followed by that of Athens. Plunder was distributed accordingly. The gods were rewarded before cities or individuals. The Greek way was to dedicate one tenth of the booty, the so-called first fruits, to the gods. The Salamis tithe consisted of various objects, including three Phoenician triremes, one at Salamis, as an offering to Ajax, and the other two as offerings to Poseidon, one at Cape Sunium in Attica and the other at the Panhellenic shrine at the Isthmus. This was the ship that Herodotus reported seeing fifty years after the battle.

The shrine of Apollo at Delphi was the holiest site in Greece and it, too, had to receive a thank-offering. The fleet at Salamis sent enough booty to Delphi to erect an almost eighteen-foot-high bronze statue of Apollo holding the stern ornament of a ship in his hand. But the priests of Delphi let it be known that the god Apollo felt shortchanged by Aegina, the biggest single beneficiary of the plunder of Salamis. The Aeginetans made amends by building a monument at Delphi consisting of three gold stars on a bronze mast, which Herodotus also saw.

After dividing the booty, the Greek allies left Salamis. They were finally going to the Isthmus. After they launched their ships and began the trip, as the island disappeared in the distance, it might have occurred to someone aboard one of the departing triremes just how much the world had changed since the night of September 24–25, when the Greek move to the Isthmus had been interrupted by the news that the enemy had surrounded them at Salamis.

Isthmia was a religious shrine, sacred to Poseidon, lord of the sea. It was also territory that belonged to Corinth. Isthmia lay just beyond the makeshift wall thrown up a month earlier to stop the Persians. Here, the ongoing threat to Greece would have often intruded into men's minds. It was not the place for calm reflection, but it was where the alliance had chosen to make an important decision.

The commanders were to choose which one of them should be awarded a prize for bravery at Salamis. Each man's career, and the honor that every Greek craved, depended on the result. To win the vote would be splendid; to support a loser would be fatal. In what might have been an effort to substitute solemnity for favoritism, the commanders followed a ritual voting procedure: one by one, they were to walk up to the altar of Poseidon and each deposit his ballot.

But unfortunately, nobody rose to the occasion. Each general without exception voted for himself. But he was also asked to award second place. On this matter, a majority—though not all—voted for Themistocles. But jealousy prevented the awarding of any prize. The navy was disbanded and the commanders each sailed home, but not without a murmur making the rounds, as Herodotus reports:

> *Themistocles' name was the cry of the hour, and it was agreed that he was the smartest man in all of Greece.*

But an ambitious man like Themistocles wanted more than a murmur of support; he wanted formal recognition. He had not received it from his comrades at Salamis nor was he likely to get it from his fellow citizens in Athens. Democracy distrusts great men, and Themistocles was not ashamed about reminding Athenians of his greatness. We can detect the signs of a postwar debate in Athens as to whether Salamis was a victory of the Athenian people or of their most famous strategist. Besides, it is human nature to hate those who see our secret weakness, and Themistocles had seen his countrymen at their most vulnerable.

A revealing anecdote is told about a certain Athenian named Timodemus of the deme of Aphidna. He was an insignificant person whose jealousy of Themistocles verged on insanity but brought him into the public eye. Timodemus constantly told Themistocles that he would have been nothing had he not been an Athenian. Finally, Themistocles swatted his enemy down with a witticism: "If I came from [the tiny islet of] Belbina," Themistocles said, "I'd be nothing, but even though you are an Athenian, Timodemus, you are still nothing." Timodemus may have been a buffoon, but behind him, one suspects, there stood thousands of Athenians who each felt that in his private sacrifice—from fighting on a ship in the straits to living off the handouts of strangers in exile—he or she had made a difference. And none of them wished to bow down before a statue of Themistocles, however much he might have deserved their curtsy.

Disrespected in his own city-state, Themistocles had to go to Sparta to achieve recognition. If this seems strange, remember that the more Sparta glorified Themistocles, the less it had to honor its own hero, Eurybiades. Spartans liked the cult of personality no more than Athenians did. So they chose the perfect gesture to force Themistocles and Eurybiades to share their glory: they gave them each an olive wreath, Eurybiades for bravery and Themistocles for wisdom and dexterity. It was as much as saying that neither man could quite have won the victory alone.

The Spartans also gave Themistocles a chariot, the most beautiful available in Sparta. It was probably a fairly plain affair, given how much Spartans disliked luxury. But no one could deny the praise that was heaped on Themistocles in Sparta. The most striking thing of all was the escort that he received: three hundred picked men accompanied Themistocles to the border when he left. Herodotus knew of no other man in history to have received this honor from Sparta. And the number three hundred, of course, recalled the number of men who died with Leonidas at Thermopylae. To be sure, this tended to downplay the battle of Salamis, but let us give the man his due: the gesture also meant that the greatest military power in the history of the Greeks associated Themistocles with their finest hour.

It could not have been easy to go back to the plain homespun of democratic Athens, especially of an Athens in mourning. To the loss of its religious heart on the Acropolis, add Athens's experience of death, dislocation, and devastation. Athenians had died at Artemisium, on the Acropolis, and in the straits of Salamis; Athenians had been dragged off in slavery to the east. A society in which suffering had been spread as evenly as it had in Athens was ready to draw an unknown soldier to its breast, but it was in no mood to crown a king.

When the war began again in the spring of 479 B.C., Themistocles commanded no Athenian army. The generals of the day were his old rivals, Aristides and Xanthippus. In all likelihood, Themistocles had failed to be reelected to the annually chosen board of ten generals, but in any case, he was out of favor. It would not be the last time that a democracy dropped a dominant leader.

To jealousy and fear of ambition, we might add another reason for Themistocles' eclipse at home, and that is the dawning realization that the war was not over. Themistocles had been the architect of a naval strategy. Its brilliant success now guaranteed its eclipse. A second Salamis would not save Greece: this time, an infantry battle loomed.

To put it in more modern terms, Salamis was a Greek Gettysburg; it was not Appomattox Courthouse. Salamis was Stalingrad, not the battle of Berlin. Salamis was a decisive battle because it broke the Persian navy, but it did not drive the Persians out of Greece. Salamis brought final victory nearly into the Greeks' hands, but it was not the last battle of the war.

Contrary to what Eurybiades had predicted at Andros in the autumn of 480 B.C., the Persians did not all leave Greece. A large enemy army remained on the Greek peninsula, threatening Attica and the Peloponnese beyond, and aided and comforted by such famous Greek states as Macedon and Thebes. In the end, only a wall of Spartan spears and a sea of Spartan blood would drive them out. The result would bring glory to Sparta but not to Eurybiades, for he was an admiral and not a general. And Athens would gain glory too, for its spearmen stood in the front lines as well and fought hard, but none of that glory would go to Themistocles.

Still, glory is not the same as power. In the aftermath of the Greek victory on land at Plataea and both on land and at sea at Mycale (a battle in 479 B.C.), Themistocles' star rose again in Athens. As soon as they had driven Persia out of Greece, the Greeks turned on each other. To stand up to Sparta, the Athenians needed a leader who was not only brave, but ruthless and devious. Neither the ham-fisted heroics of Aristides nor the stubborn energy of Xanthippus was enough. Only Themistocles and his webs of intrigue would do.

Returned to power, Themistocles managed to defy Sparta and rebuild the walls of Athens (the Persians had destroyed them). He did this by lying through his teeth to the Spartans, his former friends. By using diplomacy as a delaying tactic, Themistocles kept them from discovering that Athens was rebuilding its walls—until it was too late. The Spartans were furious, but Athens protected itself from outside interference. Themistocles also got the Athenians to finish fortifying their new harbor at Piraeus, a project he had begun years before but which had not been completed.

Themistocles served during these years as the leading spokesman for the viewpoint that Athens's future lay at sea. He was a tireless advocate of naval power. He urged Athenians to move to Piraeus, to find work in the dockyards there, and to think of Athens as a maritime country. In other words, he said that the fleet of Salamis was no aberration but the real Athens.

Themistocles was a revolutionary and creative thinker. But like many a prophet, he lacked honor in his homeland. His political base in the 470s was narrow, and he did not play a major role in setting up the new naval confederacy of Delos that Athens established in 477 B.C. The leadership in Athens passed to other shoulders.

And yet Themistocles was truly the father of the new Athens. He had founded the fleet and so had saved his country. But by raising Athens's power to new heights, Themistocles also sowed the seeds of a new conflict. Fifty years after Salamis, the two former allies against Persia would lead the entire Greek world into a new and even more destructive conflict. The Peloponnesian War (431–404 B.C.) was brutal enough to make many long for the good old days of the barbarian invasion.

For two months at the moment of their civilization's greatest danger, Themistocles and Eurybiades had put rivalry aside. Their common effort saved Greece. But only for a while: Greek indifference to the long-term dangers of competition ultimately doomed it. The image of an Athenian and a Spartan standing side by side, each crowned with a victor's wreath, would not be seen again.

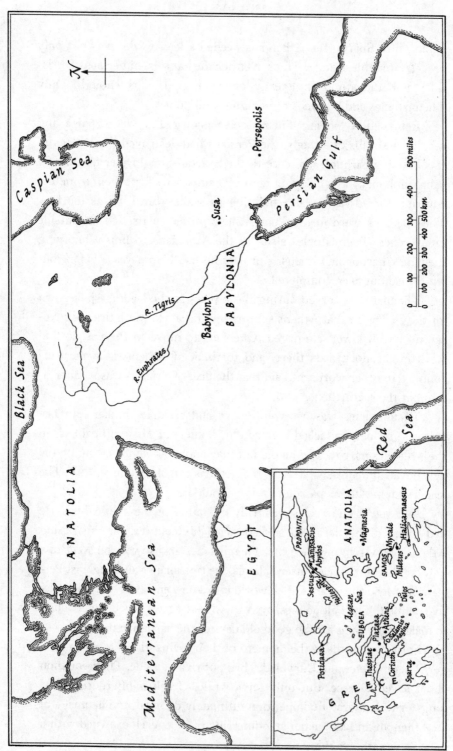

Greece and the Ancient Near East

EPILOGUE

≋

SUSA

He stands at the doorway of the throne room. He is poised to begin the next act in a life that already has enough drama for the most demanding muse. Themistocles is more than two thousand miles from home, but he has not seen home in years. First he was exiled from Athens in a season of political infighting. Then he was accused of treason and had to run for his life. He traveled from one end of the Greek world to the other; he begged, bribed, flirted, networked, tricked, threatened, befriended, and finally flattered his way to Persia. He has made the latest gamble in a life full of risks. Now it is time to see if it will pay off: Themistocles is about to meet the Great King. The date is probably early in the year 464 B.C. The place is the royal palace in the city of Susa, which, along with Persepolis, was a capital.

Themistocles had suffered the fate of many a politician in a democracy. The people like their leaders to rise high and to fall fast. The longer a successful politician stays on the scene, the more the public worries about what he wants. A man as cunning as Themistocles made people nervous, and it did not help to have him build a temple in Athens to Artemis of Good Advice, as if to trumpet his own genius. His political enemies were glad to unite against him, and in the late 470s he was ostracized. He lived in exile in Argos, a Spartan enemy in the Peloponnese. A few years later, Sparta claimed to find evidence that Themistocles was a Persian agent, and he fled Argos. After many adventures, he reached Susa.

With his round face and his coarse and fleshy features, Themistocles did not look like what the Persian king might have expected. How different he appeared from the statues brought back from Athens by the Persian army; those statues all had long, lean faces with tidy features. The Greek visitor who stood at the entrance to the royal audience hall looked more like a brute than a hero.

But the young king knew perfectly well who the Greek was. Artaxerxes had not been on the throne long, but he had been thoroughly briefed by his advisers. He had become king after the assassination in August 465 B.C. of his father, His Royal Majesty of Blessed Memory, Xerxes son of Darius, King of Kings. Xerxes was murdered in a court intrigue. And now, Artaxerxes, seated on his throne, was about to receive his father's old foe. Of all the double-dealing Greeks who stank of the salt air of the Aegean Sea, none was more treacherous than Themistocles.

Artaxerxes surely knew it. Neither he nor his advisers was likely to have been fooled by the letter written to him by Themistocles, in which the Athenian claimed that he had saved Xerxes in 480 B.C. by talking the Greeks out of destroying the bridges over the Hellespont. At the sight of Themistocles, Artaxerxes might have wanted to get up and grab a spear from one of his bodyguards and run the rotten Athenian through. But then, he probably also knew that the old Greek would be full of precious secrets. And having Themistocles on the Persian payroll was a propaganda bonanza. And so young Artaxerxes received in the hall of the heir of Cyrus the Great the worst enemy that his beloved father had ever faced.

The Greeks might have been surprised to know it, but the Persians probably mourned Xerxes as a great man. During his reign, Xerxes was a builder who constructed the greatest of the royal palaces at the city of Persepolis. He was a warrior who crushed rebellions in Egypt and Babylon. And he was a strategist who might have been remembered in Persia not as the man who lost a war with Greece but, rather, as the king who rectified the western border. Xerxes understood, as others did not, that the forces of the empire were spread too thin. It was necessary to pull back the imperial borders in the West. But first, he taught the Greeks a lesson.

The Great King's expedition to the land of the Greek barbarians truly represented one of the greatest achievements in history, or so the Persians might have thought. With the help of heaven, the King of Kings bridged the Hellespont. He gathered so many troops and ships that they darkened the horizon. After forcing every city in his path to offer him its hospitality, His Majesty crushed the Spartan army at Thermopylae and killed the evil king Leonidas. Then he took Athens, burned to the ground the temples of the false and lying gods, devastated the land, and sold into slavery all the inhabitants who had not fled. Having subjected to his will every land from Thrace to the Isthmus of Corinth, His Majesty imposed tribute and returned in the finest of form to Anatolia.

There were, of course, the usual errors made by the Great King's slaves. The unfortunate Mardonius lost his life in an ambush by Greek barbarians when his army was withdrawing after its pacification campaign. And Artaxerxes had heard something about a skirmish of ships near some island called Salamis, in which the king of Sidon had been embarrassed by certain Greek captains. But after making a show of force, the Persian army had withdrawn behind secure borders.

In 477 B.C. Athens had created a new naval alliance of Greek city-states. It was formed on the island of Delos, located in the central part of the Aegean Sea and sacred to the god Apollo. Historians usually refer to the alliance as the Delian League. This alliance consisted of about 150 Greek city-states of the Aegean islands, Euboea and the northeastern coast of Greece, the Sea of Marmara, and the west coast of Anatolia. Athens held the rank of leader of the alliance. Many of these city-states had formerly been subjects of the Great King.

Persia required its subjects to pay tribute. Athens did the same thing. To be effective, the Delian League needed to have a strong fleet, and naval power was expensive. So with the exception of a few member states, who contributed warships or men, all of the members of the Delian League paid tribute to Athens. The Greek city-states substituted one imperial power for another.

From its very founding, the Delian League committed itself to expansion. Not only did its members promise to defend Greece against any new attack by Persia, they also swore to attack the lands of the Great King in order to avenge the damage done to Greece by Xerxes in 480 B.C. and to acquire booty.

The Delian League was created and grew at Persia's expense, but the Persians might have taken it in stride. They might have seen things like this: just because the Persian imperial treasury had liquidated the cost of maintaining tyrants in Greek cities like Samos and Miletus, which now belonged to the Delian League, a certain amount of nonsense had been bruited about as to the liberation of the Ionians. The Greeks might babble on, but the Persian satrap of Ionia still sat in Sardis. Persian horsemen continued to ride the rich river valleys of Anatolia that run inland from the Aegean Sea. Some Greek cities on the Anatolian coast still paid the Great King's annual tribute; what difference did it make if some of them also paid out protection money to the Athenians?

Meanwhile, the strategy of His Late Majesty, may his name be blessed, had worked beautifully. The Greek barbarians had been left to do what they did best: kill each other. Athens was building up a naval empire in the Aegean Sea, while the Spartans fumed and plotted a war against the rising power of Athens before it became too late.

Artaxerxes could not know it, but the Persian Empire would last another 150 years after Salamis. There would be no more expansion, but after the losses to Athens of the 470s and 460s, the Persians would manage to hold on to their empire, with only the occasional rebellion to suppress here and there. The Delian League lasted just seventy-five years. After it disappeared in 404 B.C., the Great King used a combination of diplomacy and bribery to keep the Greeks divided and off guard. Only the rise of a new power, Macedonia, led by its kings Philip and Alexander, finally brought down the Persian Empire in 330 B.C.

Meanwhile, the Persians could have smiled knowingly at the saying that imitation is the sincerest sort of flattery. No sooner was the Delian League founded than it began to look a lot like the Persian Empire. Athenian allies rose in revolt as Persian allies had done in the past. Athenian generals sailed out with fleets to fight rebels, whom they then executed or enslaved just as the Persians had tried to do to Athenians at Salamis. Athenian politicians began to put on imperial airs, writing memos not about their "allies" but "the cities Athens controls." Athenian consumers developed a taste for Persian clothes and Persian art—but that only made sense, because imperial powers are naturally attracted to each other.

Within two generations of creating one of the world's first democracies, Athens had achieved the remarkable feat of also creating the world's first imperial democracy. At home, Athens stood for freedom and equality. Abroad, Athens did not hesitate to use any means necessary in order to enforce the authority of the league that it led. After making a heroic stand against Xerxes in the name of freedom, Athens had discovered that in order to maintain its freedom, it would have to make difficult compromises abroad.

Salamis, it has been said, was a great battle because, without that victory, the world would have been deprived of the glory that was Greece. But that underestimates the resiliency and the drive of Greek civilization.

If the Greeks had lost at Salamis, Xerxes would have gone on to conquer the Peloponnese. Themistocles and the surviving Athenians would have fled to southern Italy. And there, they might well have recovered. Just as mainland Greece saved Ionia in 480 B.C. and afterward, so Greek Italy might have saved mainland Greece. Athens in exile might have roused the western Greeks to arms against the invader. Together, they might eventually have sailed back to Greece and driven out the barbarian with blood and iron.

Or perhaps the exiles would have stayed in southern Italy. They might have thrived there. So even if the Greeks had lost at Salamis, the ancient Greeks might well have gone on to create classical civilization— in exile in Italy. But they would not have invented imperial democracy.

Defeat at Salamis would not have deprived the world of Greece's glory but of its guile and greed. Salamis offered Athens the first taste of the temptation that it could not resist. Thanks to Salamis, Athens was free and Greece would be enslaved. Democracy was saved and the Athenian empire was born.

And it was precisely the contradiction of democracy and empire that made Athens so exciting for a century and more after Salamis. Athens failed to live up to its ideal of freedom, and failure generated critics. They included historians like Herodotus and Thucydides and poets like Sophocles and Euripides and Aristophanes. And they included the most cutting critic of them all: Socrates. And Socrates led to Plato, Aristotle, and the Western tradition of political philosophy. That tradition, the debate over democracy and its discontents, is the true legacy of

Salamis, and the final reason it might just have been the greatest battle of the ancient world—and certainly its greatest naval battle.

In the years after Salamis, Athens headed down the road of democracy and empire. Meanwhile, the steady stream of Greek political exiles to the Great King's court did not stop flowing. And now—to return to the scene at Susa in 464 B.C.—Artaxerxes son of Xerxes an Achaemenid the King of Kings was about to pick the finest fruit of all.

The Great King motioned for the Greek stranger to enter. Themistocles advanced. They say that Greeks were too proud and freedom-loving to bow down to the ground before the Great King as all his subjects did. We do not know how Themistocles behaved on the occasion, but afterward gossip claimed that he prostrated himself without hesitation.

That night, the story goes, Artaxerxes called out three times in his sleep: "I have Themistocles the Athenian!"

Themistocles' audience with Artaxerxes was a success. The Athenian asked for and received a year to learn the Persian language and Persian customs. When he returned to see the Great King again, he impressed Artaxerxes as a man of genius. The king made Themistocles governor of the Ionian city of Magnesia, located inland in the rich valley of the Meander River. Magnesia was to provide Themistocles "his bread," and he was also given control of the nearby city of Myos "for his meat" and of the city of Lampsacus on the Hellespont "for his wine," the Lampsacus region being famous for its wines. Themistocles' family had joined him in exile, and in Magnesia his female relatives served as priestesses of the temple of Artemis.

And so the strategist of victory over the Persian fleet at Salamis, the battle that began the transfer of the Aegean Sea from Persian to Greek control; the founder of the Athenian navy and the visionary who turned his native city from a second-rate land power into a maritime giant; the man who had humiliated Xerxes and smashed his sea power—this man now crossed the Aegean Sea to live out his life in comfortable exile with his family, an administrator in the Persian provinces and a vassal of Xerxes' son, the Great King Artaxerxes I.

Themistocles died in Magnesia in 459 B.C. Egypt had risen in revolt from Persia again, and Athens had sent ships to the Nile to help the rebels. Legend says that Themistocles poisoned himself rather than follow the Great King's order to make war on Athens. But he probably died of natural causes. A monument to Themistocles was put up in the marketplace of Magnesia. Meanwhile, his family followed his last wish by secretly bringing his bones home and reburying them in Athenian soil. Or so it was said. Certainly, Athenian law forbade the burial in Attica of a traitor, as Themistocles had been judged. But there were probably many Athenians in 459 B.C. who would have been happy to honor their old commander with a good Greek grave at home.

Themistocles was not the only veteran of Salamis to see his life take unexpected turns after the battle. Consider the Greek side first, beginning with Athenians. In 480 B.C., Themistocles' old rival Aristides still had his finest hour ahead. In August 479 Aristides commanded Athens's infantry at the battle of Plataea, thereby going down in history as one of Greece's saviors. Not long afterward, Aristides helped Themistocles trick the Spartans while Athens surrounded itself with a defensive wall. In 477, Aristides made the first assessment of tribute for the members of the Delian League. But little money stuck to his fingers, because when he died around 468, he died a poor man. He was buried at Phaleron, a fitting reminder of the night when Aristides helped tip the balance against the Persian fleet that was moored there. His son, Lysimachus, was a famous failure; his grandson, also named Aristides, probably died in active service during the Peloponnesian War.

Aeschylus went on after 480 B.C. to great glory as a dramatist. In addition to the plays *The Persians* in 472 and *Seven Against Thebes* in 467, he offered his classic trilogy *Oresteia* in 458. Afterward he visited Greek Sicily, where he died and was buried in the city of Gela in 456. Two of his sons also became dramatists.

After his victory in the battle of Mycale in 479 B.C., the Athenian general Xanthippus sailed to the Hellespont to lay siege to the city of Sestus. Sestus sits on the European side of the Hellespont, opposite the city of Abydos: the twin cities command the crossing of the strait. In fact, Sestus was the first European city entered by Xerxes when he crossed the Hellespont in 480 B.C. After a months-long siege, Sestus fell to Xanthippus and his men in the spring of 478.

Xanthippus died not long afterward (the precise year is not

known), but he left behind a very ambitious son: Pericles. A teenage refugee in 480 B.C., Pericles eventually became first man in Athens. But first he had to defeat a rival. Cimon, the clever young conservative who hung up his horse bridle before Salamis, dominated Athenian politics in the 460s. He won big victories in the East against Persia. But Pericles managed to discredit Cimon and replace him.

From 460 to 430 B.C., Pericles would lead Athens to its Golden Age. It was under Pericles that the city completed its democratic revolution. It was under Pericles as well that the Delian League became the greatest maritime empire that the Mediterranean had ever known. With the tribute collected from that empire, Pericles funded the greatest building project in Greek history: Athens rebuilt the temples on the Acropolis that Xerxes' men had destroyed in September 480. Forty-two years later, in 438 B.C., the centerpiece of that rebuilding program was dedicated—the most famous building of ancient Greece: the Parthenon.

Sicinnus, the slave of Themistocles, presumably lived out his days comfortably as a citizen of the small city-state of Thespiae in central Greece. Thespiae lies to the west of Thebes, in a fertile valley in the foothills of Mount Helicon, known in legend as the home of the Muses. In its heroic days in 480 B.C., Thespiae stood up to Xerxes and was destroyed. But the city that was rebuilt after the war had time to devote to its favorite deity, Eros, the god of love. Sicinnus, we may imagine, enjoyed life as a Thespian, telling stories about his fateful meetings with the Great King.

In the Peloponnese, Adimantus of Corinth passed on his grudge against Athens to the next generation. His son Aristeas, a charismatic military commander, led a Corinthian force of so-called volunteers in an undeclared conflict with Athens in 432 B.C. When the Peloponnesian War formally broke out soon afterward, Aristeas went on a military mission to the Great King, whose aid he wanted to enlist against Athens. But Aristeas was captured en route and executed by the Athenian state in 430 B.C.

It is unclear whether Phayllos ever made it home again to Croton, but his memory lived on. After conquering the Persian army at the battle of Gaugamela in northern Iraq in 330 B.C. Alexander the Great sent a portion of the booty to far-off Croton, in recognition of Phayllos's contribution to victory at Salamis.

Some of the other principals in the battle of Salamis leave no trace in the historical record after 480 B.C. Eurybiades of Sparta, for instance, commander of the Greek fleet, is not heard of again, nor is the hardy Aeginetan marine Pytheas of Aegina, nor the proud Aeginetan captain Polycritus, nor the Athenian ace Aminias of Pallene. On the Persian side, Tetramnestus, king of Sidon, is not attested after Salamis. The eunuch Hermotimus disappears after 480 into the winding corridors of the palaces at Persepolis and Susa.

Mardonius, the chief war hawk of Xerxes' expedition, died on the battlefield at Plataea in 479 B.C. One of his daggers ended up in Athens, on the Acropolis, as part of the Athenian share of enemy booty, a total take amounting to five hundred talents, which represented three million days' wages at the time. Mardonius's dagger weighed five and a half pounds. Apparently it was made of pure gold.

Xerxes' brother and Artaxerxes' uncle Achaemenes was still alive in 464 B.C. He was governor of Egypt (at Salamis, he had commanded the Egyptian squadron). He would die fighting an Egyptian rebellion in 459.

An anecdote survives that Xerxes rewarded Demaratus of Sparta for having told him the hard truth about the enemy's strength: he let him name the reward of his choice. Demaratus is supposed to have asked to enter the city of Sardis, the pride of Anatolia, riding in a chariot and wearing the tiara, the privilege of royalty. In other words, Demaratus asked to be recognized again as a king, and with a Near Eastern splendor unheard of in Sparta. Whether or not there is any truth in this story, it is certain that Demaratus and his descendants continued to flourish in the Persian Empire. Darius had given the Spartan exile land and the governorship of three Anatolian cities not far from Troy: Halisarna, Teuthrania, and Pergamum. And his descendants would weather every storm to maintain their grip on these cities for two centuries, until after the death of Alexander the Great.

No details survive of Artemisia's activities after 480 B.C. We do not know how or when she died. But the dynasty that she had worked so hard to promote during Xerxes' expedition was still alive and well a generation later. Sometime around 460 or 450 B.C., her son or nephew Lygdamis ruled as king of Halicarnassus, as an inscription of that date shows. His position was a tribute to his survival skills. Up and down the west coast of Anatolia in the 470s and 460s B.C., the Athenian navy drove out the Persians and the rulers who supported them. One by one the kings, princes, and tyrants fell, except, that is, for a few supple rulers who managed to switch allegiances as easily as a hunter might switch arrows. Lygdamis of Halicarnassus was one of the success stories.

If Herodotus had managed to have his way, Lygdamis would have been a failure. As a young man in Halicarnassus, the future historian joined a rebellion against the ruling house. But the rebellion failed and Herodotus went into exile—and the rest is history.

NOTES

In citing ancient authors, I follow the abbreviations of the standard reference work, *The Oxford Classical Dictionary* 3rd ed. (Oxford: Oxford University Press, 1999). I cite the titles of ancient works, however, in English translation.

TIMETABLE OF EVENTS RELATING TO THE BATTLE OF SALAMIS, 480 B.C.

xiii *All dates approximate:* This chronology is based on ancient sources and modern scholarship. It aims to follow Herodotus's narrative, which is a coherent and credible story but unfortunately vague or contradictory in regard to a few dates. In those cases, I follow scholars who offer the fewest changes to Herodotus.

AN IMPORTANT NOTE ABOUT THE SHIPS

xvii *Triremes were sleek ships:* Most of the technical data cited in this section comes from the experience of *Olympias*, a hypothetical reconstruction of a fourth century B.C. Athenian trireme, built and rowed in the 1980s and 1990s. I have also taken into account criticism and revisions since then.

xix *"speed and wheeling about":* Plutarch, *Life of Cimon* 12.2.

xx O opop, O opop *and* ryppapai . . . "Bre-ke-ke-kex, ko-ax, ko-ax": Aristophanes, *Frogs* 208–209, 1073.

PROLOGUE: PIRAEUS

1 *summer morning in 430 B.C.:* It is plausible that Herodotus was in Athens at that date, as discussed by J. L. Myres, *Herodotus, Father of History* (Oxford: Clarendon Press, 1953), 14–16. I have imagined his journey aboard ship but not the view.

2 *a man in his fifties:* Herodotus's traditional birth date is 484 BC. For a discussion of the biographical tradition, see J. Gould, *Herodotus* (London: Weidenfeld & Nicolson, 1989), 4–18.

2 *he had a long beard:* See, for example, the marble portrait bust in the Metropolitan Museum of Art, New York.

2 *cloak draped over a tunic:* I imagine Herodotus in the typical garb of a Greek adult male.

3 *"divine Salamis":* Herodotus 7.141.4.

3 *victors erected two trophies:* Hdt. 8.121.

4 *huge demographic fact:* The estimated human population of the earth in 500 B.C. was about 100 million. See Colin McEvedy and Richard Jones, *Atlas of World Population History* (Harmondsworth, Eng.: Penguin, 1978), 343. Today, the human population is about 6 billion. The figure of 300,000 represents 0.3 percent of 100 million, while 0.3 percent of 6 billion is 18 million.

8 *"What follows is an exhibition":* Hdt. 1.1.1.

CHAPTER ONE: ARTEMISIUM

12 *"I may not know how to tune the lyre":* Plutarch, *Life of Themistocles* 2.3.

13 *"When the Athenians lived under a tyranny":* Herodotus 5.78.

19 *"monster storm":* Hdt. 7.188.3.

22 *"When the Phoenicians are lined up opposite":* Sosylus of Lacedaemon, Felix Jacoby, *Die Fragmente der Griechischen Historiker, Zweiter Teil, Zeitgeschichte, B. Spezialgeschichten, Autobiographien und Memoiren. Zeittafeln* (Berlin: Weidmannsche Buchhandlung, 1929), no. 176, frg. 1.2, pp. 904–905

25 *"Corpses and the wreckage of the ships":* Hdt. 8.12.1–2.

25 *"Destroy the Greek fleet":* Hdt. 8.15.2.

25 *"The barbarians shall not pass":* Hdt. 8.15.2.

26 *"it was all done by the god":* Hdt. 8.13.1.

29 *"With numerous tribes":* Plutarch, *Life of Themistocles* 8.3. Trans. John Dryden.

29 *"There the sons of Athens set":* Plutarch, *Life of Themistocles* 8.2. Trans. John Dryden = Pindar frg. 93, Alexander Turyn, *Pindari Carmina, cum fragmentis* (Cambridge, Mass.: Harvard University Press, 1952), 302.

30 *"Men of Ionia":* Hdt. 8.22.1–2.

30 *subtle serpent:* Plutarch, *Life of Themistocles* 29.1.

CHAPTER TWO: THERMOPYLAE

36 *"many people but few men"*: Herodotus 7.210.2.

36 *"ruler of heroes"*: R. Schmitt, "Achaemenid Dynasty," *Encyclopedia Iranica*, vol. 1 (London: Routledge & Kegan Paul, 1983), 417.

36 *"I am skilled both in hands and in feet"*: XP1OP (Xerxes Persepolis Inscription letter "l," in Old Persian), trans. Achaemenid Royal Inscriptions Project (Chicago: Oriental Institute, University of Chicago, 1998), http://www-oi.uchicago.edu/cgi-bin/aritextbrowse.pl?text=xpl&language=op&banner=yes&translation=yes.

38 *"interwoven with white"*: Curtius 3.3.17. Trans. John Yardley, *Quintus Curtius Rufus, The History of Alexander* (Penguin: New York, 1984), 31. The reference is to King Darius III in 331 B.C. as he led his army out to march against Alexander the Great.

38 *"This is indeed my capability"*: XP1OP, trans. Achaemenid Royal Inscriptions Project.

40 *"make the land of Persia border only on the sky"*: Hdt. 8γ1–2.

41 *"I give much to loyal men"*: XP1OP, trans. Achaemenid Royal Inscriptions Project.

43 *"suggests that Xerxes built the canal"*: See a summary of excavations at http://www.gein.noa.gr/xerxes_canal/ENG_XERX/ENGWEB.htm.

45 *"When Xerxes was campaigning against Greece"*: Polyaenus, *Stratagems* 7.15.1.

46 *"those who wear the belt (banda) of vassalage"*: after Schmitt, "Achaemenid Dynasty," 419.

46 *"to find the eldest son of Pythius"*: Hdt. 7.39.3. Xerxes may have had his father in mind, as usual, since Darius had ordered that all of Oeobazus's sons be killed when that Persian tried to keep the boys out of the Scythian expedition in 513 B.C. (Hdt. 4.84). Xerxes' punishment was both more lenient and more grisly than his father's.

47 *"household and tyrannical rule"*: Hdt. 7.52.2.

50 *"if you spring from this island"*: Hdt. 7.235.3.

CHAPTER THREE: ATHENS

54 *The distance between Thermopylae and Athens*: See C. Hignett, *Xerxes' Invasion of Greece* (Oxford: Clarendon Press, 1963), 195–196.

54 *about ten miles a day*: Alexander the Great's army averaged a marching rate of thirteen miles a day, including one day's halt per week to rest

the animals. At that rate, Xerxes' army would have reached Athens within eleven days of leaving Thermopylae. But Alexander's small and efficient army had no camp followers. On his retreat from Greece in the autumn of 480 B.C., Xerxes traveled ca. 550 miles from Athens to the Hellespont in forty-five days, that is, at a rate of about twelve miles per day (see p. 224). But the retreating army did not have to stop to make conquests, and they represented only a part of the summer's invasion force, since the rest had remained in Thessaly (Herodotus 8.115.1).

57 *Tithraustes:* Diodorus Siculus 11.60.5; Plutarch, *Life of Cimon* 12.5.

57 *Salganeus of Boeotia:* Strabo, *Geography* 9.2.9, cf. 1.1.17.

58 *"a nothing":* Hdt. 8.106.3.

59 *only a hole for urination:* a brutal but well-attested form of castration. See Vern Bullough, "Eunuchs in History and Society," in Shaun Tougher, ed., *Eunuchs in Antiquity and Beyond* (London: Duckworth, 2002), 1–2.

63 *"O wretches":* Hdt. 7.140.2.

63 *"Far-seeing Zeus":* Hdt. 7.141.3–4.

65 *"they stayed behind":* Hdt. 7.139.6.

68 *"May Zeus who dwells in the sky":* Theognis 757–764.

69 *"fraught with grief, sorrow, and lamentation":* Archaeological Museum of Kerameikos, Athens, Inventory I.318.

69 *a bronze statue of Apollo:* Consider the Piraeus Apollo, a bronze statue discovered beneath the modern city, and dated either 530–520 or 500–480 B.C. Piraeus Museum, Inv. 4645.

69 *Iranian cylinder seal:* Metropolitan Museum of Art, New York, Inv. L.1992.23.8.

70 *"a long time":* Hdt. 8.52.2.

71 *"they opened the gates and murdered the suppliants":* Hdt. 8.52.5.

CHAPTER FOUR: SALAMIS

73 *He is dressed:* See the sixth century B.C. bronze statuette of a Spartan in the Wadsworth Atheneum, Hartford, Connecticut.

74 *Salamis's population:* The current population of Salamis is ca. 34,000. See http://salamina.gr/english/information.htm.

74 *every last Greek on Salamis was at odds with all the others:* This is informed speculation based on the whispers among the commanders (and perhaps the crews) over Eurybiades' plans (Herodotus 8.74.2) as well as on the well-known reputation of ancient Greek sailors for

unruliness.

75 *"Pounded by the sea":* Sophocles, *Ajax* 598.

77 *Cynosura:* On the identification, see J. F. Lazenby, *The Defence of Greece, 490–479 B.C.* (Warminster, Eng.: Aris & Phillips, 1993), 177.

77 *Psytalleia:* For the identification of Psytalleia with the modern Greek Lipsokoutali rather than St. George, see C. Hignett, *Xerxes' Invasion of Greece* (Oxford: Clarendon Press, 1963), 397–402. Also see Lazenby, *Defence of Greece,* 179.

77 *"bulwark":* Homer, *Iliad* 3.226–229.

78 *public baths:* See Pseudo-Demosthenes 50.34–35.

79 *"amounted to thirty tens":* Aeschylus, *Persians* 339–340

80 *"the eyesore of Piraeus":* Aristotle, *Rhetoric* 1411a.

82 *the great Athenian statesman Solon:* His statue stood in Salamis in 345 B.C. (Aeschines, *Against Timarchus* 25), but since Solon was a great Athenian hero from the time of his archonship in 594 B.C., we may imagine it standing in 480 B.C. as well.

82 *Cyrus the Great:* Hdt. 1.153.2.

83 *an Athenian messenger:* I assume, following Agostino Masaracchia, *Erodoto, La battaglia di Salamina: libro VIII delle Storie/Erodoto* (Milan: Fondazione Lorenzo Valla, A. Mondadori, 1977), 183, that Hdt. 8.50 and 8.56 belong to one and the same message.

83 *thorubos:* Hdt. 8.56.1.

84 *probably moored in Paloukia Bay:* as Constantin N. Rados argues in *La Bataille de Salamine* (Paris: Fontemoing & Cie., 1915), 290.

84 *Mnesiphilus:* Many doubt this anecdote because it drips venom against Themistocles (see Hignett, *Xerxes' Invasion,* 204). But even Themistocles needed help sometimes; besides, by heightening the drama, the story underlines Themistocles' resilience. See C. J. Fornara, *Herodotus: An Interpretive Essay* (Oxford: Clarendon Press, 1971), 72, n.19.

85 *where the Spartan fleet was probably moored:* Rados, *Bataille de Salamine,* 290.

85 *"Of all the men we know":* Thucydides 5.105.4.

86 *"At the games":* Hdt. 8.59.

87 *"Strike but listen":* Plutarch, *Life of Themistocles* 11.3.

87 *"on the wide open sea":* Hdt. 8.60α.

87 *"Fighting a naval battle in the narrows":* Hdt. 8.60β.

88 *"What are you doing":* Plutarch, *Life of Themistocles* 11.5.

88 *"If you stay here":* Hdt. 8.62.1.

89 *"They had jousted with words":* Hdt. 8.64.1.

CHAPTER FIVE: PHALERON

93 *sparkle with gold jewels:* I imagine Artemisia wearing the jewelry found in the fourth century B.C. tomb of an elite woman of Halicarnassus, the so-called Carian Princess. See http://www.bodrum-museum.com/depts/carian.htm.

93 *a story about her leaping to her death:* reported by the second century A.D. writer Ptolemy Hephaestion, whose *New History* is summarized at Photius 190.

95 *"I did not lack for courage":* Herodotus 8.68.α1.

95 *"I must especially marvel":* Hdt. 7.99.1.

95 *"the king . . . of every country and every language":* a foundation tablet from Persepolis, cited in James E. Pritchard, ed., *Ancient Near Eastern Texts Related to the Old Testament,* 3rd. ed. (Princeton: Princeton University Press, 1969), 316–317.

95 *"only king to give orders to all other kings":* ibid.

95 *The day after he sacked the Acropolis:* This is a guess, based on the assumption that Xerxes wanted to move quickly while the Greeks were terrified and depressed (Hdt. 8.56).

96 *"man's will":* Hdt. 7.99.1.

96 *magnificent natural harbor:* See Vitruvius 2.8.10–15, Strabo 13.1.59; Lucian, *Dialogues of the Dead* 24.

98 *Persian men proved themselves on the battlefield:* Hdt. 3.136.

98 *"They were rather indignant":* Hdt. 8.93.2.

98 *Aristophanes: Lysistrata* 675.

98 *rogues' gallery of Persian enemies:* This consisted of a series of statues at Sparta, including one of Artemisia. See Pausanias, *Guide to Greece* 3.11.3.

99 *the Phoenicians held the western end:* as Constantin N. Rados argues in *La Bataille de Salamine,* (Paris: Fontemoing & Cie., 1915), 287–288, based on the arrangement of these squadrons in the battle of Salamis, Hdt. 8.85.

100 *wooden toolbox from a Byzantine ship:* from the Yasi Ada wreck, now in the Bodrum Museum, Turkey.

100 *"Spare the ships":* Hdt. 8.68.α.

101 *"Good men have bad slaves":* Hdt. 8.68.γ.

102 *wooden palisades and walls of haphazardly piled stones:* Intensive archaeological surveys of the Isthmus have found fortification walls of several different eras but not a trace of walls from 480 B.C., which is further evidence that what the Peloponnesians built then was flimsy and perishable. See Timothy E. Gregory, *The Hexamilion and the Fortress* (Princeton, N.J.: The American School of Classical Studies at Athens, 1993).

103 *One expert modern estimate concludes:* T. Cuyler Young, "480/479 B.C.— A Persian Perspective," *Iranica Antica* 15 (1980): 229.

104 *build a bridge:* See the excellent discussion in C. Hignett, *Xerxes' Invasion of Greece* (Oxford: Clarendon Press, 1963), 415–417.

104 *"The further the Persian went into Greece":* Hdt. 8.66.2.

104 *"In my opinion, at any rate, the Persians were not less":* Hdt. 8.66.1.

104 *"it was all done by the god":* Hdt. 8.13.1.

106 *Presumably they took up their formations just outside the entrance:* No ancient source tells us where the Persian fleet got into its battle formation, but if they had entered the channel, the Greeks would have rushed to their ships in alarm, and there is no record of that.

106 *The Greeks on Salamis saw the full force of the fleet:* Cf. Hdt. 8.78.

106 *the terror of the Persian advance:* Hdt. 8.71.1, 8.108.1. For the possible role of psychological warfare in Persian moves on the day before the battle of Salamis, see J. F. Lazenby, *The Defence of Greece, 490–479 B.C.* (Warminster, Eng.: Aris & Phillips, 1993), 165–166.

CHAPTER SIX: FROM SALAMIS TO PHALERON

112 *"the men who were wasting their time":* Ephorus, as reported by Diodorus Siculus 11.16.3.

112 *"land that had been captured by the spear":* Herodotus 8.74.2.

113 *"A Greek man from the Athenian host":* Aeschylus, *Persians* 355–360.

113 *"When he [Sicinnus] arrived":* Hdt. 8.75.2.

114 *"He [Themistocles] sent him [Sicinnus] to Xerxes secretly":* Plutarch, *Life of Themistocles* 12.4–5.

117 *the Persians let him go:* See the argument by J. F. Lazenby, *The Defence of Greece 490–479 B.C.* (Warminster, Eng.: Aris & Phillips, 1993), 169–170.

117 *"guile of the Greek man":* Aeschylus, *Persians* 360–361. See the translation by Seth Benardete, "Greek guile," in *Aeschylus II.* 2nd ed., The

Complete Greek Tragedies (Chicago: University of Chicago Press, 1991), 61.

119 *"the middle of the night"*: Hdt. 8.76.4.

119 *"quick, reckless, unscrupulous"*: Plutarch, *Life of Aristides* 2.2.

120 *"the best and most just man"*: Hdt. 8.79.1.

120 *"Aristides and Themistocles were the worst"*: Polyaenus, *Stratagems* 1.30.8–32.2.

121 *"We are shut in by the enemy in a circle"*: Hdt. 8.79.4.

122 *"The barbarian triremes"*: Plutarch, *Life of Themistocles* 8.2.

122 *"You should know that the Medes"*: Hdt. 8.80.1.

122 *"If I say it"*: Hdt. 8.79.2.

122 *"shoving each other with their words"*: Hdt. 8.78.1.

122 *"The entire camp of the Greeks is shut in"*: Hdt. 8.81.1.

CHAPTER SEVEN: FROM PHALERON TO SALAMIS

125 *Eshmunazar:* or the monarch known as Tabnit. See David M. Lewis, "Persians in Herodotus," in P. J. Rhodes, ed., *Selected Papers in Greek and Near Eastern History* (Cambridge: Cambridge University Press, 1997), 355.

126 *"great Sidon"*: Joshua 11:8.

126 *"the mother of Canaan"*: Françoise Briguel-Chatonnet and Eric Gubel, *Les Phéniciens aux origines du Liban* (Paris: Gallimard, 1998), 72.

126 *"the first-born of Canaan"*: Genesis 10:15, 19.

127 *"experience in naval deeds inherited from its ancestors"*: Diodorus Siculus 11.18.1, referring to Phoenicians in general.

127 *Megabazus and Prexaspes:* Megabazus may have held a hereditary position as "the admiral," to judge from Persian documents, while Prexaspes' father, Aspathines, appears as quiver-bearer on Darius's tomb and may have been the official in charge of Persepolis. See Lewis, "Persians in Herodotus," 358–359.

128 *sh-l-m:* See "Salamis," in A. Pauly, G. Wissowa, and W. Kroll, eds., *Real-Encyclopädie der klassischen Altertumswissenschaft*, vol. 20 (Stuttgart: A. Druckenmüller Verlag 1958, 1914): cols. 1826–1827.

128 *"to cut the Greeks off in Salamis"*: Herodotus 8.76.2.

129 *120-plus-nautical-mile-per-day voyage:* Thucydides 8.101. Cf. Xenophon, *Anabasis* 6.4.2.

131 *The Persian navy was:* Aeschylus, *Persians* 74–75, 39–42, 52–55, 59–60.

133 *"On the long ships, rank encouraged rank"*: Aeschylus, *Persians* 380–381.

134 *"Arrange the close array of ships"*: Aeschylus, *Persians* 366–368.

134 *later historian*: Diodorus Siculus 11.17.2.

135 *"was posted between Ceos and Cynosura"*: Hdt. 8.76.2.

135 *"held the entire passage with its ships all the way to Munychia"*: Hdt. 8.76.1.

135 *"encircling" the Greeks or "surrounding" them or "guarding"*: Hdt. 8.76.1, 8.81.1.

136 *"But when they bridge with boats"*: Hdt. 8.77.1.

137 *"They did everything in an undertone"*: Hdt. 8.76.3.

137 *in 388 B.C.*: Xenophon, *Hellenica* 5.1.5.

138 *"the Phoenicians . . . held the western wing"*: Hdt. 8.85.1.

139 *"They didn't get even a little sleep"*: Hdt. 8.76.3.

139 *"The lords of the ships"*: Aeschylus, *Persians* 382–383.

139 *Herodotus reports an anecdote*: Hdt. 8.118.

CHAPTER EIGHT: SALAMIS

143 *fishermen*: On Salamis today, the fishermen still trade theories about the battle of Salamis in the coffeehouses. I speculate that their ancient counterparts grumbled about the loss of access to harbors.

143 *Themistocles' itchy fingers*: Plutarch, *Life of Themistocles* 4.2, 24.4.

143 *pale and overweight*: Plato, *Republic* 556d–e.

143 *gripes about rowing masters*: Xenophon, *Oeconomicus* 21.3.

144 *"are not called slaves nor subjects of any man"*: Aeschylus, *Persians* 242.

145 *the rowers turned to one another and shook hands*: Lysias, *Funeral Oration* 2.37.

146 *lengthy inscription*: Inscriptiones Graecae, 3rd ed., vol. I, no. 1032 = Inscriptiones Graecae, 2nd ed., vol. II, no. 1951.

148 *"the dark-eyed ships"*: Aeschylus, *Persians* 559, *Suppliants* 773.

148 *"prow that looks at the way ahead"*: Aeschylus, *Suppliants* 716–718.

149 *owl*: Plutarch, *Life of Themistocles* 12.1. Plutarch places the story the night before (i.e., September 23–24), but it is hard to see when Themistocles might be addressing many people from his deck on that night. Plutarch does not vouch for the truth of the story.

149 *Themistocles' sacrifice*: Plutarch, *Life of Themistocles* 13.2, *Life of Aristides* 9.1.

150 *sunrise*: On September 25 in Athens the sun rises at 7:15 A.M. and day breaks about an hour earlier, around 6:15 A.M.

151 *"All his words contrasted the better"*: Herodotus 8.83.

151 *"finished his speech resoundingly"*: Most scholars translate the Greek

phrase simply as "he closed his speech," but the verb used by Herodotus, *kataplēssō*, is exceedingly strong.

153 aura: My analysis is based on a consultation with Dr. Michael Petrakis, Director of the Institute for Environmental Research & Sustainable Development, National Observatory of Athens. See also J. Neumann, "The Sea and Land Breezes in the Classical Greek Literature," *Bulletin of the American Meteorological Society* 54 (1973): 6–8; Jamie Morton, *The Role of the Physical Environment in Ancient Greek Seafaring* (Leiden: Brill, 1999), 97–99.

153 *"a brisk breeze . . . from the sea"*: Plutarch, Life of Themistocles 14.2.

153 *"rose high in their sterns, and had bulwarks"*: "Bulwarks" is literally "high-roofed in regard to the decks," which may refer to the bulwarks needed to protect the forty marines crowded on deck. Plutarch, *Life of Themistocles* 14.2.

153 *"they had light drafts and lay low in the water"*: Plutarch, *Life of Themistocles* 14.2.

154 *"lord of the oar"*: Aeschylus, *Persians* 378.

154 *"rich in hands and rich in rowers"*: Aeschylus, *Persians* 84.

154 *"to join in battle with their triremes' rams"*: Aeschylus, *Persians* 336.

154 *"to shut out the invincible wave with sturdy walls"*: Aeschylus, *Persians* 90.

154 *"The city of Athena will be rescued by the gods"*: Aeschylus, *Persians* 347.

CHAPTER NINE: SALAMIS STRAITS: MORNING

157 *Gobryas:* a Persian noble, he was Ariabignes' maternal grandfather and one of the seven conspirators who put Darius on the throne. See esp. Herodotus 3.78, 4.130–134, 7.97.

158 *"He had a seat"*: Aeschylus, *Persians* 466–467.

158 *"come down on the enemy with thunder"*: David G. Chandler, *The Military Maxims of Napoleon* (New York: Macmillan, 1997), 111–112.

159 *"a song-like shout"*: Aeschylus, *Persians* 388–390.

160 *"holy cry"*: Aeschylus, *Seven Against Thebes* 268–270.

160 *"All the barbarians"*: Aeschylus, *Persians* 391–394.

160 *Aristides Quintilianus:* Aristides Quintilianus, *On Music* 2.6; Homer, *Iliad* 21.388. A *salpinx* from fifth century B.C. Greece has been found: its cylinder consists of thirteen parts made of ivory, while its bell and mouthpiece are made of bronze.

160 *"the regular stroke of the rushing oars together"*: Aeschylus, *Persians* 396.

160 *clearly visible to the Persians:* As argued by J. F. Lazenby, *The Defence of Greece, 490–479 B.C.* (Warminster, Eng.: Aris & Phillips, 1993), 184, there is no need to put the Greeks around a bend in the channel merely because the Persians heard them before they saw them.

160 *Only a few minutes had passed:* Things happened quickly, says Aeschylus, *Persians* 398.

161 *"When they [the Greeks] launched their ships":* Hdt. 8.83.2.

161 *"First the right wing":* Aeschylus, *Persians* 399–400.

161 *"bronze-rammed floating chariots":* Timotheus of Miletus, *The Persians*, as cited in A. Podlecki, *The Life of Themistocles: A Critical Survey of the Literary and Archaeological Evidence* (Montreal: McGill-Queen's University Press, 1975), 63–64.

164 *"a mighty battle cry"* . . . *"O sons of the Greeks"* . . . *"the Persian tongue":* Aeschylus, *Persians* 401–407.

165 *He owned land and a house in Attica:* For the points in this sentence, see the Themistocles Decree.

165 *from a standing start to nine or ten knots:* Compare the results of the sea trials of *Olympias* from 1987 to 1992, keeping in mind that the speeds fall short of those apparently achieved in antiquity. See J. S. Morrison, J. F. Coates, and N. B. Rankov, *The Athenian Trireme: The History and Reconstruction of an Ancient Greek Warship*, 2nd ed. (Cambridge: Cambridge University Press, 2000), 262–264.

166 *Depending on whether:* See J. T. Shaw, "Steering to Ram: The Diekplous and Periplous," in J. T. Shaw, ed., *The Trireme Project: Operational Experience 1987–90: Lessons Learnt*, Oxbow Monograph No. 31 (Oxford: Oxbow Books, 1993), 100.

167 *"law of hands":* Hdt. 8.89.1.

168 *"Gentlemen, just how long":* Hdt. 8.84.2.

168 *"Greek ship":* Aeschylus, *Persians* 409.

168 *"a common problem in ancient warfare":* Thucydides 7.44.1.

168 *"wails, cries":* Thuc. 7.71.4.

169 *a great light:* All these details are found in Plutarch, *Life of Themistocles* 15.1.

170 *"can say little precisely":* Hdt. 8.87.1.

170 *"at first the flood":* Aeschylus, *Persians* 412.

170 *"The barbarians . . . did not remain drawn up":* Hdt. 8.86.

171 *As an Athenian admiral put it later:* Phormio, cited at Thuc. 2.87.

171 *"struck the barbarians' ships":* Plutarch, *Life of Themistocles* 14.2.

171 *"the boat-wrecking breezes (aurai)"*: Timotheus of Miletus, *Persians* 791.132. My translation; see J. H. Hordern, ed., *The Fragments of Timotheus of Miletus.* (Oxford: Oxford University Press, 2002). Timotheus also refers to "the swift and soaking *aura*," ibid., 81.

172 *"was inflicted on one side"*: Timotheus of Miletus, *Persians* 791.7-13. Trans. J. H. Hordern, ibid.

173 *a later story:* Diodorus Siculus 11.19.4.

174 *unnamed Persian "admiral":* Diodorus Siculus 11.85.5.

174 *"Ariamenes":* Plutarch, *Life of Themistocles* 14.3.

CHAPTER TEN: SALAMIS STRAITS: AFTERNOON

176 *"the utterly ruinous rams":* Aeschylus, *Persians* 562.

176 *"The arrow":* Aeschylus, *Persians* 278–279, cf. 269–271.

176 *"by the single sweep of the oar":* Aeschylus, *Persians* 976.

176 *situational awareness:* Mike Spick, *The Ace Factor: Air Combat & The Role of Situational Awareness* (Annapolis, Md.: Naval Institute Press, 1988), xii.

176 *"Nothing is true in tactics":* Commander Randy "Duke" Cunningham, U.S. Navy, Vietnam, as cited in Robert L. Shaw, *Fighter Combat, Tactics and Maneuvering* (Annapolis, Md.: Naval Institute Press, 1985), x.

178 *Since his feet were fixed to the floor:* In the absence of ancient evidence, this is only an assumption, but one based on the likelihood that rowers would go flying upon ramming unless their feet were fixed.

179 thorubos: Herodotus 8.87.2.

179 *More Persians died:* Hdt. 8.89.2

179 *"They all hastened":* Aeschylus, *Persians* 422–426.

180 *"sojourners in a harsh land":* Aeschylus, *Persians* 319.

180 *"wretched with their struggling hands":* Aeschylus, *Persians* 977.

180 *unknown writer:* Pseudo-Aristotle, *Mechanica* 850b.

180 *Lucian: Navigation* 6.

183 *"Master," they asked the Great King:* Hdt. 8.88.2.

183 *"Shut up! Don't tell this story to anyone":* Hdt. 8.65.5–6.

184 *"I have a list of many names of captains":* Hdt. 8.85.2.

185 *"Is it really Artemisia?":* Hdt. 8.88.2.

185 *a fabulous story about a serpent:* reported by the second century A.D. writer Ptolemy Hephaestion, whose *New History* is summarized at Photius 190.

185 *"distinguishing mark":* Hdt. 8.88.2.

186 *a set of Greek signal flags:* Polyaenus, *Stratagems* 8.53.1, 3.

188 *"covers burning with fire":* Timotheus of Miletus, *Persians* 791.26–30. Trans. J. H. Hordern; J. H. Hordern, ed., *The Fragments of Timotheus of Miletus* (Oxford: Oxford University Press, 2002).

188 *"the strong and smoky fire":* Timotheus of Miletus, *Persians* 791.183–185. My translation. Timotheus is not a fully reliable source.

188 *"My men have become women":* Hdt. 8.88.3.

CHAPTER ELEVEN: SALAMIS STRAITS: EVENING

191 *"the emerald-haired sea":* Timotheus of Miletus, *Persians* 791.31–34. Trans. J. H. Hordern; J. H. Hordern, ed., *The Fragments of Timotheus of Miletus* (Oxford: Oxford University Press, 2002).

192 *"spray [that] foamed":* Timotheus of Miletus, *Persians* 791.61–64., cf. 791.82–85. My translation.

192 *"naked and frozen":* Timotheus of Miletus, *Persians* 791.98–99. My translation.

192 *The Persians did not give up their resistance:* Plutarch, *Life of Themistocles* 15.2, a detail that may have been drawn from Simonides' poem about Salamis.

192 *"At first the flood":* Aeschylus, *Persians* 412–422.

192 *"The barbarian Persian army":* Timotheus of Miletus, *Persians* 791.86–89. Trans. J. H. Hordern.

194 *"brave man":* Herodotus 8.95.1.

194 *"best of the Athenians":* Hdt. 8.79.1.

195 *"When God had given":* Aeschylus, *Persians* 455–464.

197 *"Better plate your horns with bronze":* Hdt. 6.50.

197 *"When the barbarians were put to flight":* Hdt. 8.91.1.

197 *"The passage":* Hdt. 8.76.1, 91.1.

198 *"Medizers, are we, Themistocles?":* a paraphrase of Hdt. 8.92.2.

198 *He threw the attackers in disorder:* The word *thorubos* is used here, too. Hdt. 7.181.1.

198 *"He proved to be the bravest man that day":* Hdt. 7.181.1.

200 *"Democritus was the third":* Simonides in D. A. Campbell, *Greek Lyric*, vol. 3., Loeb Classical Library (Cambridge, Mass.: Harvard University Press, 1991), no. XIX, cited by Plutarch, *The Malice of Herodotus* 36.869d.

201 *"sent by divine intervention":* Hdt. 8.94.4.

201 *"Stranger, once we lived":* Plutarch, *The Malice of Herodotus* 39.870e =

Campbell, *Greek Lyric*, vol. 3, no. XI.

202 *"When all Greece was balanced"*: Plutarch, *The Malice of Herodotus* 39.870e = Campbell, *Greek Lyric*, vol. 3, no. XII.

202 *"This grave is Adimantus' "*: Plutarch, *The Malice of Herodotus* 39.870f = Campbell, *Greek Lyric*, vol. 3, no. X.

202 *"The rowers of Diodorus"*: Plutarch, *The Malice of Herodotus* 39.870f = Campbell, *Greek Lyric*, vol. 3, no. XIII.

202 *"throw themselves heart and soul into the fight against the barbarians"*: Plutarch, *The Malice of Herodotus* 39.871a. My translation.

202 *Ancient comics made hay:* Jeffrey Henderson, *The Maculate Muse: Obscene Language in Attic Comedy*, 2nd ed. (New York: Oxford University Press, 1991), 170.

203 *"These statues of women"*: Simonides, cited by Plutarch, *The Malice of Herodotus* 39.871b, and by Athenaeus, *Sophists at Dinner* 13.573c–e, in Campbell, *Greek Lyric*, vol. 3, no. XIV.

204 *"chiefs"*: Aeschylus, *Persians* 297.

204 *An author of the Roman era:* Diodorus Siculus 11.19.3.

205 *"Be sure of this"*: Aeschylus, *Persians* 431–432.

205 *"The shores of Salamis"*: Aeschylus, *Persians* 273–274.

205 *"The sea-dyed"*: Aeschylus, *Persians* 275–277.

205 *"Lost from a ship of Tyre"*: Aeschylus, *Persians* 964–965.

205 *"And the starry sea"*: Timotheus of Miletus, *Persians* 791.97. Trans. J. H. Hordern.

206 *"Since the Greeks fought"*: Hdt. 8.86.1.

208 *"exhibited achievements worthy of mention"*: Hdt. 8.92.1.

208 *"an exhibition of . . . great and astonishing achievements"*: Hdt. 1.1.1.

CHAPTER TWELVE: PHALERON

213 *bronze medicine chests:* found in Roman Naples, but since the city was a Greek colony, the chests may reflect earlier, Greek practice.

213 *"A healer"*: Homer, *Iliad* 11.514–515.

214 *"Our struggle is not"*: Herodotus 8.100.2.

214 *"The Persians have"*: Hdt. 8.100.4.

214 *"all tore their tunics"*: Hdt. 8.99.

215 *"worse than a woman"*: Hdt. 9.107.1.

215 *"the admiral of the fleet"*: Polyaenus, *Stratagems of War* 8.53.2, *Excerpts of Polyaenus* 53.4.

215 *"the admiral"*: See David M. Lewis, "Persians in Herodotus," in P. J. Rhodes, ed., *Selected Papers in Greek and Near Eastern History* (Cambridge: Cambridge University Press, 1997), 358–359.

215 *the Roman era:* Diodorus Siculus 11.2.2; Strabo 9.2.9.

216 *Acarnania:* the general Demosthenes (not the famous orator), after the battle of Olpae in 426 B.C. Thucydides. 3.114.

217 *"If you and your house survive"*: Hdt. 8.102.3.

220 *"Ares"*: Timotheus of Miletus, *Persians* 790. My translation.

220 *"Send money"*: Hdt. 9.2.3.

221 *"They had been struck"*: Hdt. 8.130.2–3.

223 *"Diopeithes"*: The inscription and the argument for the circumstances it commemorates can both be found in Werner Gauer, *Weihgeschenke aus den Perserkriegen* (Tübingen: Verlag Ernst Wasmuth, 1968), 40–41, 74, 134.

224 *partial eclipse:* Hdt. 9.10.3. The eclipse can be securely dated to October 2. If Cleombrotus was in fact about to attack the Persians, he was following a policy contrary to that suggested by Eurybiades, who wanted to give the Persians no reason to continue fighting; see the next chapter.

224 *forty-five days:* Hdt. 8.115.1. Herodotus might be referring to just the trip from Thessaly to the Hellespont, in which case another two to three weeks need to be added for the journey from Athens to Thessaly.

224 *tough trip:* Aeschylus, *Persians* 480–514. Aeschylus makes Xerxes' return journey even more disastrous, but the story does not deserve the respect owed to the poet's eyewitness description of the battle.

CHAPTER THIRTEEN: ANDROS

229 *"the salvation of Greece"*: Herodotus 7.139.5.

230 "Help yourself, for you are not Themistocles": Plutarch, *Life of Themistocles* 18.2.

230 *"swift ships"*: Russell Meiggs and David M. Lewis, eds., *A Selection of Greek Historical Inscriptions to the End of the Fifth Century* B.C., rev. ed. (Oxford: Clarendon Press, 1988, no. 26, 54–57.

231 *"So let each stand his ground firmly"*: Tyrtaeus, frg. 10 West, in M. L. West, *Iambi et Elegi Graeci ante Alexandrum Cantati*, vol. 2 (Oxford: Clarendon Press, 1972), 174–175; Michael Sage, trans., *Warfare in Ancient Greece: A Sourcebook* (London: Routledge, 1996), 34.

233 *"Forced to fight"*: Hdt. 8.109.2.

233 *"a great cloud of men"*: Hdt. 8.109.2.

238 *"Themistocles' name"*: Hdt. 8.124.1.

239 *"If I came from"*: Hdt. 8.125.2.

EPILOGUE: SUSA

245 *The Great King's expedition:* The Greek orator Dio Chrysostom tells a similar story in 11.147–149.

246 *"allies" but "the cities Athens controls":* Russell Meiggs, *The Athenian Empire* (Oxford: Clarendon Press, 1971), 171.

248 *"I have Themistocles the Athenian!":* Plutarch, *Life of Themistocles* 28.4.

248 *"his bread":* Thucydides 1.138.5; Plutarch, *Life of Themistocles* 29.7.

251 *Demaratus is supposed to have asked to enter the city of Sardis:* Seneca, *On Benefits* 6.31.11–12. According to Plutarch, *Life of Themistocles* 29.5–6, the Great King angrily refused Demaratus's request.

251 *as an inscription of that date shows:* Russell Meiggs and David M. Lewis, eds., *A Selection of Greek Historical Inscriptions to the End of the Fifth Century B.C.*, rev. ed. (Oxford: Clarendon Press, 1988), no. 32, 69–72.

SOURCES

The reader who wants to learn more about the battle of Salamis is in for a treat and an effort. In what follows I list only the main works that have been of use in the making of this book. The information below is by no means a complete record of the works and sources I have consulted.

ANCIENT SOURCES

The indispensable starting point is Herodotus, in particular, the eighth book, but each part of Herodotus has to be understood in the context of the whole work. Good recent translations in English include John Marincola's revision, with introduction and notes, of Aubrey de Sélincourt's version (Herodotus, *The Histories: New Edition* [Harmondsworth, Eng.: Penguin, 1996]), and Robin Waterfield's translation, with introduction and notes by Carolyn Dewald (Herodotus, *The Histories* [Oxford: Oxford University Press, 1998]). The historical commentary on Herodotus by W. W. How and J. Wells, *A Commentary on Herodotus*, 2 vols. (Oxford: Oxford University Press, 2000 [1928]), is too short and too old but nonetheless very good. Focusing more on literary than historical issues, Agostino Masaracchia offers a good commentary on the eighth book of Herodotus in *Erodoto, La battaglia di Salamina: libro VIII delle Storie /Erodoto* (Milan: Fondazione Lorenzo Valla, A. Mondadori, 1977).

The starting point for my inquiry is the conviction that Herodotus is a great historian, offering by and large a fair and accurate account. A superb defense of Herodotus's accuracy can be found in W. Kendrick Pritchett, *The Liar School of Herodotus.* (Amsterdam: J. C. Gieben, 1993). Perhaps the most important of the witnesses for the prosecution, that is, the accusers of Herodotus as a falsifier and myth maker, is Detlev Fehling, *Herodotus and His Sources: Citation, Invention, and Narrative Art*, trans. by J. G. Howie (Leeds,

Eng.: Francis Cairns, 1989). A good, brief introduction to Herodotus is John Gould, *Herodotus* (New York: St. Martin's, 1989). A short but thoughtful study of Herodotus on Xerxes' invasion is Gabriella Bodei Giglioni, *Erodoto e I sogni di Serse. L'invasione persiana dell' Europa.* Saggine 55. (Rome: Donzinelli Editore, 2002). For the impact of the Peloponnesian War on Herodotus's thinking, see C. J. Fornara, *Herodotus: An Interpretive Essay* (Oxford: Clarendon Press, 1971), 75–91.

The second most important ancient source about Salamis is Aeschylus's play *The Persians.* Good translations include Janet Lembke and C. J. Herington, *Aeschylus: Persians* (Oxford: Oxford University Press, 1991) and Seth Benardete in David Grene and Richmond Lattimore, eds., *Aeschylus II,* 2nd ed. The Complete Greek Tragedies (Chicago: University of Chicago Press, 1991). For a historical and literary commentary see H. D. Broadhead, *The Persae of Aeschylus* (Cambridge: Cambridge University Press, 1960).

The third most important work is Plutarch's *Life of Themistocles,* available, in Greek and in English translation, along with two other relevant texts, his *Life of Aristides* and *Life of Cimon,* in *Plutarch, Lives,* vol. 2: *Themistocles and Camillus, Aristides and Cato Major, Cimon and Lucullus,* trans. Bernadotte Perrin (Cambridge, Mass.: Harvard University Press, 2001 [1914]). Plutarch's *Life of Themistocles* should ideally be read along with the very good notes in Frank J. Frost, *Plutarch's Themistocles: A Historical Commentary,* rev. ed. (Chicago: Ares Publishers, 1998) or in Carlo Carena, Mario Manfredini, and Luigi Piccirilli, Plutarco, *Le Vite di Temistocle e di Camillo* (Milan: Fondazione Lorenzo Valla: A. Mondadori, 1996). The student of Salamis should also see the critique of Herodotus in Plutarch's essay "On the Malice of Herodotus," now available with introduction, Greek and English texts, and commentary in A. J. Bowen, *Plutarch: The Malice of Herodotus* (Warminster, Eng.: Aris & Phillips, 1992).

Next in importance among ancient authors comes Diodorus Siculus, whose account of Artemisium and Salamis can be read in English translation in C. H. Oldfather, trans., *Diodorus of Sicily,* vol. 4 (Cambridge, Mass.: Harvard University Press, 1939), 155–175 (11.12.1–19.6). This Sicilian Greek lived in the era of the emperor Augustus and compiled a universal history of the Mediterranean world. It is thought that Diodorus drew his account of Salamis from the now missing work of Ephorus of Cyme, a fourth century B.C. Greek historian.

Thucydides' *Peloponnesian War* not only contains important information about Themistocles and Salamis, but it is a gold mine of material about trireme strategy and tactics. An excellent English edition is Robert Strassler, ed., *The Landmark Thucydides: A Comprehensive Guide to the Peloponnesian War* (New York: Free Press, 1996).

The Themistocles Decree can be read in translation in M. Crawford and D. Whitehead, eds., *Archaic and Classical Greece* (Cambridge: Cambridge University Press, 1983). 224–225, no. 112.

What is left of Timotheus's poem may be read in Greek and English in J. H. Hordern, ed. and trans., *The Fragments of Timotheus of Miletus* (Oxford: Oxford University Press, 2002). The few lines of Choerilus of Samos's epic on Xerxes' invasion may be read in Greek in A. Bernabé, *Poetarum epicorum graecorum: fragmenta et testimonia*, part 1 (Stuttgart: Teubner, 1996). Simonides is available in Greek and English in Deborah Boedeker and David Sider, *The New Simonides: Contexts of Praise and Desire* (Oxford: Oxford University Press, 2001). See also Anthony J. Podlecki, "Simonides: 480," *Historia* 17.3 (1968): 257–275.

There are many useful tidbits of information about Salamis, Artemisium, and trireme warfare in general in Polyaenus, *Stratagems of War*, ed. and trans. Peter Krentz and Everett L. Wheeler, 2 vols. (Chicago: Ares Publishers, 1994). Much can be gleaned about oared-ship warfare in Greece from the Byzantine naval manuals (in Greek), especially that of Syrianus Magister (ca. A.D. 400–600), in Alphonsus Dain, *Naumachia* (Paris: "Les Belles Lettres," 1943).

Among the other ancient writers whom I have frequently consulted in the research for this book are Lysias, Xenophon, Justin 2.12.3, Onasander, Pausanias, and Strabo, all of whom are available in Greek-English or Latin-English versions in the Loeb Classical Library (Harvard University Press).

MODERN STUDIES OF SALAMIS

So much has been written about the battle of Salamis, and it is of such high quality, that one approaches the scholarly literature with respect, gratitude, and humility. The best book-length study, too often overlooked, is Constantin N. Rados, *La Bataille de Salamine* (Paris: Fontemoing & Cie., 1915). A scholar of ancient and medieval naval warfare, a Greek with a deep knowledge of the land, a wit, a skeptic, and a prose stylist, an officer of the French Légion d'Honneur, Rados writes with erudition and carries conviction. The most succinct and persuasive account of the battle is J. F.

Lazenby, *The Defence of Greece, 490–479 B.C.* (Warminster, Eng.: Aris & Phillips, 1993), 151–197. My account of the battle is most in accord with Rados's and Lazenby's. It also depends heavily on the magisterial research of C. Hignett, *Xerxes' Invasion of Greece* (Oxford: Clarendon Press, 1963), esp. 193–239; and of W. K. Pritchett, "Towards a Restudy of the Battle of Salamis," *American Journal of Archaeology* 63 (1959): 251–262 and "Salamis Revisited," in *Studies in Ancient Greek Topography*, part 1 (Berkeley: University of California Press, 1965), 94–102.

Although they offer rather different reconstructions of the battle from mine, Burn, Green, and Hammond, and the team of Morrison, Coates, and Rankov each make distinguished contributions to the scholarship of Salamis. See A. R. Burn, *Persia and the Greeks: The Defense of the West, 546–478 B.C.*, 2nd ed. (Stanford: Stanford University Press, 1984), esp. 450–475. See Peter Green, *The Greco-Persian Wars* (Berkeley: University of California Press, 1996), 60–64, 146–48, 162–63. See N.G.L. Hammond, "The Battle of Salamis," *Journal of Hellenic Studies* 76 (1956): 32-54; "On Salamis," *American Journal of Archaeology* 64 (1960): 367–368; "The Expedition of Xerxes," in *Cambridge Ancient History*, vol. 4, 2nd ed.: *Persia, Greece, and the Western Mediterranean c. 525 to 479 B.C.* (Cambridge: Cambridge University Press, 1988), 569–588. See J. S. Morrison, J. F. Coates, and N. B. Rankov, *The Athenian Trireme: The History and Reconstruction of an Ancient Greek Warship*, 2nd ed. (Cambridge: Cambridge University Press, 2000), 55-61. I have also profited from discussions by Josiah Ober and Victor Davis Hanson in, respectively, Barry S. Strauss and Josiah Ober, "Xerxes of Persia and the Greek Wars: Why the Big Battalions Lost," in *The Anatomy of Error, Ancient Military Disasters and Their Lessons for Modern Strategists* (New York: St. Martin's, 1990), 17–43; Victor Hanson, "Freedom—'Or to Live As You Please,'" in *Carnage and Culture: Landmark Battles in the Rise of Western Power* (New York: Anchor Books, 2001), 27–59.

Among older works, I have also profited from Giulio Giannelli, *La spedizione di Serse da Terme a Salamina* (Milan: Società Editrice "Vita e Pensiero," 1924) and G. B. Grundy, *The Great Persian War and Its Preliminaries; A Study of the Evidence, Literary and Topographical* (New York: Scribner's, 1901).

Other important works in English on the battle of Salamis in recent decades includes Jack Martin Balcer, *The Persian Conquest of the Greeks, 545–450 B.C.* (Xenia 38) (Konstanz: Univ.-Verl. Konstanz, 1995), 257–270;

C. W. Fornara, "The Hoplite Achievement at Psytalleia," *Journal of Hellenic Studies* 86 (1966): 51-55; P. W. Wallace, "Psytalleia and the Trophies of the Battle of Salamis," *American Journal of Archaeology* 73 (1969): 293–303; K. R. Walters, "Four Hundred Athenian Ships at Salamis?" *Rheinisches Museum* 124 (1981): 199–203; A. J. Holladay, "The Forethought of Themistocles," *JHS* 107 (1987): 182–187; J. F. Lazenby, "Aischylos and Salamis," *Hermes* 116 (1988): 168–185. For war-gaming the battle of Salamis, see Richard B. Nelson, *The Battle of Salamis* (London: Luscombe, 1975).

In a forthcoming book, I argue that Athens would have eventually recovered its power even had it lost at Salamis. See "The Resilient West: Salamis Without Themistocles, Classical Greece Without Salamis, and the West Without Greece," in P. E. Tetlock, R. N. Lebow, and G. Parker, eds., *Unmaking the West: Counterfactual Thought Experiments in History* (forthcoming).

ANCIENT SHIPS AND NAVAL BATTLES

The fundamental introduction to ancient seafaring is Lionel Casson, *Ships and Seamanship in the Ancient World* (Baltimore: Johns Hopkins University Press, 1995). Another good introduction is Robert Gardiner, ed., *The Age of the Galley: Mediterranean Oared Vessels Since Pre-Classical Times*, Conway's History of the Ship (Annapolis, Md.: Naval Institute Press, 1995). An important recent study is Jamie Morton, *The Role of the Physical Environment in Ancient Greek Seafaring* (Leiden: Brill, 2001).

For an introduction to the ancient trireme in the context of ancient oared ships, see J. S. Morrison and R. T. Williams, *Greek Oared Ships, 900–322 B.C.* (Cambridge: Cambridge University Press, 1968); Lucien Basch, *Le Musée imaginaire de la marine antique* (Athens: Institut héllenique pour la préservation de la tradition nautique, 1987); H. T. Wallinga, *Ships and Sea Power Before the Great Persian War: The Ancestry of the Ancient Trireme* (Leiden: Brill, 1993). J. S. Morrison and J. F. Coates, *Greek and Roman Oared Warships, 399–31 B.C.* (Oxford: Clarendon Press, 1994), focuses on the Hellenistic period but offers some important insights on classical trireme warfare. Outdated in large part but still useful in some respects is Cecil Torr, *Ancient Ships*, ed. Anthony J. Podlecki (Chicago: Argonaut, 1964). W. L. Rogers, *Greek and Roman Naval Warfare: A Study of Strategy, Tactics, and Ship Design from Salamis (480 B.C.) to Actium (31 B.C.)* (Annapolis, Md.: United States Naval Institute, 1937). For classical Athenian triremes and their crews, see M. Amit, *Athens and the Sea: A Study in Athenian Sea Power* (Brussels: Latomus, Revue d'Études Latines, 1965) and Borimir Jordan, *The Athenian Navy in the Classical Period,* Classical Studies 13 (Berkeley: University of California, 1975).

The study of *Olympias* begins with J. S. Morrison, J. F. Coates, and N. B. Rankov, *The Athenian Trireme: The History and Reconstruction of an Ancient Greek Warship,* 2nd ed. (Cambridge: Cambridge University Press, 2000). Morrison and Coates designed *Olympias,* the hypothetical trireme reconstruction. Although in some ways flawed (as its designers acknowledge, to their credit), *Olympias* is of the first order of importance for historians. See Morrison and Williams, *Greek Oared Ships.* Reports on *Olympias'*s trials can be found in J. S. Morrison and J. F. Coates, eds., *An Athenian Trireme Reconstructed: The British Sea Trials of* Olympias, 1987, BAR International Series 486 (Oxford: B.A.R., 1989) and in J. T. Shaw, ed., *The Trireme Project: Operational Experience 1987–90: Lessons Learnt,* Oxbow Monograph No. 31 (Oxford: Oxbow Books, 1993). Some useful anecdotal insights from Olympias can be found in Frank Welsh, *Building the Trireme* (London: Constable, 1988). For critiques of *Olympias,* see John Hale, "The Lost Technology of Ancient Greek Rowing," *Scientific American,* May 1996, 66–71; A. F. Tilley, "Warships of the Ancient Mediterranean," *The American Neptune* 50 (1990): 192–200.

On slaves as rowers see Peter Hunt. *Slaves, Warfare, and Ideology in the Greek Historians*. (Cambridge: Cambridge University Press, 1998); Donald R. Laing, "A New Interpretation of the Athenian Naval Catalogue, IG II^2 1951," Ph.D. diss. Cincinnati, 1960.

On trireme tactics see J. F. Lazenby, "The Diekplous," *Greece & Rome* 34.2 (1987): 169–178; Ian Whitehead, "The Periplous," *G & R* 34.2 (1987): 178–185; A. J. Holladay, "Further Thoughts on Trireme Tactics," *G & R* 35.3 (1988): 149–151; J. S. Morrison. "The Greek Ships at Salamis and the *Diekplous,*" *Journal of Hellenic Studies* 111 (1991): 196–200; and my "Democracy, Kimon, and the Evolution of Athenian Naval Tactics in the Fifth Century B.C.," in Pernille Flensted-Jensen, Thomas Heine Neilsen, and Lene Rubinstein, eds., *Polis & Politics: Studies in Ancient Greek History Presented to Mogens Herman Hansen on His 60th Birthday* (Copenhagen: Museum Tusculanum Press, University of Copenhagen, 2000), 315–326.

On the esprit de corps of the crew of an Athenian trireme, see my "The Athenian Trireme, School of Democracy," in Josiah Ober and Charles Hedrick, eds., *DEMOKRATIA: A Conversation on Democracies, Ancient and*

Modern (Princeton: Princeton University Press, 1996), 313–325. On how men died in ancient naval battles, see my "Perspectives on the Death of Fifth-Century Athenian Seamen," in Hans Van Wees, ed., *War and Violence in Ancient Greece* (London: Duckworth, 2000), 261–283. For thoughts on ancient boats and modern rowing, see my *Rowing Against the Current: On Learning to Scull at Forty* (New York: Scribner, 1999).

On ships' eyes, see Troy J. Nowak, "A Preliminary Report on *Ophthalmoi* from the Tektaş Burnu Shipwreck," *International Journal of Nautical Archaeology* 30.1 (2001): 86–94.

ANCIENT WARFARE

The five volumes of W. Kendrick Pritchett's *Greek State at War* (Berkeley: University of California Press, 1971–1991), are required reading for the nuts and bolts of classical Greek warfare, with an emphasis on fighting on land.

On hoplite warfare, see Victor Davis Hanson, *The Western Way of War: Infantry Battle in Classical Greece*, 2nd ed. (Berkeley: University of California Press, 2000). On fire arrows and other unconventional weapons, see Adrienne Mayor, *Greek Fire, Poison Arrows & Scorpion Bombs: Biological and Chemical Warfare in the Ancient World* (New York: Overlook Press, 2003).

On the rate of march by ancient armies, see Donald W. Engels, *Alexander the Great and the Logistics of the Macedonian Army.* (Berkeley: University of California Press, 1978), pp. 153–156. On the supply of Persia's forces at Phaleron, see T. Cuyler Young, "480/479 B.C.—A Persian Perspective," *Iranica Antica* 15 (1980): 213–239. On military cuisine, see Nick Sekunda, "Food and Drink—Greek Military Cuisine," http: www.hoplitesco.uk/pdf /hoplite_food_and_drink.pdf, taken from *Osprey Military Journal* 4.1. (Oxford: Osprey Publishing Ltd., 2002), 3–6. On pre-battle sacrifice, see Michael Jameson, "Sacrifice Before Battle," in Victor Davis Hanson, ed., *Hoplites: The Classical Greek Battle Experience* (London: Routledge, 1991), 197–227. On the trumpet, see Peter Krentz, "The *Salpinx* in Greek Battle," in ibid., 110–120.

PEOPLE AND PLACES

Excellent photos, maps, and commentary (in German) commentary about the sites mentioned by Herodotus can be found in Dietram Müller,

Topographischer Bildkommentar zu den Historien Herodotos. Griechenland im Umfang des heutigen griechischen Staatsgebiets (Tübingen: Ernst Wachsmuth Verlag, 1987).

For a thoughtful, scholarly introduction to the Greek world before and during the Persian invasion, see Robin Osborne, *Greece in the Making, 1200–479 B.C.* (London: Routledge, 1996), esp. 243–350.

On Themistocles, see A. Podlecki, *The Life of Themistocles: A Critical Survey of the Literary and Archaeological Evidence* (Montreal: McGill-Queen's University Press, 1975); Robert Lenardon, *The Saga of Themistocles* (London: Thames & Hudson, 1978).

For an introduction to the Themistocles Decree and the debate among scholars, see Russell Meiggs and David M. Lewis, eds., *A Selection of Greek Historical Inscriptions to the End of the Fifth Century, B.C.*, rev. ed. (Oxford: Oxford University Press, 1988), no. 23, 48–52; M. Crawford and D. Whitehead, *Archaic and Classical Greece* (Cambridge: Cambridge University Press, 1983) no. 112, 224–224.

On the Athenian empire, see Russell Meiggs. *The Athenian Empire* (Oxford: Clarendon Press, 1971). For the Persianization of Athens after 479 B.C., see Margaret C. Miller, *Athens and Persia in the Fifth Century B.C.: A Study in Cultural Receptivity* (Cambridge: Cambridge University Press, 1997).

On Athenian energy as a result of democracy, see Brook Manville and Josiah Ober, *A Company of Citizens: What the World's First Democracy Teaches Leaders About Creating Great Organizations* (Boston, Harvard Business School Press, 2003).

On the debate on democracy as the great legacy of classical Athens, see Josiah Ober, *Political Dissent in Democratic Athens: Intellectual Critics of Popular Rule* (Princeton: Princeton University Press, 1998).

On the topography of Salamis, see Yannos G. Lolos, "Notes on Salaminian Harbors," in *Tropis III: 3rd International Symposium on Ship Construction in Antiquity,* proceedings ed. Harry Tzalas (Delphi: Hellenic Institute for the Preservation of Nautical Tradition, 1995), 291–297. See also Martha C. Taylor, *Salamis and the Salaminioi: The History of an Unofficial Athenian Demos* (Amsterdam: J. C. Gieben, 1997).

A very good introduction to Sparta by a distinguished scholar is Paul Cartledge, *The Spartans: The World of the Warrior-Heroes of Ancient Greece.* (Woodstock and New York: Overlook Press, 2003).

The fundamental work on Achaemenid Persia is Pierre Briant, *From Cyrus to Alexander : A History of the Persian Empire,* trans. Peter B. Daniels (Winona

Lake, Ind.: Eisenbrauns, 2002). A sample of his thoughts on the Achaemenid army can be found in "The Achaemenid Empire," in Kurt Raaflaub and Nathan Rosenstein, eds., *War and Society in the Ancient and Medieval Worlds: Asia, The Mediterranean, Europe, and Mesoamerica* (Washington, D.C.: Center for Hellenic Studies, Trustees for Harvard University; distributed by Harvard University Press, 1999), 105–128. An excellent brief introduction to Achaemenid Persia is available in Josef Wiesehöfer, *Ancient Persia from 550 B.C. to 650 A.D.*, trans. by Azizeh Azodi (London: I. B. Tauris Publishers, 1996), pp. 1–101. See also the clear and succinct article by R. Schmitt, "Achaemenid Dynasty," in *Encyclopedia Iranica*, vol. 1 (London: Routledge & Kegan Paul, 1983), 414–426. Although superseded in some ways, still worth reading is A. T. Olmstead, *History of the Persian Empire* (Chicago: University of Chicago Press, 1959 [1948]). For an introduction to the evidence on Achaemenid Persia, see Maria Brosius, ed. and trans., *The Persian Empire from Cyrus II to Artaxerxes I.* Lactor 16. (London: London Association of Classical Teachers, 2000). An important reinterpretation of Xerxes is H. Sancisi-Weerdenburg, "The Personality of Xerxes, King of Kings," in L. de Meyer and E. Haerinck, eds., *Archaeologica iranica et orientalis: Miscellanea in honorem Louis Vanden Berghe*, vol. 1 (Gent: Peeters Presse, 1989), 549–561.

On Phoenicia in the Persian period, see, Sabatino Moscati, ed., *The Phoenicians.* (New York: Rizzoli, 2000); M. Gras, P. Rouillard, and J. Teixidor, *L'univers phénicien*, rev. ed. (Paris: Hachette, 1995).

On sixth and fifth century B.C. Egypt and its navy, see A. B. Lloyd, "Triremes and the Saïte Navy," *Journal of Egyptian Archaeology* 58 (1972): 268–279; and "Were Necho's Triremes Phoenician?" *Journal of Hellenic Studies* 95 (1975): 45–61.

On the Halicarnassus of Artemisia and Herodotus, see Simon Hornblower, *Mausolus* (Oxford: Clarendon Press, 1982), 1–33. On Artemisia, see R. Munson, "Artemisia in Herodotus," *Classical Antiquity* 7.1 (1988): 91–106.

On Hermotimus the eunuch, see Simon Hornblower, "Panionios of Chios and Hermotimos of Pedasa (Hdt. 8.104–6)," in Peter Derow and Robert Parker, eds., *Herodotus and His World* (Oxford: Oxford University Press, 2003), 37–57.

REFERENCE

There is a wealth of useful and concise information in Simon Hornblower and Anthony Spawforth, eds., *The Oxford Classical Dictionary*, 3rd ed. (Oxford:

Oxford University Press, 1999). The standard and voluminous classical encyclopedia (in German) is A. Pauly, G. Wissowa, and W. Kroll, eds., *Real-Encyclopädie der klassischen Altertumswissenschaft* (Stuttgart: A. Druckenmüller Verlag, 1958– [1893–]). Scholarly essays on a variety of historical topics in the late sixth and early fifth centuries B.C. can be found in John Boardman, N.G.L. Hammond, D. M. Lewis, and M. Ostwald, eds., The Cambridge Ancient History., 2nd ed., vol. 4: *Persia, Greece and the Western Mediterranean c. 525 to 479 B.C.* (Cambridge: Cambridge University Press, 1988).

MISCELLANEOUS

Most of the clothing described herein, from Herodotus's cloak to Xerxes' gold torque, represents educated guesses based on common practices in ancient dress. For ancient Greek clothing, see M. M. Evans and E. B. Abrahams, *Ancient Greek Dress*, ed. Dorothy M. Johnson (Chicago: Argonaut, 1964). For Persian clothing, see Pierre Briant, *From Cyrus to Alexander: A History of the Persian Empire*, trans. Peter B. Daniels (Winona Lake, Ind.: Eisenbrauns, 2002), 187, 217, 299–300, 523–524; Margaret C. Miller, *Athens and Persia in the Fifth Century B.C.: A Study in Cultural Receptivity* (Cambridge: Cambridge University Press, 1997), 153–187. I imagine Artemisia wearing the jewelry found in the fourth century B.C. tomb of an elite woman of Halicarnassus, the so-called Carian Princess. The finds are now in the Bodrum Museum, Turkey. See http://www.bodrum-museum.com/depts/carian.htm. On perfume and cosmetics, see Mikhal Dayagi-Mendels, *Perfumes and Cosmetics in the Ancient World* (Jerusalem: Israel Museum, 1989). On the arms and armor of Spartan and other Greek warriors, see Anthony Snodgrass, *Arms and Armour of the Greeks* (Ithaca: Cornell University Press, 1967); Nicholas Sekunda, *Warriors of Ancient Greece* (Botley, Eng.: Osprey Publishing Ltd., 1986) and *The Spartans* (Botley, Eng.: Osprey Publishing Ltd., 1998).

On eunuchs, see Lloyd Llewellyn-Jones, "Eunuchs and the Royal Harem in Achaemenid Persia," in Shaun Tougher, ed., *Eunuchs in Antiquity and Beyond* (London: Duckworth, 2002), pp. 19–49.

On the precious objects in Xerxes' and Mardonius's tents as well as on Xerxes' throne at Salamis, see Dorothy Burr Thompson, "The Persian Spoils in Athens," in Saul S. Weinberg, ed., *The Aegean and the Near East: Studies Presented to Hetty Goldman on the Occasion of Her Seventy-Fifth Birth-*

day (Locust Valley, N.Y.: J. J. Augustin, 1956), 281–291, and Miller, *Athens and Persia*, 29–41.

On situational awareness, see Mike Spick, *The Ace Factor: Air Combat & the Role of Situational Awareness* (Annapolis, Md.: Naval Institute Press, 1988).

ACKNOWLEDGMENTS

In writing this book I have gathered enormous debts, some to organizations and even more to people. Boris Rankov has been exceptionally generous with his time and expertise about *Olympias*, triremes, and rowing. Victor Davis Hanson has been kind enough to let me engage him in a long-running debate about the consequences of the battle of Salamis. Over the years, John Hale and Donald Kagan have each shared his considerable knowledge of ancient ships and naval warfare. Josiah Ober is an incomparable thinker on the subject of democracy and warfare. Adrienne Mayor combines an editor's eye with a scholar's learning. Mark Levine on a bad day knows more about storytelling than most of us do in a good year; he has been a generous and supportive friend from the earliest stages of this project.

John Lee, Meredith Small, and the late Aaron Strauss generously read chapters in draft version, and they each dispensed superb editorial advice. Paul Cartledge was kind enough to take part in a stimulating seminar on the Persian Wars. Elizabeth Greene and Simon Hornblower shared unpublished material with me.

Pierre Briant, Burke Carson, Judith Dupré, Laurel Freas, Timothy Gregory, John Hyland, Fred Kagan, Michelle Moyd, Bill Patterson, Hayden Pelliccia, Ingrid Rowland, Philip Sabin, Elizabeth Shepherd, and Erla Zwingle each shared his or her expertise at various stages of my research. I would also like to thank Sandra Bernstein and the late Alvin Bernstein, Joan Jacobs Brumberg, Giovanni Giorgini, Dede Hatch, Ned Lebow, Johanna Li, Deirdre Martin, Tim Merrick, Nat and Marcia Ober, Katerina Papoulia, David Rakowski, Daniel Schwarz, Tiffany Stansfield, and Gail Holst Warhaft.

In Greece, I received invaluable help in regard to triremes and naval history from Rear Admiral A. Dimitsas of the Hellenic Navy and from Rosie Randolph. For information about fishermen on Salamis today I would like to thank Antiopi Argyriou and Marisa Koch. For information about winds and weather in and around Salamis I am grateful to Dr. Michael Petrakis, Director of the Institute for Environmental Research & Sustainable Development, National Observatory of Athens. I would also like to thank Zafira Haïdou and the staff of the Nautical Museum of Greece, Piraeus.

In Turkey, I received generous assistance from Oguz Alpozen of the Bodrum Museum of Underwater Archaeology, from archaeologist Poul Pedersen, from naval archaeologist Harun Özdas, from Carian scholar Koray Konuk, and from George Bass, Don Frey, Elizabeth Greene, and the staff of the Institute of Nautical Archaeology in Bodrum.

Howard Morhaim is as sage and supportive a literary agent and friend as any author could ever ask for. He has helped me every step of the way. Robert Bender is an insightful and dedicated editor whose guidance has improved this manuscript immeasurably. Paul Sidey is as wise and discerning an editor as he is witty and patient.

It is a pleasure to acknowledge the various institutions that have helped me. The Department of History of Cornell University has been a stimulating and supportive academic home for many years and was kind enough to grant me leave from teaching to work on this book. Cornell's Department of Classics and its Peace Studies Program each also provide intellectual nourishment. With its superb collection and its supportive staff, the Cornell University Library has proven indispensable for my research. I am delighted to thank a generation of Cornell students for their questioning and encouragement.

The American School of Classical Studies in Athens is one of the world's greatest centers of knowledge about ancient Greece. I was lucky enough to spend two years there. The MacDowell Colony in Peterborough, New Hampshire, awarded me a month's residency in winter 2003, where I was able to write in an ideal setting. Without the Cascadilla Boat Club in Ithaca, New York, I would know very little about oars and boats.

I will always be grateful to the people of Greece and Turkey for their generosity and hospitality.

My greatest debt is to my family. I can never thank my parents enough. My wife and children patiently bore both my absences to do research and my distracted and inattentive presence while I was home writing.

Acknowledgments

For that, and for much more than I can say, I am grateful to my wife, Marcia, and to my children, Sylvie and Michael. Without Marcia's support, encouragement, and advice, this book could not have been written. Michael's intense and agile manipulation of video games recalls the skill of the ancient pilot. Sylvie is a constant reminder that there is more to life than war, and so I dedicate this book to her.

INDEX

285